An Investment Framework for Nutrition

DIRECTIONS IN DEVELOPMENT
Human Development

An Investment Framework for Nutrition

Reaching the Global Targets for Stunting, Anemia, Breastfeeding, and Wasting

Meera Shekar, Jakub Kakietek, Julia Dayton Eberwein, and Dylan Walters

© 2017 International Bank for Reconstruction and Development / The World Bank
1818 H Street NW, Washington DC 20433
Telephone: 202-473-1000; Internet: www.worldbank.org

Some rights reserved

1 2 3 4   20 19 18 17

This work is a product of the staff of The World Bank with external contributions. The findings, interpretations, and conclusions expressed in this work do not necessarily reflect the views of The World Bank, its Board of Executive Directors, or the governments they represent. The World Bank does not guarantee the accuracy of the data included in this work. The boundaries, colors, denominations, and other information shown on any map in this work do not imply any judgment on the part of The World Bank concerning the legal status of any territory or the endorsement or acceptance of such boundaries.

Nothing herein shall constitute or be considered to be a limitation upon or waiver of the privileges and immunities of The World Bank, all of which are specifically reserved.

Rights and Permissions

This work is available under the Creative Commons Attribution 3.0 IGO license (CC BY 3.0 IGO) http://creativecommons.org/licenses/by/3.0/igo. Under the Creative Commons Attribution license, you are free to copy, distribute, transmit, and adapt this work, including for commercial purposes, under the following conditions:

Attribution—Please cite the work as follows: Shekar, Meera, Jakub Kakietek, Julia Dayton Eberwein, and Dylan Walters. 2017. *An Investment Framework for Nutrition: Reaching the Global Targets for Stunting, Anemia, Breastfeeding, and Wasting.* Directions in Development. Washington, DC: World Bank. doi:10.1596/978-1-4648-1010-7. License: Creative Commons Attribution CC BY 3.0 IGO

Translations—If you create a translation of this work, please add the following disclaimer along with the attribution: *This translation was not created by The World Bank and should not be considered an official World Bank translation. The World Bank shall not be liable for any content or error in this translation.*

Adaptations—If you create an adaptation of this work, please add the following disclaimer along with the attribution: *This is an adaptation of an original work by The World Bank. Views and opinions expressed in the adaptation are the sole responsibility of the author or authors of the adaptation and are not endorsed by The World Bank.*

Third-party content—The World Bank does not necessarily own each component of the content contained within the work. The World Bank therefore does not warrant that the use of any third-party–owned individual component or part contained in the work will not infringe on the rights of those third parties. The risk of claims resulting from such infringement rests solely with you. If you wish to reuse a component of the work, it is your responsibility to determine whether permission is needed for that reuse and to obtain permission from the copyright owner. Examples of components can include, but are not limited to, tables, figures, or images.

All queries on rights and licenses should be addressed to World Bank Publications, The World Bank Group, 1818 H Street NW, Washington, DC 20433, USA; fax: 202-522-2625; e-mail: pubrights@worldbank.org.

ISBN (paper): 978-1-4648-1010-7
ISBN (electronic): 978-1-4648-1011-4
DOI: 10.1596/978-1-4648-1010-7

Cover photo: Child with mother, Dhaka, Bangladesh. © UN Photo/Kibae Park (https://www.flickr.com/photos/un_photo/5370298016/in/gallery-124797079@N07-72157646200180442/). Used with the permission of UN Photo/Kibae Park. Further permission required for reuse.
Cover design: Debra Naylor, Naylor Design, Inc.

Library of Congress Cataloging-in-Publication Data has been requested.

Contents

Foreword	*xv*
Acknowledgments	*xvii*
About the Authors and Contributors	*xix*
Abbreviations	*xxi*
Glossary	*xxiii*

	Executive Summary	1
	Nutrition Targets: Investment Case	1
	Estimated Financing Needs	3
	Key Recommendations	5
	Call to Action	8
	References	8
Chapter 1	**Reaching the Global Nutrition Targets: Stunting and Other Forms of Malnutrition**	**11**
	Meera Shekar, Julia Dayton Eberwein, Anne Marie Provo, Michelle Mehta, and Lucy Sullivan	
	Key Messages	11
	Objectives of the Report	12
	Why Invest in Nutrition?	12
	Global Response	16
	Analytical Framework	19
	Measuring Progress	20
	Building on Previous Estimates of Financing Needs to Scale Up Nutrition	21
	Consultative Process: The Technical Advisory Group	23
	Scope of This Report	23
	Notes	24
	References	24
Chapter 2	**Overview of Methods**	**29**
	Jakub Kakietek, Julia Dayton Eberwein, Dylan Walters, and Meera Shekar	
	Key Messages	29

	Country Sample Selection	29
	Evidence-Based Interventions and Delivery Platforms	33
	Estimating Unit Costs on the Basis of Program Experience	33
	Assumptions on the Pace of Scale-Up	34
	Estimating Total Financing Needs for Each Target	35
	Estimating Impacts	35
	Benefit-Cost Analyses	36
	Data Sources	37
	Notes	38
	References	38
Chapter 3	**Reaching the Global Target for Stunting**	**41**
	Meera Shekar, Jakub Kakietek, Julia Dayton Eberwein,	
	Jon Kweku Akuoku, and Audrey Pereira	
	Key Messages	41
	Stunting Prevalence and Progress to Date	41
	The Effects of Stunting	45
	Interventions That Reduce Stunting	47
	Analytic Approaches Specific to the Stunting Target	50
	Results	55
	Discussion	62
	Notes	65
	References	65
Chapter 4	**Reaching the Global Target for Anemia**	**71**
	Dylan Walters, Jakub Kakietek, Julia Dayton Eberwein, and	
	Meera Shekar	
	Key Messages	71
	Anemia and Its Effects	72
	Causes of Anemia	72
	Interventions That Effectively Prevent Anemia	72
	Analytic Approaches Specific to the Anemia Target	76
	Results	83
	Discussion	90
	Notes	91
	References	92
Chapter 5	**Reaching the Global Target for Breastfeeding**	**97**
	Dylan Walters, Julia Dayton Eberwein, Lucy Sullivan, and	
	Meera Shekar	
	Key Messages	97
	Optimal Breastfeeding and Its Benefits	98
	The State of Breastfeeding Worldwide	98

	Interventions That Effectively Promote Breastfeeding	100
	Analytic Approaches Specific to the Breastfeeding Target	102
	Results	106
	Discussion	113
	Notes	114
	References	114
Chapter 6	**Scaling Up the Treatment of Severe Wasting**	**117**
	Jakub Kakietek, Michelle Mehta, and Meera Shekar	
	Key Messages	117
	Wasting and Its Effects	118
	Treatment of Severe Acute Malnutrition in Children	120
	Analytic Approaches Specific to the Wasting Target	120
	Results	126
	Discussion	130
	Notes	134
	References	134
Chapter 7	**Financing Needs to Reach the Four Global Nutrition Targets: Stunting, Anemia, Breastfeeding, and Wasting**	**139**
	Jakub Kakietek, Meera Shekar, Julia Dayton Eberwein, and Dylan Walters	
	Key Messages	139
	Method for Aggregating Financing Needs across All Four Targets	140
	Total Financing Needs to Achieve All Four Targets	140
	Estimated Impacts: Method for Aggregating across Targets	144
	Three Potential Packages for Financing: The Full Package, the Priority Package, and the Catalyzing Progress Package	146
	Discussion	152
	Notes	154
	References	155
Chapter 8	**Financing the Global Nutrition Targets**	**157**
	Mary Rose D'Alimonte, Hilary Rogers, and David de Ferranti	
	Key Messages	157
	Current Levels of Spending on Nutrition	158
	Financing the Scale-Up to Reach the Global Targets	166
	Discussion	171
	Notes	174
	References	177

Chapter 9	**Reaching the Global Targets for Stunting, Anemia, Breastfeeding, and Wasting: Investment Framework and Research Implications**	181
	Meera Shekar, Julia Dayton Eberwein, Jakub Kakietek, and Michelle Mehta	
	Key Messages	181
	Rationale for Investing in Nutrition	182
	An Investment Framework for Nutrition	183
	Discussion	189
	Limitations and Constraints	191
	Policy Implications and Recommendations	194
	Note	197
	References	197
Appendix A	Technical Advisory Group Membership	199
Appendix B	Baseline Intervention Coverage Rates, by Target	201
Appendix C	Intervention Unit Costs and Data Sources for Unit Costs	209
Appendix D	Current Government Investments in Nutrition	221
Appendix E	Current Official Development Assistance for Nutrition across Aid Categories	227

Boxes

ES.1	A Big Bang for the Buck: The Benefits of Investing in Nutrition	6
1.1	What Is Malnutrition?	12
1.2	Scaling Up World Bank Support to End Stunting: An Imperative for Developing Economies	18
9.1	Peru's Success in Reducing Stunting	185
9.2	Senegal's Nutrition Policy Development Process: A Work in Progress	186
9.3	The Vietnam Experience: Investing in Breastfeeding Promotion and Anemia Reduction	187
9.4	Achieving High Coverage of Nutrition-Specific Interventions: Lessons from Vitamin A Supplementation	188

Figures

ES.1	Four World Health Assembly Global Targets for Nutrition	2
ES.2	Benefits of Investing in Global Nutrition Targets	4
ES.3	An Affordable Package of Nutrition-Specific Interventions to Meet Four Nutrition Targets	5

BES1.1	The Dramatic Benefits of Investing in Nutrition	6
1.1	Investments in Nutrition Build Human Capital and Boost Shared Prosperity	13
1.2	Gray Matter Infrastructure: Early Childhood Nutrition as a Determinant of Lifelong Cognitive Development	14
1.3	Key Global Responses on Nutrition	17
1.4	A Framework for Achieving Optimum Nutrition	20
2.1	Incremental Percentage of the Global Burden of Stunting and Number of Additional Countries Included in the Analyses	30
3.1	Global and Regional Trends of Child Stunting under Age 5 Years, 1990–2014	43
3.2	Trends in Number of Children under Age 5 Years Stunted, by Region, 1990–2014	43
3.3	Stunting Rates, by Wealth Quintile, Selected Countries	44
3.4	The Lives Saved Tool and Underlying Model Used to Estimate Impact on Stunting	54
3.5	Annual Financing Needs to Meet the Stunting Target by 2025	57
3.6	Ten-Year Total Financing Needs to Meet the Stunting Target, by Region	58
3.7	Estimated Total Financing Needs to Meet the Stunting Target, by Region	59
3.8	Ten-Year Total Financing Needs to Meet the Stunting Target, by Country Income Group	59
3.9	Costs and Impacts of a 10-Year Scale-Up of Interventions to Reach the Stunting Target	60
4.1	Conceptual Model of Determinants of Anemia	73
4.2	Underlying Model Used to Estimate the Impact of Interventions on Anemia in Women	81
4.3	Annual Financing Needs to Meet the Anemia Target, 2016–25	84
4.4	Ten-Year Total Financing Needs to Meet the Anemia Target, by Region	86
4.5	Ten-Year Total Financing Needs to Meet the Anemia Target, by Country Income Group	86
4.6	Sensitivity Analysis for 10-Year Total Financing Needs to Meet the Anemia Target	87
4.7	Costs and Impacts of a 10-Year Scale-Up of Interventions to Meet the Anemia Target	88
4.8	Sensitivity Analyses of the Impact of Interventions to Meet the Anemia Target	89
5.1	Conceptual Framework for an Enabling Environment That Supports Breastfeeding	99
5.2	Annual Financing Needs to Meet the Breastfeeding Target	108
5.3	Ten-Year Total Financing Needs to Meet the Breastfeeding Target, by Region	109

5.4	Ten-Year Total Financing Needs to Meet the Breastfeeding Target, by Country Income Group	109
5.5	Sensitivity Analyses for 10-Year Total Financing Needs to Meet the Breastfeeding Target	110
5.6	Projected Exclusive Breastfeeding Prevalence and Child Deaths Averted with Scale-Up of Interventions to Meet the Breastfeeding Target	111
5.7	Sensitivity Analyses of the Estimated Impact of Interventions on Exclusive Breastfeeding Rates	112
6.1	Total Annual Financing Needs for the Treatment of Severe Acute Malnutrition under Constant and Declining Unit Cost Assumptions, 2016–25	123
6.2	The Lives Saved Tool Model of the Impact of the Treatment of Severe Acute Malnutrition on Mortality in Children under Age 5 Years	124
6.3	Ten-Year Total Financing Needs for the Treatment of Severe Acute Malnutrition, by Region	127
6.4	Ten-Year Total Financing Needs for the Treatment of Severe Acute Malnutrition, by Country Income Group	127
6.5	Total Annual Financing Needs to Scale Up the Treatment of Severe Acute Malnutrition, 2016–25	128
7.1	Ten-Year Total Financing Needs to Meet All Four Targets, Breakdown by Target	142
7.2	Ten-Year Total Financing Needs to Meet All Four Targets, by Region	143
7.3	Ten-Year Total Financing Needs to Meet All Four Targets, by Country Income Group	143
8.1	Official Development Assistance for Basic Nutrition Disbursed between 2006 and 2013	162
8.2	Current Financing for the Costed Package of Interventions by Governments and Official Development Assistance in 2015, by Target	164
8.3	Baseline Official Development Assistance Financing for Nutrition, by Region and Income Group	166
8.4	Business as Usual in Nutrition Financing: A $56 Billion Shortfall	170
8.5	The Global-Solidarity Financing Scenario: The $70 Billion Required for Scale-Up Mobilized	170
9.1	Benefits of Investing in Global Nutrition Targets	183
9.2	Reductions in Prevalence of Stunting, Selected Countries	184
B9.1.1	Key Factors in Peru's Success in Reducing Stunting	186
B9.4.1	Vitamin A Supplementation Coverage among Children Ages 6–59 months, Selected Countries, 1999–2013	189
9.3	A Call to Action	196

Map

3.1	Stunting Rates among Low- and Middle-Income Countries as of 2015	42

Tables

1.1	Six World Health Assembly Global Targets for Nutrition	21
1.2	Studies That Estimate Global Financing Needs for Scaling Up Nutrition Interventions	22
2.1	Number of Sample Countries, Percentage of Burden, and Multiplier Used to Extrapolate to All Low- and Middle-Income Countries	31
2.2	Countries Included in the Estimates of the Four Targets	31
2.3	Process for Estimating Unit Costs and Dealing with Missing Unit Cost Data	34
3.1	Interventions to Reach the Stunting Target	51
3.2	Minimum, Maximum, and Mean Unit Costs for Interventions to Meet the Stunting Target (Annual)	56
3.3	Total Financing Needs to Meet the Stunting Target	57
3.4	Total Costs, Cost per Case of Stunting Averted, and Cost per Death Averted	61
3.5	Benefit-Cost Ratios of Scaling Up Interventions to Meet the Stunting Target, 3 and 5 Percent Discount Rates	62
3.6	Comparison across Three Studies of Unit Costs and Annual Financing Needs for Nutrition Interventions	63
3.7	Population Covered and Unit Costs to Meet the Stunting Target in the Full Sample, Sub-Saharan Africa, and South Asia	64
4.1	Recommended Iron and Folic Acid Dosages for Nonpregnant and Pregnant Women	74
4.2	Anemia Severity Thresholds in Women	76
4.3	Interventions to Reach the Anemia Target	77
4.4	Assumed Delivery Platforms for Iron and Folic Acid Supplementation for Women, by Secondary School Enrollment and Poverty Status	79
4.5	Minimum, Maximum, and Mean Unit Costs of Interventions to Meet the Anemia Target (Annual)	83
4.6	Ten-Year Total Financing Needs to Meet the Anemia Target	85
4.7	Total Cost, Cost per Case-Year of Anemia Averted, and Costs per Death Averted	89
4.8	Benefit-Cost Ratios of Scaling Up Interventions to Meet the Anemia Target, 3 and 5 Percent Discount Rates	90
5.1	Interventions to Meet the Breastfeeding Target	100
5.2	Minimum, Maximum, and Mean Unit Costs to Meet the Breastfeeding Target (Annual)	107
5.3	Total Financing Needs to Meet the Breastfeeding Target	107

5.4	Benefit-Cost Ratios of Scaling Up Interventions to Meet the Breastfeeding Target, 3 and 5 Percent Discount Rates	112
6.1	Differential Impact of Treatment of Severe Acute Malnutrition on Mortality by Underlying Prevalence of Disease Risk Factors	125
6.2	Estimated Impact over 10 Years of the Treatment of Severe Acute Malnutrition	129
6.3	Benefit-Cost Ratios of Scaling Up Treatment of Severe Acute Malnutrition, 3 and 5 Percent Discount Rates	129
6.4	Benefit-Cost Ratios of Scaling Up Treatment of Severe Acute Malnutrition, by Number of Episodes per Year	130
6.5	Comparison of Cost Estimates of the Treatment of Severe Acute Malnutrition	131
6.6	Mortality Estimates for Severe Acute Malnutrition	132
7.1	Ten-Year Total Financing Needs to Meet All Four Targets	141
7.2	Estimated Impacts of Meeting All Four Targets, 2025, Compared with 2015 Baseline	144
7.3	Benefit-Cost Ratios of Scaling Up Interventions to Meet All Four Targets, 3 and 5 Percent Discount Rates	146
7.4	Cost per Outcome, by Intervention	147
7.5	Potential Delivery Platforms for Scaling Up High-Impact Interventions	148
7.6	Total Financing Needs for Immediate Scale-Up of a Set of Priority Interventions	149
7.7	Total Financing Needs for Catalyzing Progress Package of Interventions	151
7.8	Cost Effectiveness, by Intervention Package	151
7.9	Benefits and Total Financing Needs, by Intervention Package	152
7.10	Three Scale-up Packages: Total 10-Year Resources Required and Interventions Included	153
8.1	Financing Principles Used to Close the Resource Gap under the Global-Solidarity Scenario	169
9.1	Additional Financing Needs to Reach All Four Targets, Selected Years	190
A.1	TAG Membership	200
B.1	Stunting Target: Percentage of Target Population Covered by Relevant Intervention at Baseline, by Country	202
B.2	Anemia Target: Percentage of Target Population Covered by Relevant Intervention, by Country	204
B.3	Breastfeeding Target: Percentage of Target Population Covered by Relevant Intervention at Baseline, by Country	206
B.4	Wasting Target: Percentage of Target Population Covered by Relevant Intervention at Baseline, by Country	207
C.1	Unit Costs of Interventions to Meet the Stunting Target	209

C.2	Unit Costs of Interventions to Meet the Anemia Target	215
C.3	Unit Costs of Interventions to Meet the Breastfeeding Target	217
C.4	Unit Costs of Interventions to Treat Severe Acute Malnutrition	217
D.1	Estimates of Government Expenditure on Nutrition Programs, Various Sources	222
E.1	Summary of Purpose Codes Included in the Analysis	228
E.2	Average Segmentation of Basic Nutrition (Purpose Code 12240) Disbursements in 2013, by Intervention/Activity in 60 Countries	229

Foreword

The World Bank Group is committed to the twin goals of eliminating extreme poverty and boosting shared prosperity. Although significant progress has been made, with global poverty rates having declined to less than 10 percent for the first time in history, childhood stunting—a leading measure of undernutrition and overall well-being—remains a silent emergency of a magnitude as large as that of the AIDS epidemic: it affects 159 million children with negative consequences, including illness, deaths, learning outcomes, poverty, and diminished productivity. The links between early childhood nutrition and human capital have been well recognized for some time. This book identifies a set of actions that, taken together, could allow the world to reach the global nutrition targets for stunting, anemia in women, and exclusive breastfeeding for infants, as well as for scaling up the treatment of severe wasting. Doing so would bring many benefits to children's nutrition in the immediate term, their long-term health and well-being, and their future productivity as vibrant adult members of society. Investing in this set of actions requires almost $70 billion over 10 years from domestic resources, official development assistance (ODA), and the private sector.

Unlike many other development investments, investments in nutrition are durable, inalienable, and portable. *Durable* because investments made during the critical 1,000-day window of opportunity last a lifetime without ever needing to be replenished. *Inalienable* and *portable* because they belong to that child no matter what and wherever she or he goes. Even more important are the findings in this book that these investments in nutrition are among the best in development, with a return of between $4 and $35 for every $1 invested.

This book identifies ways to raise the needed financial resources to scale up actions to address the global targets. It will be vital to combine traditional financing—ranging from additional domestic government and ODA resources to reallocating existing government resources from less cost-effective investments to highly effective investments in nutrition—with innovative financing mechanisms, such as the Power of Nutrition and the Global Financing Facility in Support of Every Woman, Every Child.

The time for action is now. Let us come together as an international community and drive down malnutrition rates. Childhood years are limited, and each day that passes without action to address stunting and improve other nutrition outcomes diminishes the growth and prosperity of countries around the world.

Timothy Grant Evans
Senior Director, Health, Nutrition, and Population
Global Practice
World Bank Group

Acknowledgments

This book was led by Meera Shekar, with Jakub Kakietek, Julia Dayton Eberwein, and Dylan Walters. The overall work was a joint effort between the World Bank Group, the Results for Development Institute, and 1,000 Days, with financial support from the Bill & Melinda Gates Foundation and the Children's Investment Fund Foundation.

The Results for Development Institute team who developed the financing scenarios for this work was led by Robert Hecht, with Shan Soe-Lin, Mary Rose D'Alimonte, Hilary Rogers, Stephanie Heung, and Daniel Arias. David de Ferranti provided technical guidance, and Jack Clift provided support and peer review in the preparation of chapter 8.

The 1,000 Days team was led by Lucy Sullivan with Danielle Porfido.

Ellen Piwoz from the Bill & Melinda Gates Foundation and Augustin Flory from the Children's Investment Fund Foundation provided valuable technical guidance. Jon Kweku Akuoku, Audrey Pereira, Rebecca Heidcamp, and Michelle Mehta (World Bank); Thu Do (Results for Development Institute); and Robert Greener and Clara Picanyol (Oxford Policy Management) provided useful inputs to the analysis. Hope Steele edited the book.

The authors are grateful to Keith Hansen, Vice President of Human Development at the World Bank Group; and Tim Evans, Senior Director for the Health, Nutrition, and Population Global Practice at the World Bank Group, for their guidance and support.

Peer-review comments were provided by Harold Alderman (International Food Policy Research Institute), Ellen Piwoz, Luc Laviolette (World Bank), and Marelize Gorgens (World Bank). In addition, Sue Horton (University of Waterloo), Julia Kravasec (United Nations Children's Fund), Monika Bloessner (World Health Organization), and Neil Watkins and Nora Coghlan (Bill & Melinda Gates Foundation) provided very valuable technical advice on advocacy-related issues.

The team is deeply grateful to the members of the Technical Advisory Group for their contributions to this work (see appendix A for group members). Additional inputs from colleagues who attended the February 22, 2016, full-day meeting are also greatly appreciated (also see appendix A for a list of meeting participants).

Consultations with development partners, especially the International Coalition for Advocacy on Nutrition, colleagues at the U.K. Department for International Development and the World Health Organization, and others provided further guidance for the book. The authors are extremely grateful for the advice and inputs from all those who contributed their valuable time.

About the Authors and Contributors

About the Authors

Meera Shekar is Global Lead for Nutrition in the Health, Nutrition, and Population Global Practice. Meera has lived and worked across the globe and has extensive operational experience in Bangladesh, Bolivia, Ethiopia, Guatemala, India, the Philippines, Sri Lanka, Tanzania, Uzbekistan, and Vietnam. Before joining the World Bank in 2003, she led the United Nations Children's Fund's Health, Nutrition, and Water and Sanitation teams in the Philippines and Tanzania. Meera has a PhD in international nutrition, epidemiology, and population studies from Cornell University.

Jakub Kakietek is a health economist in the World Bank's Health, Nutrition, and Population Global Practice. He has more than 10 years of experience designing, implementing, and managing analytic and technical assistance projects in high-, middle-, and low-income countries. His work has focused on economic and impact evaluation in the areas of nutrition, obesity, and HIV/AIDS. He holds a MS in health economics from the London School of Economics and an MPH and PhD in political science from Emory University.

Julia Dayton Eberwein is a consultant in the Health, Nutrition, and Population Global Practice at the World Bank. In addition to her work in the field of nutrition, she has consulted on the effect of HIV/AIDS, health program evaluation, and cost-effectiveness analysis. She has been a research associate at the Population Council and a postdoctoral fellow at Yale University's Center for Interdisciplinary Research on AIDS. She has a PhD in health economics from Yale University and an MPA from the Middlebury Institute of International Studies.

Dylan Walters is a consultant in the Health, Nutrition, and Population Global Practice at the World Bank. He is a PhD candidate at the Canadian Centre for Health Economics and the Institute of Health Policy, Management, and Evaluation at the University of Toronto. He has worked as a research consultant for Alive and Thrive in Southeast Asia and with the Canadian Coalition of Global Health Research, as well as managed large human resource capacity-building programs for the SickKids Centre for Global Child Health.

About the Contributors

Anne Marie Provo is a research analyst in the Health, Nutrition, and Population Global Practice at the World Bank.

Michelle Mehta is a consultant in the Health, Nutrition, and Population Global Practice at the World Bank.

Jon Kweku Akuoku is a consultant in the Health, Nutrition, and Population Global Practice at the World Bank.

Audrey Pereira is a consultant in the Health, Nutrition, and Population Global Practice at the World Bank.

David de Ferranti is the president and chief executive officer of Results for Development Institute in Washington, DC.

Mary Rose D'Alimonte is a program officer for the Results for Development Institute in Washington, DC.

Hilary Rogers is a senior program associate for the Results for Development Institute in Washington, DC.

Lucy Sullivan is the executive director for 1,000 Days in Washington, DC.

Abbreviations

AIDS	acquired immune deficiency syndrome
BCR	benefit-cost ratio
CIFF	Children's Investment Fund Foundation
CRS	Creditor Reporting System
DALY	disability-adjusted life year
DfID	U.K. Department for International Development
DHS	Demographic and Health Surveys
FAO	Food and Agriculture Organization of the United Nations
FFI	Food Fortification Initiative
GAIN	Global Alliance for Improved Nutrition
GDP	gross domestic product
GFF	Global Financing Facility
HIV	human immunodeficiency virus
IBRD	International Bank for Reconstruction and Development
ICAN	International Coalition for Advocacy on Nutrition
IDA	International Development Association
IFNA	Initiative on Food and Nutrition Security in Africa
IQ	intelligence quotient
IU	international unit
JICA	Japan International Cooperation Agency
LiST	Lives Saved Tool
MICS	Multiple Indicator Cluster Surveys
MIS	Malaria Indicator Surveys
MUAC	mid-upper arm circumference
NHM	National Health Mission
ODA	official development assistance
OECD	Organisation for Economic Co-operation and Development
RHS	Reproductive Health Surveys
RSOC	Rapid Survey of Children

SDG	Sustainable Development Goal
SUN	Scaling Up Nutrition
TAG	Technical Advisory Group
UNICEF	United Nations Children's Fund
UNIMAP	UNICEF Multiple Micronutrient Preparation
USAID	U.S. Agency for International Development
WASH	water, sanitation, and hygiene
WDI	World Development Indicators
WHA	World Health Assembly
WHO	World Health Organization
WHZ	weight-for-height z-score
WPP	World Population Prospects

All dollar amounts are U.S. dollars unless otherwise indicated.

Glossary

A **benefit-cost ratio** summarizes the overall value of a project or proposal. It is the ratio of the benefits of a project or proposal, expressed in monetary terms, relative to its costs, also expressed in monetary terms. The benefit-cost ratio takes into account the amount of monetary gain realized by implementing a project versus the amount it costs to execute the project. The higher the ratio, the better the investment. A general rule is that, if the benefit from a project is greater than its cost, the project is a good investment.

Capacity development for program delivery is a process that involves increasing in-country human capacity and systems to design, deliver, manage, and evaluate large-scale interventions (World Bank 2010). This includes developing skills by training public health personnel and community volunteers to improve the delivery of services. These efforts typically accompany program implementation or, when possible, precede program implementation. In this analysis, we allocate 9 percent of total programmatic costs to capacity development for program delivery.

Cost-benefit analysis is an approach to economic analysis that weighs the cost of an intervention against its benefits. The approach involves assigning a monetary value to the benefits of an intervention and estimating the expected present value of the net benefits, known as the *net present value*. Net benefits are the difference between the cost and monetary value of benefits of the intervention. The net present value is defined mathematically as:

$$\text{Net present value} = \sum_{t=1}^{T} \frac{C_t}{(1+r)^t} - C_0$$

where C_t is net cash inflows, C_0 is the initial investment, the index t is the time period, and r is the discount rate. A positive net present value, when discounted at appropriate rates, indicates that the present value of cash inflows (benefits) exceeds the present value of cash outflows (cost of financing). Interventions with net present values that are at least as high as alternative interventions provide greater benefits than interventions with net present values equal to or lower than alternatives. The results of cost-benefit analysis can also be expressed in terms of the benefit-cost ratio.

Cost-effectiveness analysis is an approach to economic analysis that is intended to identify interventions that produce the desired results at the lowest cost. Cost-effectiveness analysis requires two components: the total cost of the intervention and an estimate of the intervention's impact, such as the number of lives saved. The cost-effectiveness ratio can be defined as:

$$\text{Cost-effectiveness ratio} = \frac{\text{total cost of implementing the intervention}}{\text{impact of the intervention on a specific outcome}}$$

The analysis involves comparing the cost-effectiveness ratios among alternative interventions with the same outcomes. The intervention with the lowest cost per benefit is considered to be the most cost-effective intervention among the alternatives.

A **DALY** is a **disability-adjusted life year**, which is equivalent to a year of healthy life lost due to a health condition. The DALY, developed in 1993 by the World Bank, combines the years of life lost from a disease (YLL) and the years of life spent with disability from the disease (YLD). DALYs count the gains from both mortality (how many more years of life lost due to premature death are prevented) and morbidity (how many years or parts of years of life lost due to disability are prevented). An advantage of the DALY is that it is a metric that is recognized and understood by external audiences such as the World Health Organization (WHO) and the National Institutes of Health (NIH). It helps to gauge the contribution of individual diseases relative to the overall burden of disease by geographic region or health area. Combined with cost data, DALYs allow for estimating and comparing the cost-effectiveness of scaling up nutrition interventions in different countries.

A **discount rate** refers to a rate of interest used to determine the current value of future cash flows. The concept of the time value of money suggests that income earned in the present is worth more than the same amount of income earned in the future because of its earning potential. A higher discount rate reflects higher losses to potential benefits from alternative investments in capital. A higher discount rate may also reflect a greater risk premium of the intervention.

The **Lives Saved Tool (LiST)** is an estimation tool that translates measured coverage changes into estimates of mortality reduction and cases of childhood stunting averted. LiST is used to project how increasing intervention coverage would impact child and maternal survival. It is part of an integrated set of tools that make up the Spectrum policy modeling system.

Monitoring and evaluation (M&E), operations research, and technical support for program delivery are all elements of cost-effective and efficient program implementation. **Monitoring** involves checking progress against plans through the systematic and routine collection of information from projects and programs in order to learn from experience to improve practices and activities in the future, to ensure internal and external accountability of the resources used and the results obtained, and to make informed decisions on the future of the intervention. Monitoring is a periodically recurring task. **Evaluation** is the assessing, as systematically and objectively as possible, of a completed project or intervention (or a phase of an ongoing project). **Operations research** aims to inform the program designers about ways to deliver interventions more effectively and efficiently. **Technical support** entails ensuring that training, support, and maintenance for the physical elements of the intervention are available. In this costing exercise, we allocate 2 percent of total intervention costs for M&E, operations research, and technical support.

Nutrition-sensitive interventions are those that have an indirect impact on nutrition and are delivered through sectors other than health, such as the agriculture; education; and water, sanitation, and hygiene sectors. Examples include biofortification of food crops, conditional cash transfers, and water and sanitation infrastructure improvements.

Nutrition-specific interventions are those that address the immediate determinants of child nutrition, such as adequate food and nutrition intake, feeding and caregiving practices, and treatment of disease. Examples include promotion of good infant and young child nutrition, micronutrient supplementation, and deworming.

ODA refers to **official development assistance** and similar kinds of aid. This comprises aid from bilateral assistance agencies (and the high-income countries to which they belong), multilateral organizations (such as the development banks), and a wide variety of charitable institutions (including large international nongovernmental organizations).

Sensitivity analysis is a technique that evaluates the robustness of findings when key variables change. It helps to identify the variables with the greatest and least influence on the outcomes of the intervention, and it may involve adjusting the values of a variable to observe the impact of the variable on the outcome.

Stunting is an anthropometric measure of low height-for-age. It is an indicator of chronic undernutrition and is the result of prolonged food deprivation and/or disease or illness. It is measured in terms of z-score (or standard deviation score); a child is considered stunted with a height-for-age z-score of −2 or lower.

Underweight is an anthropometric measure of low weight-for-age. It is used as a composite indicator to reflect both acute and chronic undernutrition, although it cannot distinguish between them. It is measured in terms of z-score (or standard deviation score); a child is considered underweight with a weight-for-age z-score of −2 or lower.

Wasting is an anthropometric indicator of low weight-for-height. It is an indicator of acute undernutrition and the result of more recent food deprivation or illness. It is measured in terms of z-score (or standard deviation score). A child with a weight-for-height z-score of −2 or lower is considered wasted.

Executive Summary

As of 2015, 159 million children under the age of five were chronically malnourished or stunted, underscoring a massive global health and economic development challenge (UNICEF, WHO, and World Bank 2015). In 2012—in an effort to rally the international community around improving nutrition—the 176 members of the World Health Assembly endorsed the first-ever global nutrition targets, focusing on six areas: stunting, anemia, low birthweight, childhood overweight, breastfeeding, and wasting. These targets aim to boost investments in cost-effective interventions, spearhead better implementation practices, and catalyze progress toward decreasing malnutrition. Some of the targets (stunting and wasting) are further enshrined within the United Nations' Sustainable Development Goal 2 (SDG 2), which commits to ending malnutrition in all its forms by the year 2030.

These analyses estimate financing needs for the targets for stunting, anemia in women, exclusive breastfeeding for infants, and wasting among young children (see figure ES.1). The analyses are not able to estimate the financing needs to achieve the wasting target, mainly because of a lack of sufficient evidence on interventions to prevent wasting. Instead, the analyses estimate costs for the scale-up of the treatment of severe wasting. Two of the global nutrition targets—those for low birthweight and for child overweight—are not included in these analyses either because there are insufficient data on the prevalence of the condition (low birthweight) or because of a lack of consensus on effective interventions to reach the goal (child overweight).

Nutrition Targets: Investment Case

Ending malnutrition is critical for economic and human development. Childhood stunting, an overarching measure of long-term malnutrition, has life-long consequences not just for health, but also for human capital and economic development, prosperity, and equity. Being stunted in early childhood reduces schooling attainment, decreases adult wages, and makes children less likely to escape poverty as adults (Fink et al. 2016; Hoddinott et al. 2008, 2011; Martorell et al. 2010). Conversely, reductions in stunting are estimated to potentially increase

Figure ES.1 Four World Health Assembly Global Targets for Nutrition

Source: WHO 2014.

overall economic productivity, as measured by gross domestic product (GDP) per capita, by 4–11 percent in Africa and Asia (Horton and Steckel 2013). Thus nutrition interventions are consistently identified as one of the most cost-effective development actions (Horton and Hoddinott 2014). Furthermore, investments in early nutrition yield permanent and inalienable benefits.

Although the investment case for nutrition is strong, efforts to reach the nutrition SDG targets are constrained by a range of factors including insufficient financing, complexity in terms of implementation (that is, how to bridge disciplines and sectoral borders), and determining the methods and costs (both financial and human resources) involved in monitoring SDG targets. In relation to nutrition's contribution to this whole-of-society approach to development, these challenges are exacerbated because of the major gaps in knowledge regarding the costs and resources required for scaling up these interventions. Two earlier studies have estimated the total costs of scaling up nutrition interventions (Bhutta et al. 2013; Horton et al. 2010). However, those studies estimate the cost of a comprehensive package of evidence-based interventions affecting child undernutrition at large but do not focus on achieving specific outcomes (see chapter 1 for a discussion of these studies). Furthermore, neither of these studies provides estimates of the costs of reaching the global nutrition targets, including the SDG targets. In addition, no previous study has systematically linked the costs with the potential for impact and the interventions' returns on investment, nor assessed the financing shortfall between what is required and what is currently being spent at the global level. Finally, no prior study has presented a comprehensive global analysis of domestic financing from governments and official development assistance (ODA). This report aims to close these knowledge gaps by providing a more comprehensive estimate of costs as well as financing needs, linking them both to expected impacts, and laying out a potential financing framework. An in-depth understanding of current nutrition investments, future needs and their impacts, and ways to mobilize the required funds is included to move the agenda from a political commitment to a policy imperative.

Estimated Financing Needs

The expected effects of the proposed interventions on the prevalence of stunting among children, anemia in women, and rates of exclusive breastfeeding for infants are estimated, along with their impacts on mortality. Benefit-cost analyses are conducted for each intervention, translating the results into benefits in relation to stunting and anemia cases prevented, increased numbers of children breastfed, cases of wasting treated, lives saved, and potential earnings gained over adult working life. Issues of technical and allocative efficiency as they relate to the implementation of scaling-up efforts are also addressed.

This report finds that an additional investment of $70 billion over 10 years is needed to achieve the global targets for stunting, anemia in women, exclusive breastfeeding and the scaling up of the treatment of severe wasting. The expected impact of this increased investment is enormous: 65 million cases of stunting and 265 million cases of anemia in women would be prevented in 2025 as compared with the 2015 baseline. In addition, at least 91 million more children under five years of age would be treated for severe wasting and 105 million additional babies would be exclusively breastfed during the first six months of life over 10 years. Altogether, investing in interventions to reach these targets would also result in at least 3.7 million child deaths averted (see figure ES.2).

In an environment of constrained resources, if the world could not afford the $70 billion needed to achieve the targets but instead could invest in only a subset of interventions, it would have to set priorities. In this context, this report lays out two alternative packages for consideration. These packages of interventions would include scaling up interventions with the highest returns (that is, those that maximize allocative efficiency) and those that are scalable now (that is, those that maximize technical efficiency), with the caveat that investing in a smaller set of interventions would fall short of reaching some of the targets by 2025. Financing a "priority package" of interventions immediately ready to scale will require an additional investment of $23 billion over the next 10 years, or $2.3 billion per year. When combined with other health and poverty reduction efforts, this priority package would yield significant returns: an estimated 2.3 million lives would be saved and there would be 50 million fewer cases of stunting in 2025 than in 2015. A slightly more ambitious package of investments, called the "catalyzing progress package," would scale up the priority package plus provide a more phased-in expansion of the other interventions to strengthen delivery mechanisms and support research and program implementation. It is assumed that, for the latter set of interventions, during the first five years, emphasis will be placed on establishing global guidelines and on operational research to

Figure ES.2 Benefits of Investing in Global Nutrition Targets

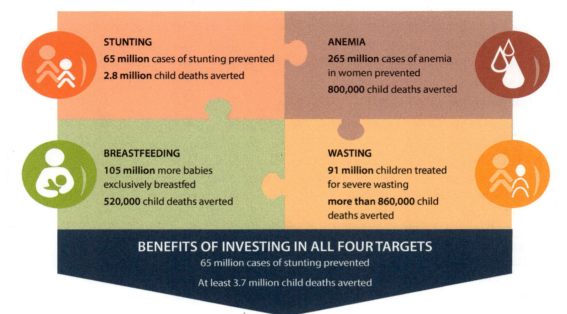

develop effective delivery platforms, or to develop less expensive products or more cost-effective technologies (such as for rice fortification). This catalyzing progress package will require an additional $37 billion over the next 10 years, or $3.7 billion per year. When combined with other health and poverty reduction efforts, this package of interventions could yield significant progress toward the global targets: an estimated 2.6 million lives would be saved and there would be 58 million fewer cases of stunting in 2025 than in 2015.

In terms of financing sources—as with other areas that the SDGs aim to address—a mix of domestic on-budget allocations from country governments combined with ODA, and newly emerging innovative financing mechanisms coupled with household contributions, could finance the remaining gap. This underscores again the extent to which a whole-of-society effort is needed for financing the achievement of the nutrition targets in the context of the broader SDGs; this mix of financing is also in line with other SDG challenges.

These analyses also confirm the high returns on investment that come from investing in nutrition among children and women. Not only do investments in nutrition make one of the best value-for-money development actions, they also lay the groundwork for the success of investments in other sectors.

Achieving the targets is within reach if partners work together to immediately step up in investments in nutrition. Indeed, some countries (Peru, Senegal, and others) have shown that rapid scale-up of nutrition interventions can be achieved and lead to swift declines in stunting rates (see chapter 9 for a discussion of country achievements in reducing malnutrition).

Key Recommendations

1. **The world needs $70 billion over 10 years** to invest in high-impact nutrition-specific interventions in order to reach the global targets for stunting, anemia in women, and exclusive breastfeeding for infants and to scale up the treatment of severe wasting among young children (see figure ES.3).

   Although $7 billion per year may seem to be a large investment, it pales in comparison to the $500 billion per year (nearly $1.5 billion/day) that is currently spent on agriculture subsidies (Potter 2014) and the $543 billion per year (over $1.5 billion/day) spent on fossil fuel subsidies (International Energy Agency 2014), or $19 billion per year on HIV-AIDS (UNAIDS 2016).

   The nutrition-specific investments presented in this report are expected to have large benefits: 65 million cases of stunting and 265 million cases of anemia in women would be prevented in 2025 as compared with the 2015 baseline. In addition, at least 91 million more children would be treated for severe wasting and 105 million additional babies would be exclusively breastfed during the first six months of life over 10 years. Altogether, achieving these targets would avert at least 3.7 million child deaths. And, every dollar invested in this package of interventions would yield between $4 and $35 in economic returns (see box ES.1). This is in line with previous studies suggesting returns of $18 (Hoddinott et al. 2013).

   In an environment of constrained resources, this report lays out two alternative investment packages, with the strong caveat that investing in these sets

Figure ES.3 An Affordable Package of Nutrition-Specific Interventions to Meet Four Nutrition Targets

- Improving nutrition for pregnant mothers
- Iron and folic acid supplementation for nonpregnant women
- Improving child nutrition, including micronutrient supplementation
- Improving feeding practices, including breastfeeding
- Pro-breastfeeding social policies and national breastfeeding promotion campaigns
- Staple food fortification

~$10 per child annually
$70B over 10 years

in addition to current spending

+

Continued improvements in underlying factors:
- Water and sanitation
- Women's education, health, and empowerment
- Food availability and diversity

An Investment Framework for Nutrition • http://dx.doi.org/10.1596/978-1-4648-1010-7

Box ES.1 A Big Bang for the Buck: The Benefits of Investing in Nutrition

With many competing development objectives, the main challenge for policy makers is to decide which actions should be prioritized. One way to do this is to compare benefit-cost ratios across interventions and programs. Even though methodologies differ across studies (see Alderman, Behrman, and Puett 2016 for detailed discussion of these differences), there is a strong body of evidence that shows very high economic returns to investing in nutrition (Alderman, Behrman and Puett 2016; Copenhagen Consensus Center 2015; Hoddinott et al. 2013). The analyses in this report support that conclusion and report benefit-cost ratios well above 1, the breakeven point, under a range of assumptions (see figure BES1.1). The benefits of investments to increase rates of exclusive breastfeeding are particularly high: $35 in returns for every dollar invested. Not only are investments in nutrition one of the best value-for-money development actions, they also lay the groundwork for the success of investments in other sectors.

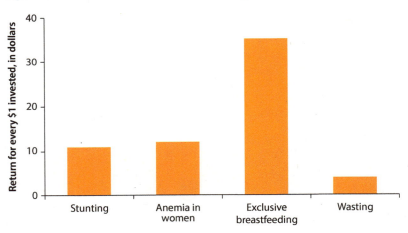

Figure BES1.1 The Dramatic Benefits of Investing in Nutrition

of interventions would fall short of reaching some of the targets by 2025. A "priority package" of immediately ready to scale interventions would require $23 billion over the next 10 years, $2.3 billion per year, or just over $4 per child. A "catalyzing progress package" would scale up the priority package plus a more phased-in expansion of some of the other interventions to strengthen delivery mechanisms, support for research and program implementation, and invest in better technologies, requiring an additional $37 billion over the next 10 years, $3.7 billion per year, or just over $5 per child. Further investments would be needed over time to build up to scaling up the full package.

An Investment Framework for Nutrition • http://dx.doi.org/10.1596/978-1-4648-1010-7

2. **Recent experience from several countries suggests that meeting these targets is feasible**, although some of the targets—especially those for reducing stunting in children and anemia in women—are ambitious and will require concerted efforts in financing, scale-up, and sustained commitment. On the other hand, the target for exclusive breastfeeding has scope to be much more ambitious.

3. **Some areas of future research need to be prioritized.** These include:

    Research on scalable strategies for delivering high-impact interventions is necessary, including how to address bottlenecks to scaling up, for example through results-based budgeting approaches or other ways of incentivizing results. Such research will not only facilitate faster scale-up, but it would also have the potential to increase the technical efficiency and delivery costs for these interventions, thereby reducing the global financing needs.

    Another critical area for future research is *the assessment of allocative efficiency*—that is, identifying the optimum funding allocation among different interventions or an allocation that maximizes the impact under a specific budget constraint. The present analyses show cost per outcome, allowing for only limited comparisons of cost-effectiveness among different interventions for the same targets.

    Research to improve the technical efficiency of nutrition spending is also urgently needed. This includes identifying new strategies for addressing complex nutritional problems such as stunting and anemia, as well as technologies to help take these solutions to scale more rapidly and at lower cost. Because of the multifactorial nature of anemia, research is under way to clearly determine what fraction of the problem can be addressed by nutrition interventions; the estimates presented in this report may need to be revised accordingly once results become available. Additionally, some micronutrient deficiencies are not included here (for example, iodine deficiencies), because these were not included in the global targets, even though they have significant impacts on morbidity, mortality, and economic productivity.

    Strengthening the quality of surveillance data, improving unit cost data for interventions in different country contexts, and building stronger data collection systems for estimating current investments in nutrition (from both domestic governments and ODA) are also crucial. Further research is needed on the costs of interventions such as maternity protection to support women in the workforce so they can exclusively breastfeed infants for the first six months. In addition, significant resources will be required to build a living database of current investments, including closely monitoring spending and ensuring accountability, and to undertake national-level public expenditure reviews.

    A dedicated effort to *understanding which interventions prevent wasting* is urgently needed. It is also essential to learn more about cost-effective strategies for managing moderate acute malnutrition, and whether or not these can contribute toward the prevention of wasting.

    More evidence is needed on the costs and impacts of nutrition-sensitive interventions—that is, interventions that improve nutrition through agriculture, social protection, and water and sanitation sectors, among others. It is evident that stunting and anemia are multifactorial and can be improved through increasing quality, diversity, and affordability of foods; increasing the control of income by women farmers; and also by reducing exposure to fecal pathogens by improved water, sanitation, and hygiene practices. However, the attributable fraction of the burden that can be addressed by these interventions is unknown. The last five years have seen a proliferation of studies to improve clarity on these issues, as well as on the use of social programs as a platform for reaching the most vulnerable. Future work in this area should take into account such new evidence as studies are published.

Call to Action

As the world stands at the cusp of the new SDGs, with global poverty rates having declined to less than 10 percent for the first time in history (World Bank 2016), there is an unprecedented opportunity to save children's lives, build future human capital and gray-matter infrastructure, and provide equal opportunity for all children to drive faster economic growth. These investments in the critical 1,000-day window of early childhood are inalienable and portable and will pay lifelong dividends—not only for the children directly affected but also for us all in the form of more robust societies—that will drive future economies.

References

Alderman, H., J. R. Behrman, and C. Puett. 2016. "Big Numbers about Small Children: Estimating the Economic Benefits of Addressing Undernutrition." *World Bank Research Observer* 31 (2).

Bhutta, Z. A, J. K. Das, A. Rizvi, M. F. Gaffey, N. Walker, S. Horton, P. Webb, A. Lartey, and R. E. Black. 2013. "Evidence-Based Interventions for Improvement of Maternal and Child Nutrition: What Can Be Done and at What Cost?" *The Lancet* 382 (9890): 452–77.

Copenhagen Consensus Center. 2015. *Smart Development Goals: The Post-2015 Consensus.* http://www.copenhagenconsensus.com/sites/default/files/outcomedocument_col.pdf.

Fink, G., E. Peet, G. Danaei, K. Andrews, D. C. McCoy, C. R. Sudfeld, M. C. Smith Fawzi, M. Ezzati, and W. W. Fawzi. 2016. "Schooling and Wage Income Losses Due to Early-Childhood Growth Faltering in Developing Countries: National, Regional, and Global Estimates." *The American Journal of Clinical Nutrition* 104 (1): 104–12.

Hoddinott, J., H. Alderman, J. R. Behrman, L. Haddad, and S. Horton. 2013. "The Economic Rationale for Investing in Stunting Reduction." *Maternal and Child Nutrition* 9 (Suppl. 2): 69–82.

Hoddinott, J., J. Maluccio, J. R. Behrman, R. Martorell, P. Melgar, A. R. Quisumbing, M. Ramirez-Zea, R. D. Stein, and K. M. Yount. 2011. "The Consequences of Early Childhood Growth Failure over the Life Course." IFPRI Discussion Paper 01073, International Food Policy Research Institute, Washington, DC.

Hoddinott, J., J. A. Maluccio, J. R. Behman, R. Flores, and R. Martorell. 2008. "Effect of a Nutrition Intervention during Early Childhood on Economic Productivity in Guatemalan Adults." *Lancet* 371 (9610): 411–16.

Horton, S., and J. Hoddinott. 2014. "Benefits and Costs of the Food and Nutrition Targets for the Post-2015 Development Agenda: Post-2015 Consensus." Food Security and Nutrition Perspective paper, Copenhagen Consensus Center Working Paper. http://www.copenhagenconsensus.com/sites/default/files/food_security_and_nutrition_perspective_-_horton_hoddinott_0.pdf.

Horton, S., M. Shekar, C. McDonald, A. Mahal, and J. K. Brooks. 2010. *Scaling Up Nutrition: What Will it Cost?* Directions in Development Series. Washington, DC: World Bank.

Horton, S., and R. Steckel. 2013. "Malnutrition: Global Economic Losses Attributable to Malnutrition 1900–2000 and Projections to 2050." In *The Economics of Human Challenges*, edited by B. Lomborg, 247–72. Cambridge, U.K.: Cambridge University Press.

International Energy Agency. 2014. *World Energy Outlook 2014*. Paris: International Energy Agency. http://www.worldenergyoutlook.org/weo2014/.

Martorell, R., B. L. Horta, L. S. Adair, A. D. Stein, L. Richter, C. H. D. Fall, S. K. Bhargava, S. K. Dey Biswas, L. Perez, F. C. Barros, C. G. Victora, and Consortium on Health Orientated Research in Transitional Societies Group. 2010. "Weight Gain in the First Two Years of Life Is an Important Predictor of Schooling Outcomes in Pooled Analyses from Five Birth Cohorts from Low and Middle-Income Countries." *Journal of Nutrition* 140: 348–54.

Potter, G. 2014. "Agricultural Subsidies Remain a Staple in the Industrial World." Vital Signs, World Watch Institute, Washington, DC. http://vitalsigns.worldwatch.org/vs-trend/agricultural-subsidies-remainstaple-industrial-world.

UNAIDS. 2016. *Fast-Track Update on Investments Needed in the AIDS Response*. Geneva: UNAIDS. http://www.unaids.org/sites/default/files/media_asset/UNAIDS_Reference_FastTrack_Update_on_investments_en.pdf.

UNICEF, WHO, and World Bank (United Nations Children's Fund, World Health Organization, and World Bank). 2015. *Joint Child Malnutrition Estimates: Levels and Trends*. Global Database on Child Growth and Malnutrition, http://www.who.int/nutgrowthdb/estimates2014/en/.

WHO. 2014. *Comprehensive Implementation Plan on Maternal, Infant and Young Child Nutrition*. Geneva: WHO. http://apps.who.int/iris/bitstream/10665/113048/1/WHO_NMH_NHD_14.1_eng.pdf?ua=1.

World Bank. 2016. *Global Monitoring Report 2015/2016: Development Goals in an Era of Demographic Change*. Washington, DC: World Bank. http://www.worldbank.org/en/publication/global-monitoring-report.

CHAPTER 1

Reaching the Global Nutrition Targets: Stunting and Other Forms of Malnutrition

Meera Shekar, Julia Dayton Eberwein, Anne Marie Provo, Michelle Mehta, and Lucy Sullivan

Key Messages

- As of 2015, 159 million children globally were stunted in their physical and cognitive development, yielding poor learning outcomes and, eventually, premature death and disability with significant long-term economic consequences for future workforces in already constrained economies.
- Low- and middle-income countries, mainly in Sub-Saharan Africa and South Asia, bear most of the burden of poor nutrition outcomes; stunting prevalence rates exceed 30 percent in these two regions, albeit some middle-income countries in other regions, such as China, Guatemala, Indonesia, and Mexico, also carry high burdens.
- These losses are largely preventable with adequate investments in proven interventions targeting the critical first 1,000 days of a child's life, from the beginning of a woman's pregnancy to her child's second birthday.
- Stunting and other forms of malnutrition can be a life sentence, but these must not be accepted as the "new normal." Although political commitment is growing rapidly for investing in the 1,000-day window of opportunity, more is needed to move this agenda from a pet cause to a common cause and from a political imperative to an economic imperative.
- To galvanize action on these issues, in 2012 the World Health Assembly set the first-ever global targets for nutrition. These focus on six areas: stunting, anemia, exclusive breastfeeding, wasting, low birthweight, and overweight; the first four of these are the focus of this report.
- This report adds to previous work in three ways: by providing a more comprehensive estimate of financing needs, by linking financing needs to impacts, and by laying out a potential financing framework for four of the six global nutrition targets.
- Given the right investments in "gray-matter infrastructure" at the right time, every child can achieve her or his full potential. The payoffs from these investments are durable, portable, and inalienable. An in-depth understanding of current nutrition investments, future needs, their impacts, and ways to mobilize the required financing is essential.

Objectives of the Report

This report aims to close remaining knowledge gaps related to the financing needs, impacts, and financing of nutrition interventions by:

- Estimating investments needed to achieve the global targets for reducing stunting in children under five, reducing anemia in women, increasing the prevalence of exclusive breastfeeding among infants; and mitigating the impacts of wasting among young children by estimating the financing needs to scale up treatment of severe wasting;
- Linking financing needs with potential for impact for the first time; and
- Proposing a financing framework for mobilizing the needed resources.

Why Invest in Nutrition?

With so many competing priorities, policy makers naturally ask why they should invest in nutrition. Current estimates suggest that all forms of malnutrition (undernutrition, micronutrient deficiencies, and overweight) cost the global economy an estimated $3.5 trillion per year, or $500 per individual, creating a major impediment for country governments in their efforts to reduce poverty and create thriving and productive communities (Global Panel 2016). Unlike investments in physical infrastructure, investments intended to reduce malnutrition (box 1.1) generate benefits that are durable, inalienable, and portable. These investments also fuel progress on all of the 17 development goals enshrined in the Sustainable Development Goals (SDGs), including education and alleviating poverty. Why is this so? Ensuring optimum nutrition—particularly early in life—can permanently alter an individual's development trajectory and maximize her or his productive potential.

Globally, more than 2 billion individuals are malnourished (IFPRI 2016). They include 159 million children who are stunted (low height-for-age), which affects not only their physical but also their cognitive development (UNICEF, WHO, and World Bank 2015). Each year, undernutrition accounts for about 45 percent of all child deaths worldwide (Black et al. 2013). Undernourished

---

Box 1.1 What Is Malnutrition?

The term *malnutrition* encompasses both undernutrition and overnutrition. Undernutrition is commonly measured by inadequate height-for-age (stunting), by inadequate weight-for-height (wasting), or by deficiencies in micronutrients such as vitamin A, iodine, zinc, and iron. Overnutrition is often measured as excessive weight-for-height (overweight and obesity) using growth reference standards for children and body mass index measurements (weight-for-height squared, or kg/m^2) for adults.

---

children who survive often suffer serious cognitive delays (Grantham-McGregor et al. 2007), yielding poor learning outcomes and schooling deficits. Ultimately, the consequences of undernutrition are premature death and disability—along with the loss of creative and intellectual energy (Lye 2016). These outcomes are compounded by billions in economic losses due to excess health care spending and lower productivity. Thus investments in nutrition provide an opportunity not only to improve nutrition indicators but also to contribute to achievement of other goals, such as increasing school completion, raising adult wages, helping children escape poverty, and increasing national gross domestic product (GDP) (figure 1.1).

Fortunately, these losses are largely preventable if adequate investments in proven interventions are made, particularly those that focus on ensuring optimum nutrition in the critical 1,000-day window between the start of a woman's pregnancy and her child's second birthday (Black et al. 2008, 2013; World Bank 2006). Not only do these investments improve the nutritional status of a population for a lifetime (see figure 1.2), but they can also stimulate gains in the efficiency of health and education spending and trigger productivity gains that further accelerate economic growth.

Stunting and other forms of malnutrition can be a life sentence; they must not be accepted as the "new normal." Although political commitment is growing rapidly for investing in the 1,000-day window of opportunity, more is needed to move this agenda from a pet cause to a common cause, and from a political imperative to an economic imperative. Given the right investments in "gray-matter infrastructure" at the right time, every child can achieve her or his full potential. And the payoffs from these investments are durable, portable, and inalienable.

Stunting (low height-for-age) is the leading population measure of chronic undernutrition and has been included as a key indicator under the SDGs (Target 2.2).[1] Moreover, stunting is a remarkable proxy for exposure to a host of early life behavioral and environmental insults that limit children's overall potential. Childhood stunting has lifelong consequences not just for health but also for

Figure 1.1 Investments in Nutrition Build Human Capital and Boost Shared Prosperity

SCHOOLING	EARNINGS	POVERTY	ECONOMY
Early nutrition programs can increase school completion by one year	Early nutrition programs can raise adult wages by 5–50%	Children who escape stunting are 33% more likely to escape poverty as adults	Reduction in stunting can increase GDP by 4–11% in Asia and Africa

Sources: Hoddinott et al. 2008, 2011; Horton and Steckel 2013; Martorell et al. 2010.

Figure 1.2 Gray Matter Infrastructure: Early Childhood Nutrition as a Determinant of Lifelong Cognitive Development

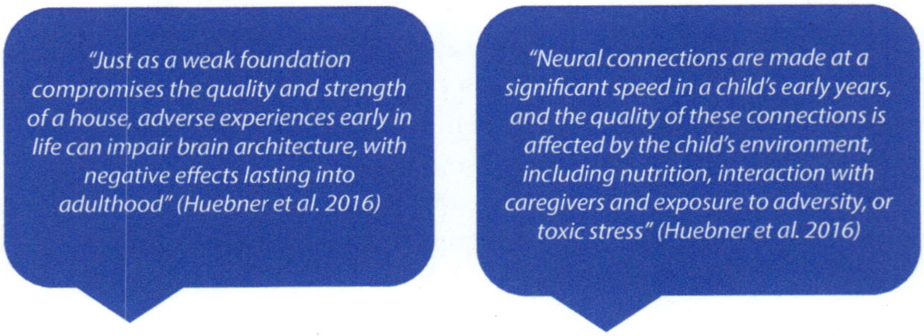

> "Just as a weak foundation compromises the quality and strength of a house, adverse experiences early in life can impair brain architecture, with negative effects lasting into adulthood" (Huebner et al. 2016)

> "Neural connections are made at a significant speed in a child's early years, and the quality of these connections is affected by the child's environment, including nutrition, interaction with caregivers and exposure to adversity, or toxic stress" (Huebner et al. 2016)

cognitive function, human capital, poverty, and equity; these early deficits reverberate across generations (Victora et al. 2010). Importantly, malnutrition often exists in an intergenerational cycle, and malnourished mothers are more than twice as likely to have stunted children as well-nourished mothers (Ozaltin, Hill, and Subramanian 2010).[2] Widespread evidence from a range of settings and using diverse empirical approaches indicates that malnutrition leads to reductions in schooling and in learning per year of school, ultimately resulting in lower earnings. Being stunted in early childhood is associated with a delayed start at school (Daniels and Adair 2004), reduced schooling attainment (Fink et al. 2016; Martorell et al. 2010), and substantially decreased adult wages when measured at both the individual (Hoddinott et al. 2008) and country level (Fink et al. 2016). One study found that young children who were stunted were 33 percent less likely to escape poverty as adults (Hoddinott et al. 2011). These consequences add up to overall GDP losses of 4 to 11 percent in Africa and Asia (Horton and Steckel 2013) (figure 1.1). Thus the direct nutrition interventions that can mitigate the burden of stunting are consistently identified as being among the most cost-effective development and global health actions (Horton and Hoddinott 2014).

Wasting (low weight-for-height) occurs when children lose weight rapidly, generally from low caloric intakes and/or repeated infections.[3] Wasting is an indicator of acute undernutrition. It can result from ongoing food insecurity in resource-poor settings involving insufficient diets in terms of quantity, quality, and diversity; suboptimal breastfeeding; and recurrent episodes of illness—for example, diarrhea (WHO 2014b). At the same time, children living through humanitarian crises, such as famine and complex emergencies, are particularly vulnerable to acute malnutrition. Wasting and infection can create a vicious cycle, whereby acute malnutrition leads to lower immune function, which increases susceptibility to infections and subsequently results in decreased appetite, nutrient malabsorption, elevated metabolic requirements, and undernutrition (WHO 2014b). Consequently, wasted children have roughly twice the risk of mortality as stunted children (WHO 2014b), and severely wasted children have an elevenfold increase in mortality risk when compared with healthy children (McDonald et al. 2013). More details are provided in chapter 6.

Micronutrient deficiencies (sometimes referred to as "hidden hunger") affect nearly 2 billion people worldwide (IFPRI 2016). Deficiencies of iodine, iron, vitamin A, zinc, and folic acid are those most commonly identified in populations and have significant impacts on health and human capital.

- **Iodine deficiency** is one of the main preventable causes of cognitive impairment among children. Maternal iodine deficiency, in particular, has grave consequences for fetal development and child intelligence quotient (IQ). Children born to mothers who were iodine deficient during pregnancy experience, on average, a loss of 12.5 to 13.5 IQ points (Bleichrodt and Born 1994; Qian et al. 2005). Iodine-deficient children lose 13 IQ points on average, making them less educable (World Bank 2006).

- **Iron deficiency** is one of the most common direct epidemiological causes of anemia globally, albeit isolated infections (especially helminthic infections) and repeated infections as a consequence of poor hygiene also have a key role to play in anemia, as do other factors. Given the multifactorial nature of anemia, research is underway to clarify what fraction of the problem can be addressed by nutrition interventions. Although anemia can affect anyone, children and women of reproductive age in low- and middle-income countries are at the greatest risk.[4] Anemia is a major contributor to maternal and perinatal mortality as well as low birthweight among children. The morbidity associated with anemia in working-age adults can lead to lower work productivity as a result of both impaired cognitive functioning and risk of infection. Furthermore, iron deficiency anemia has been associated with developmental deficits and delayed brain maturation in children under age three (Walker et al. 2011). Supplementation for pregnant women with iron and folate has been linked with improvements in cognition of the offspring at seven to nine years (Christian et al. 2010). More details are provided in chapter 4.

- **Vitamin A deficiency** in childhood is a leading risk factor for morbidity, including preventable pediatric blindness, and mortality in low-income countries. Vitamin A deficiency results from insufficient dietary consumption of vitamin A–rich foods (including animal flesh foods, liver, and green leafy vegetables) and is often exacerbated by illness (WHO 2010). Vitamin A deficiency increases the severity of measles and diarrheal and malaria infections in childhood. Conversely, vitamin A supplementation for children is linked to a 23 percent reduction in child mortality (Beaton et al. 1993).

- Zinc plays a pivotal role in immune function and growth. **Zinc deficiency** is associated with increased incidence, severity, and duration of diarrhea and, as recent evidence demonstrates, has a negative effect on child growth (Imdad and Bhutta 2011).

- **Folic acid deficiency** in mothers before or during pregnancy can lead to serious neural tube defects in their infants, resulting in cognitive and developmental delays. Folic acid supplementation reduces the risk of neural tube defects by over 70 percent (Bhutta et al. 2013). However, delivery mechanisms for supplementation have proven challenging, particularly for nonpregnant women of reproductive age.

Exclusive breastfeeding (defined as the practice of giving an infant only breastmilk for the first six months of life, with no other food, other liquids, or even water) has many widely known benefits. However, in reality, social, societal, and environmental factors make this practice challenging for millions of mothers globally. Near full scale-up of exclusive breastfeeding practices could prevent 823,000 annual deaths in children under five years (Victora et al. 2016). Non-breastfed children are nearly three to four times more likely to die of illnesses in the first six months, and there is overwhelming evidence of the positive effects of breastfeeding in preventing pneumonia and diarrhea in young children (Victora et al. 2016). Recent evidence shows that breastfeeding is also associated with higher IQs (Horta, Loret de Mola, and Vitora 2015) and, in the longer term, with enhanced labor market and economic outcomes (Lutter 2016; Rollins et al. 2016). The existence of pro-breastfeeding policies and supportive environments to protect breastfeeding as the best source of nutrition for infants is far from universal, making promotion of exclusive breastfeeding an even greater challenge. More details are provided in chapter 5.

Global Response

Over time, malnutrition rates have not declined fast enough, mainly because of the lack of global action and investment in evidence-based solutions. However, global consensus regarding the essential role of nutrition in achieving sustainable development is growing (figure 1.3). Supported by a solid and growing evidence base regarding what works to address malnutrition, key actors have gradually come to recognize the importance of investing in nutrition. In 2000, ending hunger in all its forms was included in the Millennium Development Goals. A seminal 2006 World Bank report, *Repositioning Nutrition as Central to Development*, further galvanized world leaders to recognize nutrition as a critical element of the global development agenda. The 2008 *Lancet* Series on Maternal and Child Undernutrition builds on an earlier estimate of the impact of nutrition interventions on child mortality (Jones et al. 2003) and provides answers to what interventions could have the maximum impact. This was followed by *Scaling-Up Nutrition: What Will It Cost?*, which was the first-ever effort to estimate the financing needs of scaling up key nutrition interventions (Horton et al. 2010), and then another *Lancet* Series on Maternal and Child Nutrition in 2013 (Bhutta et al. 2013).

Reaching the Global Nutrition Targets: Stunting and Other Forms of Malnutrition

Figure 1.3 Key Global Responses on Nutrition

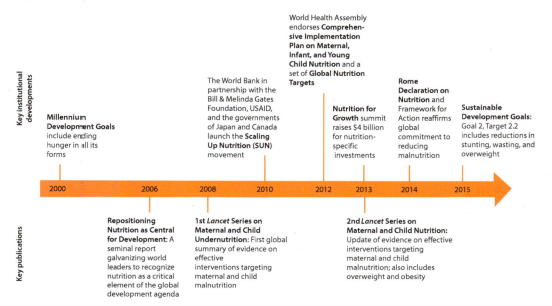

Armed with improved knowledge and increased global commitment, the Scaling Up Nutrition (SUN) movement was launched jointly at the World Bank in 2010 with the Bill & Melinda Gates Foundation, the U.S. Agency for International Development (USAID), and the governments of Japan and Canada. The political commitment raised by the SUN movement led to greater demand for investments in nutrition and a greater response from development partners and governments. In this same year, the 1,000 Days movement began, advocating for action and investment in nutrition for women and children in the critical days from conception until a child is two years old. As of 2016, the SUN network includes 57 client countries supported by over 100 partners from bilateral agencies, academia, and businesses as well as over 3,000 civil society organizations worldwide.[5]

The 2013 Nutrition for Growth event organized by the U.K. Department for International Development (DfID), the Children's Investment Fund Foundation (CIFF), and the government of Brazil was another landmark. The event yielded commitments of over $4 billion, albeit only a small number of stakeholders have reached or are on-course to reaching this commitment (IFPRI 2016). Building on this momentum, the International Coalition for Advocacy on Nutrition (ICAN) was formed to unite civil society organizations working to end malnutrition in all of its forms and advocate for the prioritization of investments and policies that save and improve lives through better nutrition.

An Investment Framework for Nutrition • http://dx.doi.org/10.1596/978-1-4648-1010-7

In April 2016, the United Nations General Assembly proclaimed a Decade of Action on Nutrition (2016–25) to provide a unique opportunity for all stakeholders to strengthen joint efforts toward ending all forms of malnutrition. Convened by the World Health Organization (WHO) and the Food and Agriculture Organization of the United Nations (FAO), the Decade of Action on Nutrition offers an opportunity for accountability for country-driven, SMART commitments to advance the global nutrition agenda within the SDGs and framed by the Rome Declaration on Nutrition.[6] A Nutrition for Growth media moment highlighting progress since 2013 was held on the margins of the Rio Summer Olympics in August 2016 and a future pledging moment is anticipated in 2017. In August 2016, as part of the sixth Tokyo International Conference on African Development (TICAD-VI) in Nairobi, the Japan International Cooperation Agency (JICA) launched a new Initiative on Food and Nutrition Security in Africa (IFNA), with a plan to scale up nutrition-specific and nutrition-sensitive actions in 10 countries in Africa.

The World Bank has been integrally engaged in many of these milestones, and momentum continues to build within the organization (box 1.2), which is catalyzing further action at national and global levels. In April 2016 and coinciding with the World Bank's Spring Meetings, global nutrition leaders gathered in Washington, DC, to discuss the main findings from the analyses in this report on costing and financing and their implications for domestic and overseas aid. Another key landmark of the World Bank's commitment to investing in nutrition was a summit on human capital featuring heads of state and ministers of finance during the 2016 Annual Meetings of the International Monetary Fund and the World Bank Group. The process of translating evidence into action and political and financial commitments through advocacy has taken time, but the current impetus is significant.

Box 1.2 Scaling Up World Bank Support to End Stunting: An Imperative for Developing Economies

Over the past decade, the World Bank has been a major contributor to the dialogue on scaling up actions to prevent stunting. More recently, this effort has been spearheaded by President Jim Yong Kim, as illustrated in these remarks:

> Economies are increasingly more dependent on digital and higher-level competencies and skills, and our investments in "grey matter infrastructure" are perhaps the most important ones we can make. In too many low- and middle-income countries, children are disadvantaged before they even set foot in school because they did not have adequate early nutrition and stimulation, or were exposed to toxic environments. Childhood stunting rates of 45 percent—and as high as 70 percent in some countries—are a stain on our collective conscience.

box continues next page

Box 1.2 Scaling Up World Bank Support to End Stunting: An Imperative for Developing Economies *(continued)*

This is a turnaround from the early to mid-2000s, when support for the nutrition agenda had waned significantly both at the country level and among development partners. In 2002–04, the World Bank's support for nutrition was at a low, with minimal staffing, very little analysis of what works, low institutional and senior management commitment, and minimal investments. This changed dramatically with the publication of the seminal report *Repositioning Nutrition as Central to Development* (World Bank 2006), which brought attention to the issue—not just within the World Bank but also among key partners and governments. Within the institution, this new attention led to a rapid and significant scale-up of staffing for nutrition financed through a special contingency fund in 2007–08. The follow-on 2010 World Bank publication *Scaling Up Nutrition: What Will It Cost?* provided the world with the first estimates of global nutrition costs, and the SUN[a] movement launched in 2010 rallied partners around the cause.

Simultaneously, the World Bank's commitment to investing in the early years (early life nutrition, early learning and stimulation, and nurturing care and protection from stress to support these agendas) is growing exponentially, in scope, scale, and coverage, led by the World Bank Group's twin goals of reducing poverty and boosting shared prosperity. Investments in reducing stunting as well as early childhood stimulation and learning are now center stage on the corporate agenda, not just in the health sector, but across several sectors, including education, water and sanitation, social protection, and agriculture. In addition to International Development Association (IDA) and International Bank for Reconstruction and Development (IBRD) resources, new resources are also becoming available to support this agenda at both global and national levels—from partners such as the Bill & Melinda Gates Foundation, CIFF, the Dangote Foundation, Tata Trusts, the Power of Nutrition,[b] and the Global Financing Facility in support of Every Woman Every Child.[c] These and many other partners, including civil society organizations, are rallying around to catalyze and reinforce the achievement of results in support of the SDGs.

a. For more information on the SUN movement, see http://www.scalingupnutrition.org.
b. For more information on the Power of Nutrition, see http://www.powerofnutrition.org.
c. For more information on the Global Financing Facility in support of Every Woman Every Child, see http://www.worldbank.org/en/topic/health/brief/global-financing-facility-in-support-of-every-woman-every-child.

Analytical Framework

The analyses presented here are informed by the conceptual framework for nutrition (see figure 1.4), which illustrates the benefits during the life course as a result of nutrition-specific and nutrition-sensitive interventions, as well as the benefits of an enabling environment. *Nutrition-specific interventions* are primarily delivered within the health sector and address the immediate determinants of child nutrition, such as breastfeeding, adequate food and nutrient intake, feeding and caregiving practices, and disease prevention and management. *Nutrition-sensitive interventions* are delivered through other sectors—for example, agriculture, water and sanitation, education, or social protection—and address the underlying or basic influencers on childhood nutrition outcomes.

Figure 1.4 A Framework for Achieving Optimum Nutrition

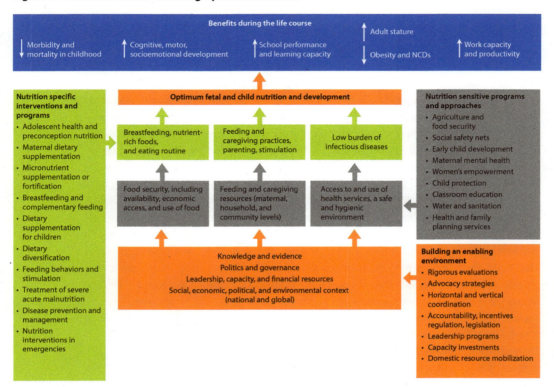

Source: Black et al. 2013, p. 16, Elsevier. Reproduced with permission from Elsevier; further permission required for reuse.

The synergy between nutrition-specific interventions and interventions in other sectors is critical to breaking the cycle of malnutrition and sustaining the gains from direct nutrition-specific interventions (World Bank 2013). This report focuses on costing, financing, and estimating the impact of nutrition-specific interventions with sufficient evidence of benefit for reaching the World Health Assembly global nutrition targets for stunting, anemia, and breastfeeding, and interventions for treating wasting.

Measuring Progress

Lessons from the Millennium Development Goal era demonstrate that clear, ambitious targets can ignite countries to action. In 2012—in an effort to rally the international community around improving nutrition—the 176 members of the World Health Assembly endorsed a *Comprehensive Implementation Plan on Maternal, Infant, and Young Child Nutrition* (WHO 2014a). The plan includes the first-ever global nutrition targets, focusing on six areas: stunting, exclusive breastfeeding, wasting, anemia, low birth-weight, and overweight (table 1.1). The World Health Assembly targets aim to boost investment in cost-effective

Table 1.1 Six World Health Assembly Global Targets for Nutrition

Nutrition target	2025 global target
1. Stunting	40% reduction in the number of children under five who are stunted
2. Anemia	50% reduction of anemia in women of reproductive age
3. Low birthweight[a]	30% reduction of low birth weight
4. Overweight[a]	No increase in childhood overweight
5. Breastfeeding	Increase the rate of exclusive breastfeeding in the first six months up to at least 50%
6. Wasting	Reduce and maintain childhood wasting to less than 5%

Source: WHO 2014a.

a. It was not possible to estimate financing needs to reach the low birthweight and overweight targets either because there are insufficient data on the prevalence of the condition (low birthweight) or because of a lack of consensus on effective interventions to reach the goal (child overweight).

interventions and catalyze progress toward decreasing malnutrition and micronutrient deficiencies. Although targets are set at the global level, member states were urged to develop national targets to facilitate a harmonized approach to measure progress toward the goals, provide accountability for actions, and develop or modify policies to achieve the goals. To help countries set targets and monitor their progress, the WHO has developed a tracking tool that allows users to explore scenarios that take into account different rates of progress (WHO 2015).[7] To sustain momentum, world leaders enshrined some of the World Health Assembly targets within the second SDG, committing to end malnutrition in all its forms by the year 2030. Indicators related to stunting, wasting, and child overweight are included in the SDG framework under Target 2.2 (IAEG-SDG 2016). Although many of these indicators are improving over time, a continuation of current trends would not allow the world to achieve the targets. For example, on the basis of current global trends, approximately 127 million children under five will be stunted by 2025; the World Health Assembly goal is to decrease this number to no more than 100 million by 2025 (WHO 2014c).

Building on Previous Estimates of Financing Needs to Scale Up Nutrition

A broad package of reproductive, maternal, newborn, and child health interventions were costed by Stenberg et al. (2014), which included some related nutrition interventions. However, that analysis did not establish links with the World Health Assembly targets—nor did it include the full package of nutrition interventions. Two previous studies have estimated the global cost of SUN interventions (Bhutta et al. 2013; Horton et al. 2010). The 2010 World Bank report *Scaling Up Nutrition* was the first systematic attempt to estimate the resources needed to scale up nutrition interventions on a global level. It focuses on estimating the financing needs (not impact) of scaling up 13 proven interventions, based in part on the findings of the 2008 *Lancet* Series on Maternal and Child Undernutrition (Bhutta et al. 2008). Financing needs were estimated using the program experience approach, and the report estimates the additional financing needs to scale up the set of interventions to be $10.3 billion per year. In the 2013 *Lancet* Series on Maternal and Child Nutrition, Bhutta et al. revisited the evidence of intervention effectiveness and estimated the financing needs of a global scale-up of interventions to address all forms of malnutrition to be about $9.6 billion per year. Similar to *Scaling Up Nutrition*, this estimate assumed a one-year scale up but, unlike *Scaling Up Nutrition*, it based financing needs on an ingredients-based approach grounded on the WHO OneHealth Tool (Bhutta et al. 2013). In addition to these global studies, several country-level costing and financing studies have contributed to the knowledge base, especially in gaining a better understanding of unit costs for nutrition interventions and in developing the methods to estimate financing needs, impacts, and benefits (IFPRI 2016; Shekar et al. 2014; Shekar, Dayton Eberwein, and Kakietek 2016; Shekar, Mattern, Eozenou et al. 2015; Shekar, Mattern, Laviolette et al. 2015).

Those studies estimated the costs of a comprehensive package of evidence-based interventions affecting different aspects of child undernutrition but did not provide estimates of the financing needs required to reach the global targets. No previous or planned study has systematically linked global financing needs with potential for impact, or assessed the shortfall between what is required and what is currently being spent to address the World Health Assembly global targets. Finally, no prior study has presented a comprehensive global analysis of donor and national government investments, or what financing scenarios may be needed to close these gaps.

The current report adds to the previous work in three unique ways: by providing a more comprehensive estimate of financing needs, by linking financing needs to impacts, and by laying out a potential financing framework (table 1.2). An in-depth understanding of current nutrition investments, future needs and

Table 1.2 Studies That Estimate Global Financing Needs for Scaling Up Nutrition Interventions

Scaling Up Nutrition (Horton et al. 2010)	Lancet Series on Maternal and Child Nutrition (Bhutta et al. 2013)	Investment Framework for Nutrition (this report)
• Focus is on estimating financing needs, not impacts • Includes interventions to address all forms of undernutrition • Assumes going from current coverage to 90% in 1 year • Program experience financing needs • Additional cost to scale-up estimated to be $10.3 billion/year	• Focus is on estimating financing needs and some impact estimations for stunting • Includes interventions to address all forms of malnutrition • Assumes going from current coverage to 90% in 1 year • Ingredients-based financing needs • Additional cost to scale-up estimated to be $9.6 billion/year	• Focus is on financing needs and impacts of four out of six Global Nutrition Targets (stunting, anemia, exclusive breastfeeding, wasting) and financing estimates • More realistic scale-up: increasing current coverage to 90% over 10 years • Declines in stunting over time are modeled rather than assumed • Program experience financing needs • Additional costs to scale-up estimated to be $49.5 billion over 10 years for stunting alone and $69.9 billion for all four targets • Several financing options included

their impact, and ways to mobilize the required funds is needed to move the agenda from political commitment to policy imperative. It should be noted that the estimates from this study are lower than the previous two because it includes a smaller set of interventions than previous estimates (that is, it excludes oral rehydration solution with therapeutic zinc and calcium supplements). This report also uses updated unit costs, which may be lower than the ones used in the previous analyses.

Consultative Process: The Technical Advisory Group

These analyses were guided by the expert advice of a Technical Advisory Group (TAG). This group comprised nutrition experts from around the world, representing country ministries of health, other implementing agencies, academia, and the donor community (see appendix A for a list of the TAG members). TAG met on four occasions to provide feedback on issues such as the selection of interventions, methodology, and data sources, and for validating assumptions made in the models. Its contribution culminated in a one-day in-person meeting to review the final methods and interpret the results (see appendix A for a list of participants).

Scope of This Report

Two of the global nutrition targets—those for low birthweight and for child overweight—are not included in the analyses because there are insufficient data, either because there are insufficient data on the prevalence of the condition (low birthweight) or because of a lack of consensus on effective interventions to reach the goal (child overweight). Financing needs are estimated for scaling up interventions to treat severe wasting, but it was not possible to estimate the financing needs of achieving the wasting target because of a lack of evidence about which interventions are effective in preventing wasting. For the remaining three targets, the analyses focus on costing a package of primarily preventive nutrition-specific interventions, which have proven to be efficacious in averting stunting and anemia, enhancing breastfeeding, and reducing child mortality.

Further, the analyses were limited to low- and middle-income countries because this is where the undernutrition problem is concentrated. In addition, high-income countries can finance their own efforts, and the financing needs and targeting strategies in these countries are likely to be different from those in low- and middle-income countries.

The remainder of this report is structured as follows: Chapter 2 describes the analytical framework for the costs, impacts, and benefit-cost analyses. Chapters 3, 4, 5, and 6 present the financing needs and impacts for reaching targets for stunting, anemia in women, and breastfeeding for infants, and for treating wasting, respectively. Chapter 7 reports on the total financing needs and benefits of scaling up to meet all targets, taking into account the fact that some interventions overlap across targets. Chapter 8 presents scenarios for scaling up financing to reach the targets by 2025. Chapter 9 discusses the findings and sets forth policy and programmatic action items for the future, Including areas for future research.

Notes

1. *Stunting* is defined among children under five years of age as being of a height that is more than two standard deviations below the median height for a child of the same age and sex (height-for-age z-score <–2) according to the WHO Growth Standard (WHO 2009).
2. The term *malnourished mothers* uses maternal short stature (<145 cm) as an indicator of maternal malnutrition.
3. *Wasting* is defined for children under five years of age as being of a weight that is more than two standard deviations below the median weight for a child of the same height and sex (weight-for-height z-score <–2) according to the WHO Growth Standard (WHO 2009).
4. The current World Health Organization thresholds for mild, moderate, and severe anemia are 110–119, 80–109, and <80 grams of hemoglobin per liter for nonpregnant women and 100–109, 70–99 and <70 grams for pregnant women (WHO 2011).
5. For more information on the SUN movement, see http://scalingupnutrition.org/.
6. SMART: specific, measureable, achievable, relevant, and time-bound.
7. The tracking tool is available online at http://www.who.int/nutrition/trackingtool/en/.

References

Beaton, G. H., R. Martorell, K. J. Aronson, B. Edmonston, G. McCabe, A. C. Ross, and B. Harvey. 1993. "Effectiveness of Vitamin A Supplementation in the Control of Young Child Morbidity and Mortality in Developing Countries." Nutrition Policy Discussion Paper 13, International Nutrition Program, Toronto, ON.

Bhutta, Z. A., T. Ahmed, R. E. Eihcblack, S. Cousens, K. Dewey, E. Glugliani, B. A. Haider, B. Kirkwood, S. S. Morris, H. P. S. Sachdeve, and M. Shekar. 2008. "What Works? Interventions for Maternal and Child Undernutrition and Survival." *The Lancet* 371 (9610): 417–40.

Bhutta, Z. A., J. K. Das, A. Rizvi, M. F. Gaffey, N. Walker, S. Horton, P. Webb, A. Lartey, and R. E. Black. 2013. "Evidence-Based Interventions for Improvement of Maternal and Child Nutrition: What Can Be Done and at What Cost?" *The Lancet* 382 (9890): 452–77.

Black, R. E., L. H. Allen, Z. A. Bhutta, L. E. Caulfield, M. de Onis, M. Ezzati, C. Mathers, J. Rivera, and the Maternal and Child Undernutrition Study Group. 2008. "Maternal and Child Undernutrition: Global and Regional Exposures and Health Consequences." *The Lancet* 371 (9608): 243–60.

Black, R. E., C. G. Victora, S. P. Walker, Z. A. Bhutta, P. Christian, M. de Onis, M. Ezzati, S. Grantham-Mcgregor, J. Katz, R. Martorell, R. Uauy, and the Maternal and

Child Nutrition Study Group. 2013. "Maternal and Child Undernutrition and Overweight in Low-Income and Middle-Income Countries." *The Lancet* 382: 427–51.

Bleichrodt, N., and M. P. Born. 1994. "A Meta-Analysis of Research on Iodine and Its Relationship to Cognitive Development." In *The Damaged Brain of Iodine Deficiency*, edited by J. B. Stanbury, 195–200. New York: Cognizant Communication.

Christian, P., L. E. Murray-Kolb, S. K. Khatry, J. Katz, B. A. Schaefer, P. M. Cole, S. C. Leclerq, and J. M. Tielsch. 2010. "Prenatal Micronutrient Supplementation and Intellectual and Motor Function in Early School-Aged Children in Nepal." *JAMA* 304 (24): 2716–23.

Daniels, M. C., and L. Adair. 2004. "Growth in Young Filipino Children Predicts Schooling Trajectories through High School." *Journal of Nutrition* 134: 1439–46.

Fink, G., E. Feet, G. Danaei, K. Andrews, D. C. McCoy, C. R. Sudfeld, M. C. Smith Fawzi, M. Ezzati, and W. W. Fawzi. 2016. "Schooling and Wage Income Losses Due to Early-Childhood Growth Faltering in Developing Countries: National, Regional, and Global Estimates." *The American Journal of Clinical Nutrition* 104 (1): 104–12.

Global Panel (Global Panel on Agriculture and Food Systems for Nutrition). 2016. "The Cost of Malnutrition: Why Policy Action Is Urgent." Technical Brief 3. http://glopan.org/sites/default/files/Costs-of-malnutrition-brief.pdf.

Grantham-McGregor, S., Y. Cheung, S. Cueto, P. Glewwe, L. Richter, B. Strupp, and the International Child Development Steering Group. 2007. "Developmental Potential in the First 5 Years for Children in Developing Countries." *The Lancet* 369 (9555): 60–70.

Hoddinott, J., J. A. Maluccio, J. R. Behman, R. Flores, and R. Martorell. 2008. "Effect of a Nutrition Intervention during Early Childhood on Economic Productivity in Guatemalan Adults." *The Lancet* 371 (9610): 411–16.

Hoddinott, J., J. Maluccio, J. R. Behrman, R. Martorell, P. Melgar, A. R. Quisumbing, M. Ramirez-Zea, R. D. Stein, and K. M. Yount. 2011. "The Consequences of Early Childhood Growth Failure over the Life Course." IFPRI Discussion Paper 01073, International Food Policy Research Institute, Washington, DC.

Horta, B. L., C. Loret de Mola, and C. G. Victora. 2015. "Breastfeeding and Intelligence: A Systematic Review and Meta-Analysis." *Acta Paediatrica* 104: 14–19.

Horton, S., and J. Hoddinott. 2014. "Benefits and Costs of the Food and Nutrition Targets for the Post-2015 Development Agenda: Post-2015 Consensus." Food Security and Nutrition Perspective paper, Copenhagen Consensus Center.

Horton, S., M. Shekar, C. McDonald, A. Mahal, and J. K. Brooks. 2010. *Scaling Up Nutrition. What Will it Cost?* Directions in Development Series. Washington, DC: World Bank.

Horton, S., and R. Steckel. 2013. "Malnutrition: Global Economic Losses Attributable to Malnutrition 1900–2000 and Projections to 2050." In *The Economics of Human Challenges*, edited by B. Lomborg, 247–72. Cambridge, UK: Cambridge University Press.

Huebner, G., N. Boothby, J. L. Aber, G. L. Darmstadt, A. Diaz, A. S. Masten, H. Yoshikawa, I. Redlener, A. Emmel, M. Pitt, L. Arnold, B. Barber, B. Berman, R. Blum, M. Canavera, J. Eckerle, N. A. Fox, J. L. Gibbons, S. W. Hargarten, C. Landers, C. A. Nelson III, S. D. Pollak, V. Rauh, M. Samson, F. Ssewamala, N. St Clair, L. Stark, R. Waldman, M. Wessells, S. L. Wilson, and C. H. Zeanah. 2016. "Beyond Survival: The Case for Investing in Young Children Globally." Discussion Paper, National Academy of Medicine, Washington, DC.

IAEG-SDG (Inter-Agency and Expert Group on Sustainable Development Goal Indicators). 2016. "Provisional Proposed Tiers for Global SDG Indicators as of March 24, 2016." Discussion document for the 3rd IAEG-SDG meeting, 30 March–1 April, 2016, Mexico City, Mexico.

IFPRI (International Food Policy Research Institute). 2016. *Global Nutrition Report 2016: From Promise to Impact: Ending Malnutrition by 2030.* Washington, DC: IFPRI.

Imdad, A., and Z. A. Bhutta. 2011. "Effect of Preventive Zinc Supplementation on Linear Growth in Children under 5 Years of Age in Developing Countries: A Meta-Analysis of Studies for Input to the Lives Saved Tool." *BMC Public Health* 11 (Suppl 3): S22.

Jones, G., R. W. Steketee, R. E. Black, Z. A. Bhutta, and S. S. Morris. 2003. "How Many Child Deaths Can We Prevent This Year?" *The Lancet* 362 (9377): 65–71.

Lutter, R. 2016. "Cognitive Performance, Labor Market Outcomes and Estimates of the Economic Value of Cognitive Effects of Breastfeeding." Unpublished manuscript, May.

Lye, S. J. 2016. "The Science of Early Development: Investing in the First 2000 Days of Life to Enable All Children, Everywhere to Reach Their Full Potential." Presentation at the World Bank Early Childhood Development Meeting, April.

Martorell, R., B. L. Horta, L. S. Adair, A. D. Stein, L. Richter, C. H. D. Fall, S. K. Bhargava, S. K. Dey Biswas, L. Perez, F. C. Barros, C. G. Victora, and Consortium on Health Orientated Research in Transitional Societies Group. 2010. "Weight Gain in the First Two Years of Life Is an Important Predictor of Schooling Outcomes in Pooled Analyses from Five Birth Cohorts from Low- and Middle-Income Countries." *Journal of Nutrition* 140: 348–54.

McDonald, C. M., I. Olofin, S. Flaxman, W. W. Fawzi, D. Spiegelman, L. E. Caulfield, R. E. Black, M. Ezzati, and G. Danaei. 2013. "The Effect of Multiple Anthropometric Deficits on Child Mortality: Meta-Analysis of Individual Data in 10 Prospective Studies from Developing Countries." *American Journal of Clinical Nutrition* 97 (4): 896–901. doi:10.3945/ajcn.112.047639.

Ozaltin, E., K. Hill, and S. V. Subramanian. 2010. "Association of Maternal Stature with Offspring Mortality, Underweight, and Stunting in Low- to Middle-Income Countries." *JAMA* 303 (15): 1507–16.

Qian, M., D. Wang, W. E. Watkins, V. Gebski, Y. Q. Yan, M. Li, and Z. P. Chen. 2005. "The Effects of Iodine on Intelligence in Children: A Meta-Analysis of Studies Conducted in China." *Asia Pacific Journal of Clinical Nutrition* 14 (1): 32–42.

Rollins, N. C., N. Bhandari, N. Hajeebhoy, S. Horton, C. K. Lutter, J. C. Martines, E. G. Piwoz, L. M. Richter, and C. G. Victora. 2016. "Why Invest, and What It Will Take to Improve Breastfeeding Practices?" *The Lancet* 387 (10017): 491–504.

Shekar, M., J. Dayton Eberwein, and J. Kakietek. 2016. "The Costs of Stunting in South Asia and the Benefits of Public Investments in Nutrition." *Maternal and Child Nutrition* 12 (Supl 1): 186–95.

Shekar, M., C. McDonald, A. Subandoro, J. Dayton Eberwein, M. Mattern, and J. K. Akuoku. 2014. "Costed Plan for Scaling Up Nutrition: Nigeria." Health, Nutrition and Population (HNP) Discussion Paper, World Bank, Washington, DC.

Shekar, M., M. Mattern, L. Laviolette, J. Dayton Eberwein, W. Karamba, and J. K. Akuoku. 2015. "Scaling Up Nutrition in the DRC: What Will It Cost?" Health, Nutrition and Population (HNP) Discussion Paper, World Bank, Washington, DC.

Shekar, M., M. Mattern, P. Eozenou, J. Dayton Eberwein, J. K. Akuoku, E. Di Gropello and W. Karamba. 2015. "Scaling Up Nutrition for a More Resilient Mali: Nutrition

Diagnostics and Costed Plan for Scaling Up." Health, Nutrition and Population (HNP) Discussion Paper, World Bank, Washington, DC.

Stenberg, K., H. Axelson, P. Sheehan, I. Anderson, A. M. Gülmezoglu, et al. 2014. "Advancing Social and Economic Development by Investing in Women's and Children's Health: A New Global Investment Framework." *The Lancet* 383 (9925): 1333–54.

UNICEF, WHO, and World Bank (United Nations Children's Fund, World Health Organization, and World Bank). 2015. *Joint Child Malnutrition Estimates*. Global Database on Child Growth and Malnutrition, http://www.who.int/nutgrowthdb/estimates2014/en/.

Victora, C. G., M. de Onis, P. C. Hallal, M. Blössner, and R. Shrimpton. 2010. "Worldwide Timing of Growth Faltering: Revisiting Implications for Interventions." *Pediatrics* 125: e473–80.

Victora, C., R. Bahl, A. Barros, G. V. A. Franca, S. Horton, J. Krasevec, S. Murch, M. J. Sankar, N. Walker, and N. C. Rollins. 2016. "Breastfeeding in the 21st Century: Epidemiology, Mechanisms and Lifelong Effect." *The Lancet* 387 (10017): 475–90.

Walker, S. P., T. D. Wachs, S. Grantham-McGregor, M. M. Black, C. A. Nelson, S. L. Huffman, H. Baker-Henningham, S. M. Chang, J. D. Hamadani, B. Lozoff, J. M. Meeks Gardner, C. A. Powell, A. Rahman, and L. Richter. 2011. "Inequality in Early Childhood: Risk and Protective Factors for Early Child Development." *The Lancet* 378 (9799): 1325–38.

WHO (World Health Organization). 2009. "WHO Child Growth Standards and the Identification of Severe Acute Malnutrition in Infants and Children: A Joint Statement by the World Health Organization and the United Nations Children's Fund." http://apps.who.int/iris/bitstream/10665/44129/1/9789241598163_eng.pdf?ua=1.

———. 2010. *Nutrition Landscape Information System (NLIS) Country Profile Indicators: Interpretation Guide*. Geneva: WHO.

———. 2011. "Haemoglobin Concentrations for the Diagnosis of Anaemia and Assessment of Severity." WHO, Geneva. http://www.who.int/vmnis/indicators/haemoglobin.pdf.

———. 2012. *Global Targets 2025*, http://www.who.int/nutrition/topics/nutrition_globaltargets2025/en/.

———. 2014a. *Comprehensive Implementation Plan on Maternal, Infant and Young Child Nutrition*. Geneva: WHO. http://apps.who.int/iris/bitstream/10665/113048/1/WHO_NMH_NHD_14.1_eng.pdf?ua=1.

———. 2014b. *Global Nutrition Targets 2025: Wasting Policy Brief*. Geneva: WHO. http://www.who.int/nutrition/publications/globaltargets2025_policybrief_wasting/en/.

———. 2014c. *Global Nutrition Targets 2025. Policy Brief Series*. Geneva: WHO. http://apps.who.int/iris/bitstream/10665/149018/1/WHO_NMH_NHD_14.2_eng.pdf?ua=1.

———. 2015 *Global Targets Tracking Tool*, http://www.who.int/nutrition/trackingtool/en/.

World Bank. 2006. *Repositioning Nutrition as Central to Development: A Strategy for Large-Scale Action*. Washington, DC: World Bank.

———. 2013. *Improving Nutrition through Multisectoral Approaches*. Washington, DC: World Bank.

CHAPTER 2

Overview of Methods

Jakub Kakietek, Julia Dayton Eberwein,
Dylan Walters, and Meera Shekar

Key Messages

- The total 10-year costs for scaling up key interventions are estimated for reaching the targets to reduce stunting among children and anemia in women, increase exclusive breastfeeding rates for infants, and mitigate the impact of wasting among children.
- For each of these four targets, the analyses cover the highest-burden countries; the results are extrapolated to all low- and middle-income countries.
- Data and methods derived from country-level costing are used to inform the analyses and determine the set of evidence-based interventions needed to meet each target.
- The impact of the additional investments on the prevalence of stunting, anemia in women, and rates of exclusive breastfeeding is estimated, along with the additional impacts on child mortality.
- Benefit-cost analyses are performed for each target individually, translating the results into benefits in terms of potential earnings gained over adult working life.

This chapter describes the general methodological approach used in estimating the costs and impacts of achieving the four World Health Assembly targets: stunting, anemia in women, and exclusive breastfeeding for infants, and mitigating the impact of wasting among young children. The methods for estimating benefit-cost ratios are also described. Target-specific methodological considerations are discussed in chapters 3 through 6. The methods used to estimate current and future financing scenarios are described separately in chapter 8.

Country Sample Selection

Although the nutritional status of women and children is a public health concern in many high-income countries, this report focuses on estimating the costs and impacts of achieving the World Health Assembly targets in low- and middle-income countries only, because this is where the burden is greatest. Concentrating on low- and middle-income countries allows for greater confidence in the estimates because information on cost, coverage, and service delivery modality in high-income countries are either not comparable or not readily accessible. Furthermore, the estimates generated here are intended to inform policy makers in low- and middle-income country governments that are considering investing in nutrition as well as official development assistance partners and philanthropic foundations that are developing investment strategies.

A sample of high-burden low- and middle-income countries is identified for each of the four targets. Figure 2.1 shows the proportion of the burden of stunting captured by a given number of countries. The figure indicates that 37 countries account for 85 percent of the global burden of stunting. On the basis of this assessment, a decision was made to systematically cut off the number of countries in the sample to a manageable number for the purpose of these analyses. Thus 37 countries are included for stunting, 26 for anemia, 27 for breastfeeding, and 24 for wasting (table 2.1). This approach allows global estimates to be developed more efficiently given the level of effort required to obtain often scant information on cost estimations and impacts.

Each sample includes the 20 countries with the highest burden of a given aspect of malnutrition (that is, the highest number of stunted children, of women of reproductive age suffering from anemia, of children under six months of age who were not exclusively breastfed, and of children under five years of age suffering from wasting). In addition, all countries with malnutrition burdens above a specific prevalence threshold are added to the respective sample of countries (see table 2.2 for threshold levels). This strategy for selecting the sample ensures that both large and small countries with high burdens of stunting are represented.

Figure 2.1 Incremental Percentage of the Global Burden of Stunting and Number of Additional Countries Included in the Analyses

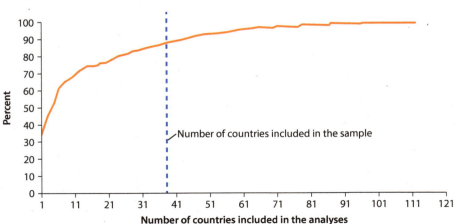

Source: IFPRI 2014.

Overview of Methods

Table 2.1 Number of Sample Countries, Percentage of Burden, and Multiplier Used to Extrapolate to All Low- and Middle-Income Countries

Target	Number of countries in the sample	Percentage of the global burden captured in the sample	Multiplier used to extrapolate the cost to estimate financing needs for all low- and middle-income countries
Stunting	37	84.3	1.19
Anemia	26	82.8	1.22
Breastfeeding	27	78.1	1.28
Wasting	24	82.9	1.21

Table 2.2 Countries Included in the Estimates of the Four Targets[a]

Global nutrition target (number of countries in the sample)	20 countries with highest absolute burden	Additional countries with highest/lowest prevalence[b]
Stunting (37 countries)	Bangladesh, China, Democratic Republic of Congo, Arab Republic of Egypt, Ethiopia, India, Indonesia, Kenya, Madagascar, Mexico, Mozambique, Myanmar, Nigeria, Pakistan, Philippines, Sudan, Tanzania, Uganda, Vietnam, Yemen	Benin, Burundi, Cambodia, Central African Republic, Eritrea, Guatemala, Lao PDR, Liberia, Malawi, Nepal, Niger, Papua New Guinea, Rwanda, Sierra Leone, Somalia, Timor-Leste, Zambia
Anemia (26 countries)	Bangladesh, Brazil, China, Democratic Republic of Congo, Arab Republic of Egypt, Ethiopia, India, Indonesia, Islamic Republic of Iran, Mexico, Myanmar, Nigeria, Pakistan, Philippines, South Africa, Tanzania, Thailand, Turkey, Uzbekistan, Vietnam	Republic of Congo, Gabon, Ghana, Mali, Senegal, Togo
Breastfeeding (27 countries)	Algeria, Bangladesh, Brazil, China, Côte d'Ivoire, Democratic Republic of Congo, Arab Republic of Egypt, Ethiopia, Iraq, India, Indonesia, Mexico, Myanmar, Nigeria, Pakistan, Philippines, Tanzania, Turkey, Vietnam, Yemen	Chad, Djibouti, Dominican Republic, Gabon, Somalia, Suriname, Tunisia
Wasting (24 countries)	Afghanistan, Bangladesh, China, Democratic Republic of Congo, Arab Republic of Egypt, Ethiopia, India, Indonesia, Iraq, Mali, Myanmar, Niger, Nigeria, Pakistan, Philippines, South Sudan, Sri Lanka, Sudan, Vietnam, Yemen	Chad, Djibouti, Eritrea, Timor-Leste

a. Stunting and wasting prevalence rates are from UNICEF, WHO, and World Bank 2015. Rates of anemia and exclusive breastfeeding are from WHO 2015.
b. For the stunting target, sample countries have a greater than 40 percent prevalence of stunting. For anemia in women, sample countries have a greater than 50 percent prevalence of anemia. For breastfeeding, sample countries have a less than 10 percent rate of exclusive breastfeeding. For wasting, sample countries have a greater than 15 percent prevalence of wasting.

An Investment Framework for Nutrition • http://dx.doi.org/10.1596/978-1-4648-1010-7

Table 2.1 lists the number of countries in each sample, the percentage of burden captured in the sample, and the multiplier used to extrapolate the sample cost to all low- and middle-income countries. Naturally there is overlap in country selection across target interventions. Twelve countries are included in all four samples, 3 are included in three samples, and 12 are included in two.

For the stunting target, estimates of financing needs are based on a sample of 37 countries. This includes 20 countries with the highest absolute burden (the highest number of stunted children) and an additional 17 countries with the highest stunting prevalence (a prevalence exceeding 40 percent, which is the WHO threshold for a "very high" stunting prevalence). These countries account for 84.3 percent of the global stunting burden. The sample for the anemia target consists of 26 countries (20 countries with the highest absolute burden and 6 countries with anemia prevalence higher than 50 percent) and accounts for 82.8 percent of the burden of anemia in women of reproductive age. The breastfeeding target sample consists of 27 countries (20 with the highest absolute burden and 7 countries with exclusive breastfeeding prevalence lower than 10 percent), which together account for 78.1 percent of the burden of non-exclusively breastfed children (0–5 months). The wasting target sample consists of 24 countries (20 countries with the highest absolute burden and 4 countries with wasting prevalence higher than 15 percent), together accounting for 82.9 percent of the burden of wasted children. The list of countries included in each sample for each target is shown in table 2.2.

Financing needs and impacts are estimated and modeled for each country. For each target, the results from the sample are then extrapolated to all low- and middle-income countries. It is assumed that the financing needs for countries outside the sample are proportional to their burden of malnutrition. For example, for the stunting target, the countries in the sample account for 84 percent of the burden of stunting in all low- and middle-income countries. Therefore it is assumed that they also account for 84 percent of the total costs. Consequently, the total cost is calculated for low- and middle-income countries by multiplying the sample cost by 1/0.84 or 1.19. This is clearly a simplification but it is consistent with the approach used in previous global nutrition costing studies (see Horton et al. 2010).

Financing needs are analyzed along two dimensions. The first is geographic. All low- and middle-income countries are grouped according to World Bank regions: Sub-Saharan Africa, Europe and Central Asia, East Asia and Pacific, Latin America and the Caribbean, Middle East and North Africa, and South Asia.[1] This geographic classification serves as a proxy for unobserved factors that may potentially affect the cost of delivering nutrition interventions (for example, development, infrastructure, and structural constraints). A classification based on geography is intuitive and has been used in the past in studies assessing the cost of implementation of nutrition interventions (Bhutta et al. 2008; Bhutta et al. 2013; Horton et al. 2010). Country income represents the second dimension for analyzing financing needs because wealth has been shown to be one of the key predictors of the cost of health service provision (Edejer et al. 2003). Variation in country wealth is examined using the World Bank country income groups: low-income, lower-middle-income, and upper-middle-income.[2]

Evidence-Based Interventions and Delivery Platforms

Two key principles guided the selection of interventions: (1) a strong evidence base must exist for effectiveness in reducing stunting in children under five years of age, reducing anemia in women of reproductive age, increasing exclusive breastfeeding, and reducing wasting;[3] and (2) the interventions must be relevant for a substantial portion of low- and middle-income countries or, as is the case with intermittent presumptive treatment of malaria in pregnancy, applicable across a specific region as a result of a high prevalence of malaria.

High-impact interventions are identified on the basis of the 2013 *Lancet* Series on Maternal and Child Nutrition and the 2016 *Lancet* Series on Breastfeeding. For stunting, wasting, and anemia, literature reviews were conducted to identify any additional evidence reviews and meta-analyses published after the publication of the *Lancet* series. The literature reviews do not identify any additional interventions that should be included in the study.

This report focuses on nutrition-specific interventions primarily because the evidence base for the impact of nutrition-sensitive interventions on stunting, anemia, breastfeeding, and wasting remains limited (Ruel et al. 2013), and therefore it is not feasible to cost these interventions, nor to fully assess their impact on the global targets. For some targets, the analyses incorporate the potential impact of nutrition-sensitive interventions for which there is evidence, but does not cost these because it is not possible to apportion a part of the cost to the nutrition outcomes specifically. For example, in the case of the water, sanitation and hygiene (WASH) interventions, even though the costs are known (Hutton 2015), because they include large infrastructure costs, it is not possible to determine what portion of these costs apply to their impact on stunting reduction. With the exception of the treatment of severe wasting, the analyses focus primarily on preventive interventions. Chapters 3 through 6 provide additional methodological details for each target.

Estimating Unit Costs on the Basis of Program Experience

The unit costs are estimated using the program experience approach where data were collected on the actual financing needs of programs, as in Horton et al. (2010) (table 2.3).[4] Unit cost data were obtained from peer-reviewed publications, gray literature, and costed national nutrition plans as well as primary data collected by the World Bank as part of a series of country-level costing studies from Sub-Saharan Africa (Shekar et al. 2014; Shekar, Dayton Eberwein, and Kakietek 2016; Shekar, Mattern, Eozenou, et al. 2015; Shekar, Mattern, Laviolette, et al. 2015). If no unit cost data are available for a given intervention in a given country, the mean unit cost for other countries in that region is used.

Table 2.3 Process for Estimating Unit Costs and Dealing with Missing Unit Cost Data

Step	Description
Step 1: Within country	• Select most recent unit costs • If a range is reported, the average of the reported range is used
Step 2: Within region	• Extrapolate unit cost data for countries where the data are missing using other countries in the same region for which data are available
Step 3: Across regions	• If data are missing for all countries in a region, extrapolate a regional unit cost estimate on the basis of application of regional unit cost multiplier • Use the estimate as the approximate unit cost for all countries in that region

If there are no unit cost data for any country in a given region, the unit costs are approximated by using the average from other regions and applying regional adjustment factors from Horton et al. (2010), if appropriate.

Assumptions on the Pace of Scale-Up

The analyses assume program coverage of each intervention increases at a constant rate over five years from current coverage rates in 2016 to 100 percent coverage rates in 2021, followed by a subsequent five-year maintenance phase with steady 100 percent program coverage between 2021 and 2025. This scale-up scenario is used to allow for the full accrual of the benefits of the interventions affecting stunting, which are delivered during the first five years of a child's life. In particular, full program coverage needs to be maintained for five years in order for the cohort of newborns to five-year-olds to fully accrue its benefits. Furthermore, the Lives Saved Tool (LiST)—the tool used to model the impact of the interventions—is a cohort model in which the likelihood of stunting depends on interventions, risk factors, and whether or not the child was stunted in the previous year. Because LiST is a cohort model, in a given year a child benefits from all interventions received in this year (direct impact of interventions) as well as interventions received in all previous years (indirect impact of interventions through reduced risk of stunting in previous years). Therefore, once all interventions are scaled up to maximum coverage, it will take five years for the cohort of newborns to accrue full benefits of the interventions.

This same pace of scale-up is used for the anemia and exclusive breastfeeding targets for two primary reasons. First, some of the interventions included in the stunting target are also included in the package of interventions needed to reach other targets (for example, counseling for mothers and caregivers on good infant and young child nutrition and hygiene practices for the exclusive breastfeeding target and antenatal micronutrient supplementation and intermittent presumptive treatment of malaria in pregnancy in malaria-endemic regions for the anemia target). Second, using the same assumptions about scale-up allows for easier aggregation and calculation of financing needs for a comprehensive intervention package (see chapter 7). However, because there is no overlap of interventions between stunting and the treatment of wasting, a linear scale-up from 2016 through 2025 is assumed for the treatment of severe wasting, as discussed in chapter 6.

To account for potential increases in marginal costs as program coverage approaches 100 percent (for example, more financing is required to access the hardest-to-reach groups), the approach adopted in Horton et al. (2010) is followed: the costs of 100 percent coverage are calculated, although the impact assessments assume that only 90 percent of the beneficiaries are reached for all interventions.

Estimating Total Financing Needs for Each Target

For each intervention in each country in each sample, the additional financing needs to scale up program coverage from the current level to 100 percent are estimated:

$$FN_y = UC * IC_y * Pop_y$$

where FN_y is the annual financing need for a given intervention in year y, UC is the unit cost, IC_y is the incremental coverage assumed for year y, and Pop_y is the target population in year y.

The total financing needs per intervention over the 10-year period are the sum of the annual financing needs. Total financing needs per country are the sum of the 10-year financing needs of all interventions for a given target. The total financing needs for the sample for each target are calculated by summing the country-level total 10-year financing needs. To take into account the program costs, an additional 9 percent of the estimate was added for capacity development, 2 percent for monitoring and evaluation, and 1 percent for policy development on top of the total direct financing needs. This assumption about the size of program costs follows the methodology used in Horton et al. (2010). However, making this blanket assumption is recognized as a limitation and an area where better data are needed.

To determine total financing needs, a multiplier equal to the inverse of the percentage of the target's burden contained in each target's country sample was applied to extrapolate the sample estimates to cover all low- and middle-income countries (see table 2.1).

Estimating Impacts

The impact analyses are based on LiST (LiST 2015) estimations. LiST is an epidemiological model for maternal and child health that allows users to estimate the impact of expanding the coverage of maternal and child health and nutrition interventions on mortality, morbidity, and the nutritional status of children under age five. LiST is used to model the impact of the interventions on stunting prevalence and on mortality in children under age five. LiST does not include interventions targeting nonpregnant women of reproductive age. It also does not model the impact of any of the interventions on that target group. Therefore a separate model was developed (using Microsoft Excel) to estimate the impact of anemia prevention interventions on the prevalence of anemia in women.

LiST is used to model mortality impacts for each intervention in each country in the samples. The country-specific results are then combined to obtain a population-weighted reduction in overall prevalence. The same relative prevalence change in low- and middle-income countries is assumed for all countries to which the results are extrapolated. The global reductions in prevalence of stunting and anemia, and the increase in exclusive breastfeeding rates, are estimated by applying these relative reductions in the sample to the 2015 baselines in all low- and middle-income countries (data from UNICEF, WHO, and World Bank 2015). For mortality reductions, the same multipliers that are used to extrapolate the financing needs are also used to estimate reductions in mortality for all low- and middle-income countries (see table 2.1).

Benefit-Cost Analyses

A benefit-cost analysis is an economic evaluation tool commonly used by policy makers, industry, and researchers to assess the monetary value of benefits of interventions relative to their costs. The benefit-cost ratios are computed in these analyses for all four targets.

For each target, maternal and child mortality averted are translated into expected earnings gains over adult working lives, up to age 65 or average country life expectancy at birth (whichever is lower). Similarly, the impact results (number of cases of stunting averted and additional children exclusively breastfed) are also translated into benefits in terms of expected earnings gained over adult working life via improvements in cognitive development. Estimations of expected increases in income as a result of the prevention of stunting are based on Hoddinott et al. (2013) and those as a result of increases in income are from Rollins et al. (2016). Reductions in anemia in women are translated into earnings gained via increased productivity within the years the intervention was received, based on methods employed in Horton and Ross (2003). Specific assumptions about these benefits are explained in chapters 3 through 6.

Beneficiary earnings projections are based on gross domestic product (GDP) per capita; labor share of income; and, for anemia, the percent share of all work that is manual labor. In an effort to keep the estimates conservative, a 3 percent per year GDP growth rate is assumed for all low- and middle-income countries, even though the average annual GDP growth rate for the countries in this sample has been approximately 5 percent over the past decade (World Bank 2016).[5] It is assumed that a maximum of 90 percent of earnings gains could be realized (Hoddinott et al. 2013) and that labor wages are responsible for 52 percent of gross national income (Lübker 2007).

Discounting is needed in this analysis because there may be up to a 65-year gap between incurring costs and yielding some of the benefits of investments in nutrition. However, the appropriate discount rate to use continues to be a topic of debate. Guidelines from the World Health Organization's Choosing Interventions that are Cost-Effective project (WHO-CHOICE) (Edejer et al. 2003) and, more recently, the Bill & Melinda Gates Foundation's Methods in Economic Evaluation Project (BMGF 2014) both advise that the base case scenarios in economic evaluations of health interventions assume a 3 percent discount rate for both costs and benefits. Three percent is argued to reflect the cost of public sector borrowing of capital at market rates (Hoddinott 2016; Wethli 2014). Recent work on economic evaluations pertaining to reducing the impact of climate change over the next hundred or more years has proposed social discount rates as low as 1.4 percent would be appropriate (Stern 2008) or time-varying discount rates that decline after many years and affect future generations (Arrow et al. 2012; Hoddinott 2016; Sunstein and Weisbach 2008). For the analyses in this report, benefit-cost ratios are presented for a base case scenario using a 3 percent discount rate on costs and benefits, as per the existing guidelines, as well as a 5 percent discount rate in the sensitivity analyses to parallel recent seminal nutrition economic analyses (Hoddinott 2016; Horton and Hoddinott 2014; Rajkumar, Gaukler, and Tilahun 2012).

Results from these analyses are presented in multiple formats—median benefit-cost ratios among all countries in the sample, the pooled benefit-cost ratios of all countries, and the subgroup of pooled benefit-cost ratios for each region and income group—to allow the reader to interpret the results as appropriate for different contexts. More accurate estimates can be developed through country-level studies and ex post benefit-cost analyses of programs within specific country contexts.

Data Sources

Data on the baseline prevalence of stunting and wasting are from UNICEF, WHO, and World Bank (2015). Data on anemia and exclusive breastfeeding prevalence are from the Global Targets Tracking Tool data set (WHO 2015). Baseline intervention coverage data are from Demographic and Health Surveys (DHS) or from Multiple Indicator Cluster Surveys (MICS). The World Population Prospects 2015 (UN DESA 2015) is used to obtain population data, including the projected 2015 population baseline and projected population growth from 2016 through 2025. Data on GDP and population living under the poverty line are from the World Development Indicators database. Other sources specific to one target are declared in the target-specific chapters that follow.

An Investment Framework for Nutrition • http://dx.doi.org/10.1596/978-1-4648-1010-7

Notes

1. For a list of countries in each region, see https://datahelpdesk.worldbank.org/knowledgebase/articles/906519.
2. For a list of countries included in each World Bank income group, see https://datahelpdesk.worldbank.org/knowledgebase/articles/906519.
3. To effectively reach targets for stunting, anemia, and breastfeeding, selected interventions are all preventive. However, with the limited research on preventing wasting, only treatment interventions are selected for mitigating wasting.
4. The other main method for estimating unit costs is the ingredients approach, which constructs the cost of an ideal service delivery model based on the cost of required inputs. See Bhutta et al. 2013.
5. Calculations based on data from World Bank 2016.

References

Arrow, K., M. Cropper, C. Gollier, B. Groom, G. M. Heal, R. G. Newell, W. D. Nordhaus, R. S. Pindyck, W. A. Pizer, P. R. Portney, T. Sterner, R. S. J. Tol, and M. L. Weitzman. 2012. "How Should Benefits and Costs Be Discounted in an Intergenerational Context? The Views of an Expert Panel." RFF Discussion Paper 12–53, Resources for the Future, Washington, DC.

Bhutta, Z. A., T. Ahmed, R. E. Black, S. Cousens, K. Dewey, E. Glugliani, B. A. Haider, B. Kirkwood, S. S. Morris, H. P. S. Sachdeve, and M. Shekar. 2008. "What Works? Interventions for Maternal and Child Undernutrition and Survival." *The Lancet* 371 (9610): 417–40.

Bhutta, Z. A., J. K. Das, A. Rizvi, M. F. Gaffey, N. Walker, S. Horton, P. Webb, A. Lartey, and R. E. Black. 2013. "Evidence-Based Interventions for Improvement of Maternal and Child Nutrition: What Can Be Done and at What Cost?" *The Lancet* 382 (9890): 452–77.

BMGF (Bill & Melinda Gates Foundation). 2014. *Methods for Economic Evaluation Project (MEEP) Final Report*. NICE International. https://www.nice.org.uk/Media/Default/About/what-we-do/NICE-International/projects/MEEP-report.pdf.

Edejer, T., R. Baltussen, T. Adam, R. Hutubessy, A. Acharya, D. B. Evans, and C. J. L. Murray, eds. 2003. *Making Choices in Health: WHO Guide to Cost-Effectiveness Analysis*. Geneva: WHO.

Hoddinott, J. 2016. "The Economics of Reducing Malnutrition in Sub-Saharan Africa." Global Panel on Agriculture and Food Systems for Nutrition Working Paper. http://glopan.org/sites/default/files/Global_Panel_Working_Paper.pdf.

Hoddinott, J., H. Alderman, J. R. Behrman, L. Haddad, and S. Horton. 2013. "The Economic Rationale for Investing in Stunting Reduction." *Maternal and Child Nutrition* 9 (Suppl. 2): 69–82.

Horton, S., and J. Hoddinott. 2014. "Benefits and Costs of the Food Nutrition Targets for the Post-2105 Agenda." Copenhagen Consensus Center Working Paper, Copenhagen, Denmark. http://www.copenhagenconsensus.com/sites/default/files/food_security_and_nutrition_perspective_-_horton_hoddinott_0.pdf.

Horton, S., and J. Ross. 2003. "The Economics of Iron Deficiency." *Food Policy* 28 (1): 51–75.

Horton, S., M. Shekar, C. McDonald, A. Mahal, and J. K. Brooks. 2010. *Scaling Up Nutrition: What Will It Cost?* Directions in Development Series. Washington, DC: World Bank.

Hutton, G. 2015. "Benefits and Costs of the Water and Sanitation Targets for the Post-2015 Development Agenda." Copenhagen Consensus Center Working Paper. http://www.copenhagenconsensus.com/sites/default/files/water_sanitation_assessment_-_hutton.pdf.

IFPRI (International Food Policy Research Institute). 2014. *Global Nutrition Report 2014.* Washington, DC: IFPRI.

LiST (Lives Saved Tool). 2015. Baltimore, MD: Johns Hopkins Bloomberg School of Public Health, http://livessavedtool.org/.

Lübker, M. 2007. *Labour Shares.* Geneva: Policy Brief, Policy Integration Department, International Labour Office.

Rajkumar, A. S., C. Gaukler, and J. Tilahun. 2012. *Malnutrition in Ethiopia. An Evidence-Based Approach for Sustained Results.* Africa Human Development Series. Washington, DC: World Bank.

Rollins, N. C., N. Bhandari, N. Hajeebhoy, S. Horton, C. K. Lutter, J. C. Martines, E. G. Piwoz, L. M. Richter, and C. G. Victora. 2016. "Why Invest, and What It Will Take to Improve Breastfeeding Practices?" *The Lancet* 387 (10017): 491–504.

Ruel, M., H. Aldernal, the Maternal and Child Nutrition Study Group. 2013. "Nutrition-Sensitive Interventions and Programmes: How Can They Help Accelerate Progress in Improving Maternal and Child Nutrition?" *The Lancet* 382 (9890): 66–81.

Shekar, M., J. Dayton Eberwein, and J. Kakietek. 2016. "The Costs of Stunting in South Asia and the Benefits of Public Investments in Nutrition." *Maternal and Child Nutrition* 12 (Suppl 1): 186–95.

Shekar, M., M. Mattern, P. Eozenou, J. Dayton Eberwein, J. K. Akuoku, E. Di Gropello, and W. Karamba. 2015. "Scaling Up Nutrition for a More Resilient Mali: Nutrition Diagnostics and Costed Plan for Scaling Up." Health, Nutrition and Population (HNP) Discussion Paper, World Bank, Washington, DC.

Shekar, M., M. Mattern, L. Laviolette, J. Dayton Eberwein, W. Karamba, and J. K. Akuoku. 2015. "Scaling Up Nutrition in the DRC: What Will It Cost?" Health, Nutrition and Population (HNP) Discussion Paper, World Bank, Washington, DC.

Shekar, M., C. McDonald, A. Subandoro, J. Dayton Eberwein, M. Mattern, and J. K. Akuoku. 2014. "Costed Plan for Scaling Up Nutrition: Nigeria." Health, Nutrition and Population (HNP) Discussion Paper, World Bank, Washington, DC.

Stern, N. 2008. *The Economics of Climate Change: The Stern Review.* Cambridge, U.K.: Cambridge University Press. http://www.cambridge.org/ca/academic/subjects/earth-and-environmental-science/climatology-and-climate-change/economics-climate-change-stern-review.

Sunstein, C., and D. Weisbach. 2008. "Climate Change and Discounting the Future: A Guide for the Perplexed." Reg Markets Center Working Paper 08–19, Harvard Law School, Cambridge, MA. http://papers.ssrn.com/sol3/papers.cfm?abstract_id=1223448.

UN DESA (United Nations, Department of Economic and Social Affairs, Population Division). 2015. *World Population Prospects: The 2015 Revision.* Custom data acquired via http://esa.un.org/unpd/wpp/DataQuery/.

UNICEF, WHO, and World Bank (United Nations Children's Fund, World Health Organization, and World Bank). 2015. *Joint Child Malnutrition Estimates.* Global

Database on Child Growth and Malnutrition, http://www.who.int/nutgrowthdb/estimates2014/en/.

Wethli, K. 2014. "Benefit-Cost Analysis for Risk Management: Summary of Selected Examples." Background Paper for the *World Development Report 2014*, World Bank, Washington, DC. http://siteresources.worldbank.org/EXTNWDR2013/Resources/8258024-1352909193861/8936935-1356011448215/8986901-1380568255405/WDR15_bp_BenefitCost_Analysis_for_Risk_Management_Wethli.pdf.

WHO (World Health Organization). 2015. Global Targets Tracking Tool, http://www.who.int/nutrition/trackingtool/en/.

World Bank. 2016. World Development Indicators (database), World Bank, Washington, DC (accessed March 1, 2016), http://data.worldbank.org/data-catalog/world-development-indicators.

CHAPTER 3

Reaching the Global Target for Stunting

Meera Shekar, Jakub Kakietek, Julia Dayton Eberwein, Jon Kweku Akuoku, and Audrey Pereira

Key Messages

- Reaching the stunting target is feasible but will require large coordinated investments in key interventions and a supportive enabling environment.
- The analyses focus on key high-impact interventions with strong evidence of effectiveness in reducing stunting. Scale-up costs are estimated for a sample of 37 high-burden countries and extrapolated to all low- and middle-income countries. The Lives Saved Tool (LiST) is used to model the impact of scale-up on stunting.
- Scaling up high-impact interventions in all low- and middle-income countries, along with expected improvements in underlying determinants of undernutrition, would lead to a 40 percent decline in the number of stunted children by 2025 and allow the world to achieve the stunting target. The total financing needed to reach this target over 10 years is $49.5 billion.
- This scale-up in intervention coverage, along with improvements in underlying determinants, would result in 65 million fewer children stunted in 2025. Furthermore, those interventions would, over 10 years, prevent about 2.8 million deaths among children under age five.

Not only does stunting mean being short for one's age but recent evidence suggests that it is also a predictor of many other developmental constraints, including cognitive deficits and future economic opportunities. In 2012 the World Health Assembly agreed on a global target to reduce the number of stunted children under age five by 40 percent by 2025. This chapter describes the methods used to estimate the financing needs for achieving this target, the estimated resources required, and the impact those investments will be expected to have on nutrition, health, and economic outcomes.

Stunting Prevalence and Progress to Date

The World Health Organization (WHO) defines *stunting* as height (or length) that is two or more standard deviations below the global WHO child growth standards reference (WHO 2016).

As of 2015, 159 million children under age five were stunted, with the highest burden concentrated in low- and middle-income countries (map 3.1; UNICEF, WHO, and World Bank 2015). Since the 1990s, the worldwide prevalence of stunting declined from 40 percent to just under 24 percent in 2014. However, stark regional differences persist, with South Asia and Sub-Saharan Africa remaining above the global average both in terms of prevalence and numbers of stunted children (figure 3.1). Indeed, South Asia is home to the largest number of stunted children worldwide (figure 3.1; UNICEF, WHO, and World Bank 2015). Thirty-seven percent of all children under five were stunted in South Asia in 2014, although the share is down from 49 percent in 1990. Even though the prevalence of child stunting in Sub-Saharan Africa fell from 49 percent in 1990 to 35 percent in 2014, the total number of stunted children in Africa increased by 12.8 million during the same period as a result of high fertility rates and lower rates of decline in stunting in Africa as compared with other regions (figure 3.2).

Of all the regions, East Asia and Pacific have made the most progress in decreasing stunting. Stunting prevalence there fell by almost three-quarters, from 42 percent to 11 percent, and the number of stunted children decreased by 64 million between 1990 and 2014. Much of that decline, however, was driven by improvements in China, and many countries—such as Indonesia, the Lao People's Democratic Republic, and Cambodia—continue to carry very high

Map 3.1 Stunting Rates among Low- and Middle-Income Countries as of 2015

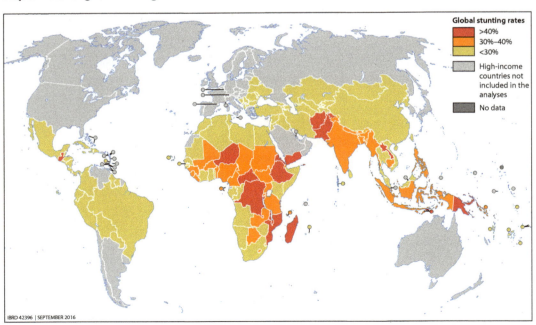

Source: Based on data from UNICEF, WHO, and World Bank 2015.

Reaching the Global Target for Stunting

Figure 3.1 Global and Regional Trends of Child Stunting under Age 5 Years, 1990–2014

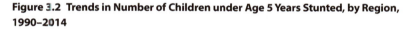

Source: UNICEF, WHO, and World Bank 2015.

Figure 3.2 Trends in Number of Children under Age 5 Years Stunted, by Region, 1990–2014

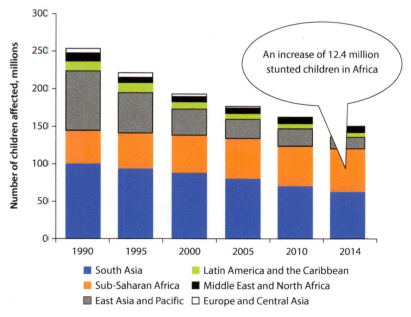

Source: UNICEF, WHO, and World Bank 2015.

An Investment Framework for Nutrition • http://dx.doi.org/10.1596/978-1-4648-1010-7

burdens of child stunting. Albeit more slowly than Asia, Europe, Latin America and the Caribbean and the Middle East and North Africa have also made considerable progress in decreasing stunting; and stunting prevalence in those regions remains well under the global average. The combined share of the number of stunted children for these three regions decreased from 30 percent to 14 percent between 1990 and 2014. On the basis of current global trends, approximately 127 million children under five will be stunted by 2025; the World Health Assembly goal is to decrease this number to no more than 100 million by 2025 (WHO 2014).

Not only do stunting rates remain high in many low- and middle-income countries, but stunting affects all echelons of society and the richest groups are not immune (figure 3.3). Across many low- and middle-income countries, a similar pattern emerges: stunting rates are highest among the poorest wealth quintiles but they are unacceptably high even in the highest wealth quintile. This finding

Figure 3.3 Stunting Rates, by Wealth Quintile, Selected Countries

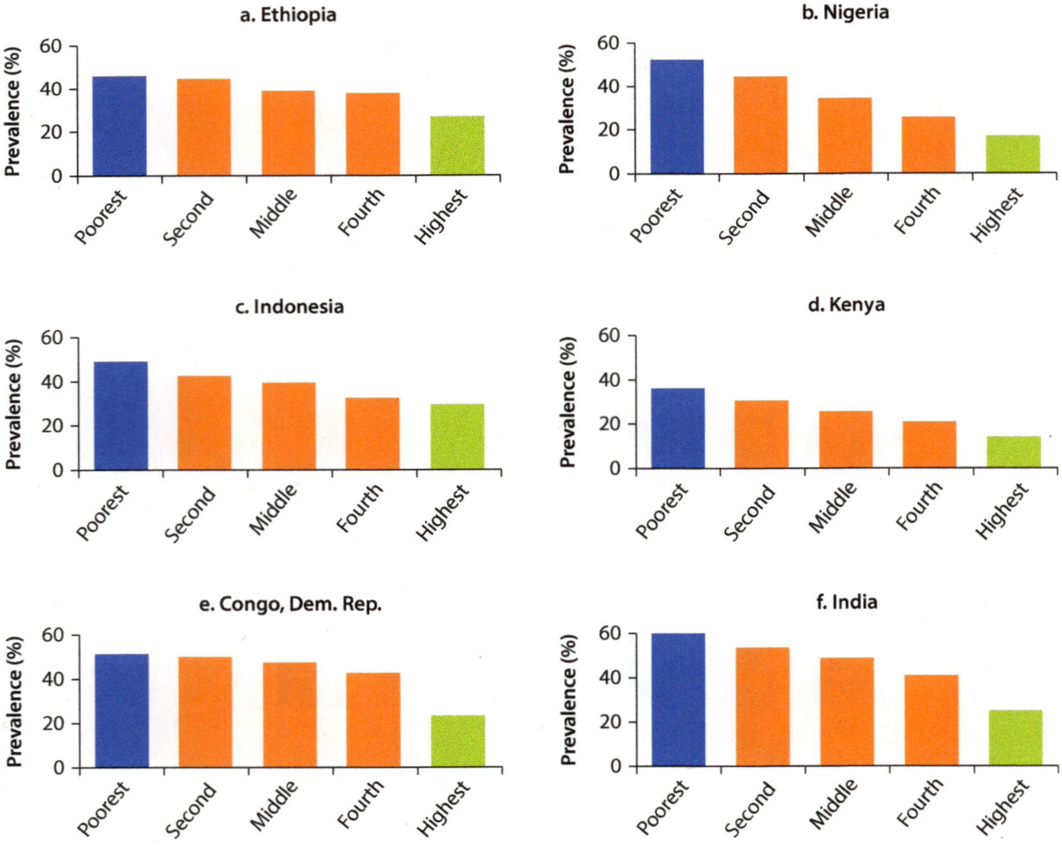

Source: UNICEF, WHO, and World Bank 2015.

debunks a commonly held view that stunting is caused by poverty alone. Instead, research shows that other factors, such as the burden of disease, access to adequate sanitation, food diversity, and optimal feeding and caregiving practices, also affect levels of stunting. Stunting-reduction strategies need to be designed with this in mind, so that free services that consume large public resources are targeted toward the poor while the better-off are provided better knowledge and information through traditional and social media.

The Effects of Stunting

Childhood stunting warrants serious policy attention because not only does it affect long-term health and cognitive ability but it is also inextricably linked to sustainable and equitable growth of a whole society. The societal costs of stunting during childhood are high and include increased mortality, increased morbidity (both in childhood and later in adulthood), decreased cognitive ability, poor educational outcomes, lost earnings, and losses to national economic productivity. Conversely, investing in nutrition provides many benefits for poverty reduction and economic growth. A recent National Academy of Medicine paper (Huebner et al. 2016) reports on the opportunities in the U.S. context: "the return on investments during the prenatal and early childhood years average between 7 and 10 percent greater than investments made at older ages" (Carneiro and Heckman 2003). "Although there are other opportunities to enhance human development, cost-effective strategic investments made during children's early years can mitigate the deleterious effects of poverty, social inequality, and discrimination, ultimately resulting in long-lasting gains that reap benefits for children and youth, families, communities, and nations" (Huebner et al. 2016, 1).

Increased Child Mortality and Morbidity

Stunting involves multiple pathological changes marked by linear growth retardation (low height-for-age z-score), which increases morbidity and mortality and decreases physical, neurodevelopmental, and economic capacity (Prendergast and Humphrey 2014). Malnutrition in the form of stunting, wasting, fetal growth retardation, suboptimum breastfeeding, and micronutrient deficiencies is an underlying cause of about 45 percent of the deaths of children under five years of age and one-fifth of maternal deaths in developing countries (Black et al. 2013). Furthermore, low gestational or preterm weight and suboptimal breastfeeding practices are among the main causes of neonatal deaths (Black et al. 2013). In several large studies reviewed by Prendergast and Humphrey (2014), a clear dose-response relationship could be seen between height-for-age z-scores and morbidity. Children with poor linear growth are more than 1.5 times more likely to contract respiratory infections and diarrhea; children with severe stunting are more than six times more likely to contract these conditions. Severely stunted children also have a threefold increased risk of mortality from other infections such as sepsis, meningitis, tuberculosis, hepatitis, and cellulitis (Prendergast and Humphrey 2014).

Irreversible Cognitive Damage and Diminished Educational Attainment

Conditions that give rise to stunting, such as poor feeding practices or persistent diarrhea, have detrimental effects on a child's brain by causing changes in the temporal sequence of brain maturation, which in turn disturb the formation of neural circuits (Udani 1992) and result in cognitive deficits (Kar, Rao, and Chandramouli 2008). Widespread evidence from a range of settings and using diverse empirical approaches indicates that malnutrition leads to negative educational outcomes. Stunted children are more likely to start school late and to repeat a grade or drop out of school (Daniels and Adair 2004; Mendez and Adair 1999). Martorell et al. (2010) show that adults who were stunted at age two completed one less year of schooling. Adair et al. (2013) estimate that improving linear growth for children under two years of age by one standard deviation adds about half a grade of school attainment. Behrman et al. (2009) report increased schooling attainment and higher test scores from improved nutrition in early childhood. In studying the provision of lipid-based nutrition supplements for malaria and diarrhea treatment, Prado et al. (2016) show that the intervention independently affected developmental scores, such as motor and language skills.

Links with Poverty

Stunting and poverty are interrelated and exacerbate each other. A recent study (Hoddinott et al. 2011) concludes that children who are not stunted at 36 months are one-third less likely to live in poor households as adults. Poverty increases the risk of stunting and other forms of undernutrition by lowering poor households' purchasing power, reducing access to basic health services, and exposing these households to unhealthy environments, thereby compromising food intake (both quality and quantity), reducing access to health services, and increasing exposure to infections. Poor households are also more likely to have frequent pregnancies, larger family sizes with high dependency ratios, more infections, and increased health care costs (Victora et al. 2003). At the same time, malnutrition contributes to poor health and poor cognitive development, resulting in poor human capital and long-term productivity losses (Horton and Steckel 2013).

Reduced Wages and Losses to GDP

Undernutrition costs developing countries billions of dollars in lost revenue through reduced economic productivity, particularly through lower wages, lower physical and mental capabilities, and more days away from work as a result of illness. At the individual level, childhood stunting is estimated to reduce a person's potential lifetime earnings by at least 10 percent (World Bank 2006). Other studies have shown that a 1 percent increase in adult height results in a 2.4 percent increase in earnings (Thomas and Strauss 1997). The economic costs of undernutrition have the greatest effect on the most vulnerable in the developing world. A recent analysis estimates these losses at 4–11 percent of gross domestic product (GDP) in Africa and Asia each year (Horton and Steckel 2013)—equivalent to about $149 billion of productivity losses each year. Most of those losses are due to cognitive deficits. Another recent study by Lin, Lutter, and Ruhm (2016) shows that cognitive performance is positively linked to future labor market outcomes in terms of increased lifetime earnings. Fink et al. (2016) also find that growth faltering in children from developing countries leads to 0.5 years lost in educational attainment, resulting in global economic losses of more than $175 billion and average loss of lifetime earnings of $1,400 per child. As the world moves from economies based on unskilled manual labor to ones based on skilled labor requiring high mental capacity, the impact of childhood stunting and other forms of undernutrition on incomes and economies will likely increase. Because stunting is concentrated in low- and middle-income countries, it will weigh heavily on the ability of these countries to benefit from technological progress and catch up with high-income countries, potentially further exacerbating global income inequalities.

Interventions That Reduce Stunting

The etiology of stunting is complex. It is caused by the lack of appropriate quality and quantity of foods, repeated bouts of disease, and/or poor birth outcomes including low birthweight and preterm delivery, which in turn may result from poor feeding behaviors and poor nutrition knowledge on the part of parents and caregivers, poor sanitation and hygiene, lack of access to health care services, low purchasing power of the household, insufficient supply of appropriate quality foods in the market, and other factors (Black et al. 2013). Preventing stunting therefore requires multifaceted and multisectoral approaches. To date the evidence base regarding the most effective strategies remains a work in progress.

There is strong evidence regarding interventions that affect the proximal determinants of stunting—the *nutrition-specific* interventions. Two *Lancet* Series on Maternal and Child Nutrition (in 2008 and 2013) provide a summary of global evidence based on systematic literature reviews and meta-analyses. In contrast, the evidence base regarding the effectiveness of interventions that target more distal determinants of stunting (the *nutrition-sensitive* approaches) remains limited (see Ruel et al. 2013 for a review). Some evidence links poor water and sanitation to a greater incidence of diarrheal diseases, which is a risk factor for stunting (Bhutta et al. 2013). Evidence of the impact of nutrition-sensitive interventions on stunting—such as improving food security and dietary diversity as well as women's education and empowerment—is more limited. Therefore this chapter focuses primarily on the nutrition-specific interventions, as outlined by Bhutta et al. 2013, where the evidence is the strongest and allows for estimating both the costs of the interventions and their impact on nutrition outcomes, including stunting.

Interventions for Pregnant Women and Mothers of Infants and Young Children

Interventions for pregnant women, such as micronutrient supplementation, affect child stunting by improving fetal growth and reducing conditions effecting growth outcomes, such as iron deficiency anemia. Current evidence on the effectiveness of these interventions focuses primarily on birth outcomes rather than on the linear growth of children. Interventions included in this study are those with proven effectiveness. Other interventions that show great promise—such as small-quantity lipid-based nutrient supplements,[1] and the provision of deworming tablets to prevent parasitic and helminth diseases—can be added as the evidence base grows.

Antenatal micronutrient supplementation. Antenatal micronutrient supplementation consists of multiple micronutrient supplements, which are broadly characterized as containing more than two micronutrients.[2] The United Nations Children's Fund Multiple Micronutrient Preparation (UNICEF UNIMAP) supplement contains 14 micronutrients, including iron, folic acid, and vitamin A, at levels appropriate for daily intake during pregnancy. Although antenatal micronutrient supplements have been shown to reduce low birthweight and small-for-gestational-age births by 11–13 percent according to a Cochrane review (Haider and Bhutta 2015), other studies have shown little direct effect on child anthropometric outcomes, with the exception of child head circumference (Lu et al. 2014). Peña-Rosas et al. (2015) found that giving pregnant women any supplementation with iron increases birthweight in infants by over 20 grams as compared to giving no supplements or supplements without iron. Nonetheless, antenatal micronutrient supplements are a low-cost and feasible way to provide essential micronutrients to improve birth outcomes, which in turn reduce the risk of stunting (Haider and Bhutta 2015). In this analysis, financing needs were estimated for antenatal micronutrient supplementation.

Counseling for mothers and caregivers on good infant and young child nutrition and hygiene practices. This intervention name is shortened throughout these analyses to *infant and young child nutrition counseling*. Optimal feeding of infants and young children includes immediate initiation of breastfeeding, early and exclusive breastfeeding until six months of age, and age-appropriate complementary feeding from 6 to 24 months with continued breastfeeding until two years of age. Good infant and young child feeding and hygiene practices are promoted at various levels: health facilities, community/home settings, and through mass media campaigns. Health facilities are the main outlet for nutrition counseling, but community health workers play an immensely important role in reaching outlying and hard-to-reach areas where the most vulnerable live. Education on complementary feeding alone, in food insecure populations, has been shown to significantly improve linear growth (height-for-age Z-scores) and weight gain (weight-for-age Z-scores) and decrease stunting rates (Lassi et al. 2013). Breastfeeding promotion and resulting increases in exclusive breastfeeding rate affect stunting by reducing diarrhea incidence. The impact estimate used in this analysis comes from Lamberti et al. (2011) who presented the effects of suboptimal breastfeeding on diarrhea incidence.

Balanced energy-protein supplementation for pregnant women Balanced energy-protein supplements refer to food supplements that contain less than 25 percent protein as their total energy content; they are intended for pregnant women who are undernourished or at risk of becoming undernourished, and promote gestational weight gain and improve birth outcomes. The 2013 *Lancet* Series on Maternal and Child Malnutrition reports a 34 percent reduction in the risk of small-for-gestational-age babies and stillbirths from 16 studies. Furthermore, data from five studies demonstrate a 32 percent reduction in the risk of low birthweight, with effects more clearly pronounced in undernourished women than in adequately nourished women (Imdad and Bhutta 2012). More recently, Ota et al. (2015) found an increase in mean birthweight and a significant reduction in the incidence of infants born small for gestational age with balanced energy protein supplementation.

Intermittent presumptive treatment of malaria in pregnancy in malaria-endemic regions. The WHO recommends at least two doses, preferably four, of intermittent presumptive treatment of malaria in pregnancy with sulfadoxine-pyrimethamine as part of routine antenatal care in areas of moderate to high malaria transmission, particularly Sub-Saharan Africa (WHO 2012). Trials of intermittent presumptive treatment of malaria in pregnancy in malaria-endemic regions to estimate their effect on birth outcomes have shown significant reductions in low birthweight and increases in mean birthweight of infants (Garner and Gülmezoglu 2006; Radeva-Petrova et al. 2014), which in turn have significant effects on stunting. Further studies have also shown that, among first and second pregnancies in malaria-prevalent areas, prevention interventions such as intermittent presumptive treatment of malaria in pregnancy were found to have a pooled protective efficacy of 35 percent on reducing low birthweight (Eisele, Larsen, and Steketee 2010). Although this intervention stands out as the only nonnutrition intervention included in the analyses, its significant impacts on birth outcomes, and thus on stunting, justifies its inclusion.

Interventions for Infants and Young Children

Vitamin A supplementation for children. Vitamin A deficiency causes visual impairment and blindness among children, and contributes to diarrheal diseases and child mortality. The WHO recommends the provision of 100,000 international units (IU) of vitamin A for infants 6–11 months of age, and 200,000 IU of vitamin A every four to six months for children age 12–59 months, in settings where night-blindness prevalence is 1 percent or higher among children 24–59 months, or where vitamin A deficiency is 20 percent or higher in infants and children age 6–59 months (WHO 2011). A Cochrane systematic review of 43 randomized controlled trials and cluster randomized controlled trials in community settings found no effect of vitamin A supplementation on linear growth (Imdad et al. 2010). However, vitamin A indirectly influences stunting, by reducing diarrheal incidence, and the effects of vitamin A supplementation on diarrhea-specific mortality among children have been well documented. Within the same systematic review, several of the trials reported a 30 percent reduction in diarrhea-specific child mortality with preventive vitamin A supplementation (Imdad et al. 2010). Results from an evaluation of 21 studies show that vitamin A supplementation reduces all-cause mortality in children 6–59 months by 25 percent and reduces diarrhea-specific mortality by 30 percent in children 6–59 months (Imdad et al. 2011).

Prophylactic zinc supplementation. Zinc is an important micronutrient that is associated with immune function, cellular growth and differentiation, and metabolism. A systematic review of 36 randomized controlled trials shows that mean height increased significantly, by 0.37 centimeters, and diarrheal incidence decreased by 13 percent in children who received prophylactic zinc supplementation for 24 weeks (Imdad et al. 2011). At present, the WHO does not have any specific recommendations on preventive zinc supplementation.

Public provision of complementary food for children. Interventions to ensure adequate nutrient intake for children 6–24 months of age can provide anywhere from 100 to 1,500 additional calories, as well as essential micronutrients, to improve height-for-weight z-scores in these children. Imdad, Yakoob, and Bhutta (2011) found that complementary food supplements with or without nutrition counseling, significantly improves weight and height z-scores. Furthermore, the provision of complementary food, with or without education, can reduce stunting by 67 percent in food-insecure populations (Lassi et. al. 2013).

Analytic Approaches Specific to the Stunting Target

This section considers the methods used in the analysis that are specific to the stunting target, looking at the applicable interventions, assumptions about delivery, the selection of sample countries, and the sources of data used as well as methods used to estimate impact. For more detail on methodology, see chapter 2.

Interventions Included in the Analyses

Seven key interventions have strong evidence of effectiveness in reducing stunting. Table 3.1 shows the pathways and estimates of the impact each intervention has on the likelihood of stunting. Four of these interventions are directed at pregnant women and mothers of infants and young children; three are directed at infants and young children (table 3.1). For women, antenatal micronutrient supplementation and infant and young child nutrition counseling would be scaled up for all pregnant women, balanced energy-protein supplementation would be scaled up for all pregnant women living under the poverty line, and intermittent presumptive treatment of malaria would be scaled up only for pregnant women living in malaria-endemic regions.[3] Vitamin A supplementation and prophylactic zinc supplementation would be scaled up for all children 6–59 months of age, and the public provision of complementary food would be scaled up for all children living under the poverty line. The *poverty line* is defined as persons living on less than $1.90 per day (World Bank 2009).[4]

Assumptions about Delivery Platforms

Several of the interventions—infant and young child nutrition counseling, vitamin A supplementation for children, and intermittent presumptive treatment of malaria in pregnancy in malaria-endemic regions—have existing large-scale delivery platforms that could be scaled up to increase coverage rates to full coverage. For other interventions, however, there is little experience with large-scale programming and so assumptions have been made about delivery platforms. For prophylactic zinc supplementation for children, for the purposes of these analyses, zinc is assumed to be delivered in a manner similar to that of multiple

Table 3.1 Interventions to Reach the Stunting Target

Intervention	Target population	Description and delivery method	Evidence of effectiveness
For pregnant women and mothers of infants and young children			
Antenatal micronutrient supplementation[a]	Pregnant women	Includes iron and folic acid, and at least one additional micronutrient, for approximately 180 days per pregnancy. Delivered as part of antenatal care.	Recent reviews of multiple micronutrient supplementation (Haider and Bhutta 2015) show significant reductions in low birthweight and small-for-gestational age of 10 percent (or effectiveness 0.10).
Infant and young child nutrition counseling	Mothers of children 0–23 months old	This intervention comprises individual or group-based counseling sessions to promote exclusive breastfeeding delivered in the community and/or health facility, depending on country context.	Reanalysis by Sinha et al. (2015) for LiST shows that receiving breastfeeding promotion increased exclusive breastfeeding in infants age 0–5 months [OR 2.5 in health system, OR 2.61 in home/community setting]. Lamberti et al. (2011) shows that infants 0–5 months had an increased relative risk of diarrhea if they are predominantly breastfed [RR 1.26, 95% CI 0.81–1.95], partially breastfed [RR 1.68, 95% CI 1.03–2.76], or not breastfed at all [RR 2.65, 95% CI 1.72–4.07]. Children 6–23 months have more than twice the risk of diarrhea if not breastfed at all [RR 2.07, 95% CI 1.49–2.88].
Balanced energy-protein supplementation for pregnant women[a]	Undernourished pregnant women living under the poverty line ($1.90/day)	This intervention provides food supplementation during pregnancy to at-risk women (with no more than 25 percent energy content contributed by proteins). Some existing delivery mechanisms are through community-based programs.	This intervention reduces the risk of low-birthweight infants and infants born small for gestational age, and as such has an indirect impact on stunting. Ota et al. (2015) have found an increase in mean birthweight [MD +40.96 g, 95% CI 4.66–77.26] and a significant reduction in the incidence of infants born small for gestational age [RR 0.79, 95% CI 0.69–0.90] with balanced energy-protein supplementation.
Intermittent presumptive treatment for malaria in pregnancy in malaria-endemic regions	Pregnant women (in malaria-endemic regions only)	This intervention provides at least two doses of sulfadoxine-pyrimethamine during pregnancy. Delivered as part of antenatal care.	Among first and second pregnancies in malaria-prevalent areas, prevention interventions such as intermittent presumptive treatment for malaria in pregnancy are found to have a pooled protective efficacy of 35 percent [95% CI 23–45%] on reducing low birthweight (Eisele, Larsen, and Steketee 2010).

table continues next page

Table 3.1 Interventions to Reach the Stunting Target *(continued)*

Intervention	Target population	Description and delivery method	Evidence of effectiveness
For infants and young children			
Vitamin A supplementation for children	Children 6–59 months old	This intervention distributes two doses per year (100,000 international units (IU) for children age 6–11 months and 200,000 IU for children age 12–59 months), either through mass campaigns or in health facilities.	Vitamin A indirectly affects stunting by influencing diarrheal incidence and mortality. Vitamin A supplementation has been shown to reduce diarrhea-specific incidence [RR 0.85, 95% CI 0.82–0.87; 13 studies] and mortality [RR 0.72, 95% CI 0.57–0.91; 7 studies] (Imdad et al. 2011).
Prophylactic zinc supplementation for children[a]	Children 6–59 months old	This intervention provides zinc (10 mg/day); 120 packets per child per year. Currently no delivery platforms exist at scale. Delivery cost estimates are based on costs to deliver multiple micronutrient powder supplementation programs.	Supplementation with 10 mg zinc/day for 24 weeks increases mean gain in height (cm) [0.37, 95% CI 0.12–0.62; 16 studies] compared with a placebo intervention (Imdad and Bhutta 2011). Zinc supplementation also reduces diarrheal incidence [RR 0.87, 95% CI 0.81–0.94] in the intervention group compared with a control group (Yakoob et al. 2011).
Public provision of complementary foods for children	Children 6–23 months old living under the poverty line ($1.90/day)	Food supplementation for children (100–1,500 kcal per day), typically including micronutrients. Some existing delivery mechanisms are through community-based programs.	Bhutta et al. (2008) find that, in food secure settings, 6–12 month old children of mothers who are not given nutrition education are 1.43 times more likely to become stunted. In food insecure settings, complementary food supplements with or without maternal nutrition education increases child stunting OR to 1.60; and no supplements or education further increases child stunting OR to 2.39.

Note: CI = confidence interval; kcal = kilocalories; MD = mean difference; OR = odds ratio; RR = relative risk; SMD = standard mean difference.
a. This intervention was awaiting updated WHO guidelines as of late 2016.

micronutrient supplementation through community-based programs. Antenatal micronutrient supplementation is assumed to be delivered through existing antenatal and postnatal services. Balanced energy-protein supplementation for pregnant women could be delivered through existing food distribution and/or social safety net programs.

Sample Selection

Stunting cost estimates are based on a sample of 37 countries, which includes 20 countries with the highest absolute burden (the number of stunted children) and additional 17 countries with the highest stunting prevalence (a prevalence exceeding 40 percent, which is the WHO threshold for a "very high" stunting prevalence) (see table 2.2 for the list of countries). The 20 countries with the highest absolute burden account for 77 percent of the burden worldwide and the 17 countries with the highest prevalence account for an additional 7 percent, so taken together this sample accounts for 84 percent of the global burden of stunting.

Data Sources

Population and population growth estimates are obtained from the UNDP World Population Prospects (UN DESA 2015a, 2015b). Current intervention coverage data are extracted from the most recent Demographic and Health Surveys. Current coverage for antenatal micronutrient supplementation, balanced energy-protein supplementation for pregnant women, and prophylactic zinc supplementation is assumed to be 0 percent because no countries implement those interventions at scale. The cost and impact of intermittent presumptive treatment of malaria in pregnancy in malaria-endemic regions are estimated only for Sub-Saharan Africa, where malaria incidence is high enough to justify this intervention.

Estimating Impact

The additional effect of the seven nutrition interventions on stunting prevalence is modeled using LiST. The specific pathways and effect estimates used in LiST are shown in figure 3.4. Overall, 37 country models are estimated and the results are combined to obtain a population-weighted reduction in the overall prevalence in the sample of countries. The same relative prevalence change is assumed to occur in the remaining low- and middle-income countries not included in the sample. Reductions in the number of stunted children in all low- and middle-income countries are calculated by applying the relative reduction in the number of stunted children in the sample to the 2014 baseline estimate of the global number of stunted children worldwide—159 million (UNICEF, WHO, and World Bank 2015).

The impact of a scale-up of interventions is estimated in terms of (1) the number of cases of stunting prevented in 2025 as compared with the 2015 baseline; (2) the percent reduction in the number of children who are stunted; and (3) the number of deaths among children averted.

It is widely recognized that linear growth is affected by both direct and indirect or underlying factors, and that improvements in the underlying determinants of malnutrition will lead to reductions in stunting prevalence. As such, the model estimates additional reductions in stunting that would be accrued from improvements in food availability and food diversity; in women's health status, education, and empowerment; and in water, sanitation, and hygiene (WASH).

For the WASH interventions, the impact on stunting was estimated using LiST for five interventions: handwashing with soap, improved excreta disposal, improved water source, hygienic disposal of children's stool, and water connection at home.

Figure 3.4 The Lives Saved Tool and Underlying Model Used to Estimate Impact on Stunting

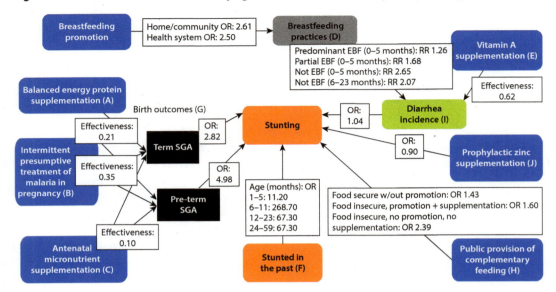

Sources: (A) balanced energy-protein supplementation: Ota et al. 2015; (B) intermittent presumptive treatment of malaria in pregnancy: Eisele, Larsen, and Steketee 2010; (C) antenatal micronutrient supplementation: Haider and Bhutta 2015; Haider, Yakoob, and Bhutta 2011; (D) breastfeeding practices: Lamberti et al. 2011; (E) vitamin A supplementation: Imdad et al. 2011; (F) stunted in the past: LiST default values based on expert opinion; (G) birth outcomes: LiST default values based on expert opinion; (H) public provision of complementary food: Bhutta et al. 2008; (I) diarrhea incidence: Bhutta et al. 2008; (J) prophylactic zinc supplementation: Bhutta et al. 2013; Yakoob et al. 2011.

For each of the 37 countries in the sample, a linear expansion of coverage is modeled from the level exhibited in 2016 to 90 percent in 2021 and maintenance of the 90 percent coverage from 2021 to 2025. These interventions were not included in the analysis of total financing needs because of the inability to proportionately allocate these costs to nutrition programming. Costs for WASH and other nutrition-sensitive interventions are likely much higher than those for the nutrition-specific interventions, and including them without proper apportionment will probably skew the costing estimates.

The magnitude of the impact of the improvements in other underlying conditions, such as food availability and food diversity, women's health status, education, and empowerment, could not be directly estimated using LiST. Recognizing that changes in these conditions will also make a significant contribution to achieving the World Health Assembly stunting target, their impact was approximated using estimates from Smith and Haddad (2015). Smith and Haddad use a country-level regression model to assess the impact of food availability (measured as average daily kilocalories consumed per capita), food diversity (measured as the percentage of total diet derived from nonstaples), women's education (measured as female secondary enrollment rate), and women's health and empowerment (measured as female-to-male life expectancy ratio) on country-level stunting prevalence. For each of the 37 countries in the sample, a trend is calculated in each of the four variables on the basis of the changes over the previous five years (2011–15), with the assumption that the same trend will continue over the 10-year period 2016–25. Using the regression coefficients reported in Smith and Haddad, reductions in stunting during 2016–25, expected if the previous five-year trend continues, are calculated. Data on women's secondary enrollment and female-to-male life expectancy ratio are from the World Development Indicators (WDI) database. Data on food availability and diversity are extracted from the Food and Agriculture Organization (FAO) food balance sheets.

The potential reductions in stunting that result from improvement in WASH and the other underlying determinants are combined with the estimates from the 37 models to obtain a population-weighted reduction in the overall prevalence in the sample of countries.

Benefit-Cost Analyses

Benefits of the scale-up of the key nutrition-specific interventions are calculated based on estimates of lives saved and cases of stunting averted obtained from the LiST model (see figure 3.4). In the base case scenario, one life saved at age five was valued as GDP per capita. One case of stunting averted is valued at 21 percent of GDP per capita based on estimates of the impact of childhood stunting on adult wages (Hoddinott et al. 2013); this result is adjusted to account for the proportion of income from wages (see chapter 2 for detailed methodology).

The economic benefits are approximated in all low- and middle-income countries using the same methods used to approximate the cost: multiply the total benefits by the inverse of the total proportion of the stunting burden in the 37 high-burden countries included in the sample (see chapter 2 for details). The benefit-cost ratio is calculated by dividing the total discounted monetary benefits that will accrue to the beneficiaries over their lifetime by the total discounted scale-up costs. As described in chapter 2, a 3 percent discount rate is used for both costs and benefits; in the sensitivity analysis, the discount rate is varied to 5 percent.

Results

This section presents the results of the analysis of the interventions described above for stunting, including costs, impacts, and benefit-cost analysis.

Unit Costs

Summary measures of the unit costs by intervention are shown in table 3.2. Micronutrient supplementation (vitamin A and prophylactic zinc for children and antenatal micronutrient supplementation) have the lowest unit costs, each at less than $4 a year (or $4 per pregnancy in the case of antenatal micronutrients). The unit cost for intermittent presumptive treatment of malaria in pregnancy in malaria-endemic regions is equally low-cost: about $2 per pregnancy. The public provision of complementary food for children entails higher unit costs, but it is important to note that these interventions are much more narrowly targeted to

Table 3.2 Minimum, Maximum, and Mean Unit Costs for Interventions to Meet the Stunting Target (Annual)
US$

Intervention	Minimum	Maximum	Mean unit cost
For pregnant women and mothers of infants			
Antenatal micronutrient supplementation	1.80	7.55	2.80
Infant and young child nutrition counseling	0.07	12.00	6.62
Balanced energy-protein supplementation for pregnant women	16.93	54.72	24.07
Intermittent presumptive treatment of malaria in pregnancy in malaria-endemic regions	2.27	2.27	2.27
For infants and young children			
Vitamin A supplementation for children	0.03	4.81	0.32
Prophylactic zinc supplementation for children	2.40	6.19	3.89
Public provision of complementary foods for children	29.03	115.28	42.93

Note: The mean unit costs are population-weighted means.

those living under the poverty line. The cost of providing one year of public provision of complementary foods for children living in poverty is about $43 per year per child, and the cost for providing balanced energy-protein supplementation for pregnant women living in poverty is about $24. Appendix C provides detailed unit costs and data sources for each target.

Estimated Total Financing Needs

The total 10-year costs of scaling up the package of the seven interventions affecting stunting are estimated to be $49.5 billion (table 3.3). This includes $44.2 billion in direct service delivery and an additional $5.3 billion for monitoring and evaluations, capacity building, and policy development. Prophylactic zinc supplementation and the public provision of complementary food for young children together account for about 60 percent of the intervention costs (32 and 29 percent, respectively). Infant and young child nutrition counseling (including breastfeeding promotion and counseling on appropriate complementary feeding) account for some 15 percent of the total cost, and balanced-energy protein supplementation for 16 percent. Antenatal micronutrient supplementation, vitamin A supplementation for children, and intermittent presumptive treatment of malaria in pregnancy in malaria-endemic regions account for the remainder of the estimated direct scale-up costs (5 percent, 2 percent, and 1 percent, respectively).

During the five-year scale-up period (2016–20), the expected resource requirement is $16.3 billion; during the five-year maintenance phase (2021–25), an additional $33.1 billion would be required (figure 3.5) (for the rationale for the two phases of scale-up, see chapter 2).

About 50 percent of the estimated global cost ($23.5 billion) is needed for the scale-up of nutrition interventions in Sub-Saharan Africa (figure 3.6), with South

Table 3.3 Total Financing Needs to Meet the Stunting Target

Intervention	Total 10-year intervention costs (US$, millions)	Share of total 10-year cost (%)
For pregnant women and mothers of infants		
Antenatal micronutrient supplementation	2,309	5
Infant and young child nutrition counseling	6,823	15
Balanced energy-protein supplementation for pregnant women	6,949	16
Intermittent presumptive treatment of malaria in pregnancy in malaria-endemic regions	416	1
For infants and young children		
Vitamin A supplementation for children	716	2
Prophylactic zinc supplementation for children	14,212	32
Public provision of complementary foods for children	12,750	29
Subtotal	**44,175**	**100**
Program (monitoring and evaluation, capacity strengthening, and policy development)	5,301	n.a.
Total	**49,476**	n.a.

Note: n.a. = not applicable.

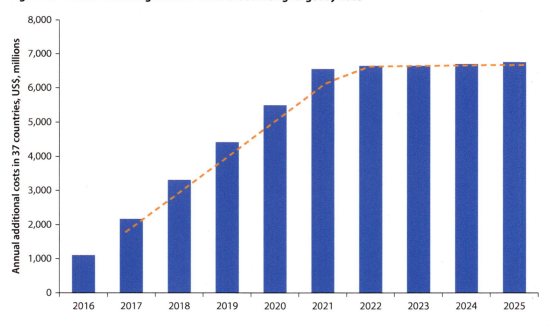

Figure 3.5 Annual Financing Needs to Meet the Stunting Target by 2025

Asia and East Asia and the Pacific each accounting for a little over 20 percent ($10.8 billion and $10.4 billion, respectively). Two countries, India and China, account for about a quarter of the global cost (26.3 percent) because of the large size of their populations of children under age five and pregnant women, the beneficiaries of the interventions included in the analyses.

An Investment Framework for Nutrition • http://dx.doi.org/10.1596/978-1-4648-1010-7

Figure 3.6 Ten-Year Total Financing Needs to Meet the Stunting Target, by Region

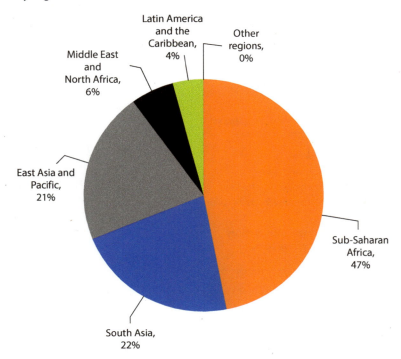

The costs in South Asia and other regions decrease from 2020 through 2025 even though the intervention coverage level is maintained through this period (see figure 3.7). This is because of the projected population declines with greater uptake of family planning programs and families having fewer children. In contrast, in Sub-Saharan Africa, the costs of these interventions increase over the same period of time because of projected population increases and slower uptake of family planning programs.

Low-income countries account for about 30 percent of the total scale-up cost (figure 3.8). Lower-middle income countries account for about 50 percent of the total scale-up cost, largely because three of the four countries with the largest populations (India, Nigeria, and Pakistan) are in that income group. Upper-middle-income countries account for about 20 percent of the total scale-up cost; this is mostly driven by China, because of its large population.

Estimated Impacts of the Scale-Up

Together, scaling up the key nutrition-specific interventions to 90 percent coverage along with expected improvements in the underlying determinants of stunting are estimated to lead to about a 40 percent decline in the number of stunted children by 2025, enabling the achievement of the global target for stunting (figure 3.9).

Reaching the Global Target for Stunting

Figure 3.7 Estimated Total Financing Needs to Meet the Stunting Target, by Region

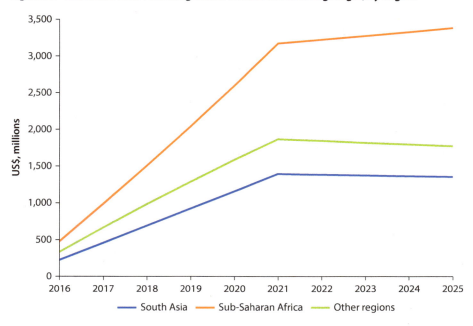

Figure 3.8 Ten-Year Total Financing Needs to Meet the Stunting Target, by Country Income Group

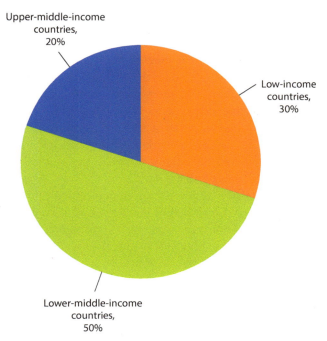

An Investment Framework for Nutrition • http://dx.doi.org/10.1596/978-1-4648-1010-7

Figure 3.9 Costs and Impacts of a 10-Year Scale-Up of Interventions to Reach the Stunting Target

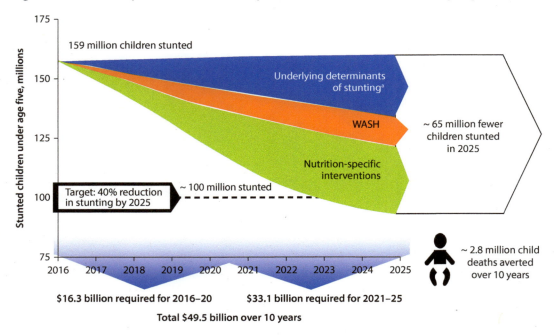

a. Includes food availability and diversity, women's education, women's empowerment and health, and water, sanitation and hygiene (WASH).

Scaling up nutrition-specific interventions would result in a reduction of 19.5 percent in the number of stunted children in the 37 high-burden countries by 2025.[5] The changes in the underlying determinants drive the remaining decline in stunting. Assuming a similar relative reduction in the other countries with the remaining 15.7 percent of the global stunting burden, this translates into 65 million fewer children stunted in 2025 than the 159 million children stunted in the beginning of 2015. In addition, the interventions would, over 10 years, prevent about 2.8 million deaths in children under five years of age.

Comparing the costs and impacts of specific interventions shows that the promotion of good infant and child nutrition and hygiene practices and vitamin A supplementation for children have the lowest cost per case of stunting averted ($273 and $266, respectively) (table 3.4).[6]

Despite having low relative impact on stunting prevalence (because vitamin A supplementation is modeled via diarrhea incidence), vitamin A supplementation is a very low-cost intervention, making it highly cost-effective. Other interventions, especially those targeting pregnant women (for example, balanced energy-protein supplementation for pregnant women) have a much higher cost per case of stunting averted and are relatively less cost-effective. It is also worth noting that some interventions that have a relatively high cost per case of stunting averted have a relatively low cost per death averted (for example, breastfeeding promotion) and vice versa (complementary feeding education). Chapter 7 offers

Reaching the Global Target for Stunting

Table 3.4 Total Costs, Cost per Case of Stunting Averted, and Cost per Death Averted

Intervention	Total 10-year costs (US$, billions)[a]	Cost per case of stunting averted (US$)	Cost per death averted (US$)
For pregnant women and mothers of infants			
Antenatal micronutrient supplementation	2.59	3,637	7,376
Infant and young child nutrition counseling (complementary feeding education and breastfeeding promotion)	7.64	467	7,353
Complementary feeding education	4.28	273	16,122
Breastfeeding promotion	3.36	4,761	4,347
Balanced energy-protein supplementation for pregnant women	7.78	29,949	37,054
Intermittent presumptive treatment of malaria in pregnancy in malaria-endemic regions	0.47	1,535	6,594
For infants and young children			
Vitamin A supplementation for children	0.8	266	4,270
Prophylactic zinc supplementation for children	15.92	988	23,642
Public provision of complementary food for children	14.28	1,724	67,787

Note: In this analysis, the two components of the infant and young child nutrition counseling—complementary feeding education and breastfeeding promotion—are evaluated separately and then together.
a. All intervention costs include additional 12 percent of overhead costs.

a more in-depth discussion of cost-effectiveness and technical and allocative efficiency of interventions targeting stunting and the other three nutrition targets considered in this report.

Benefit-Cost Analyses

Under the base case scenario, the scale-up of the key nutrition-specific interventions is estimated to generate about $417 billion in annual economic benefits over the productive lives of beneficiaries (discounted at 3 percent) in low- and middle-income countries. The bulk of the benefits (about 98 percent) would be the consequence of the cognitive losses avoided in children under age five and the resulting improvements in economic productivity. The remaining 2 percent would result from premature mortality averted by the interventions. Comparing those benefits with discounted costs yields a benefit-cost ratio of 10.5. This means that one dollar invested in stunting reduction will generate more than 10 dollars in economic returns.

Changing the discount rate from 3 percent to 5 percent changes the benefits from $417 billion to $172 billion over the productive lives of the beneficiaries, with a benefit-cost ratio varying from 10.5 to 5.0. The results are sensitive to discount rate changes because, although most of the costs are incurred immediately and are not much affected by discounting, most of the benefits accrue in the future and thus are affected by discounting much more than the costs (see table 3.5). However, it needs to be noted that, even

Table 3.5 Benefit-Cost Ratios of Scaling Up Interventions to Meet the Stunting Target, 3 and 5 Percent Discount Rates

	3% discount rate			5% discount rate		
Group	Present value benefit (US$, billions)	Present value cost (US$, billions)	Benefit-cost ratio	Present value benefit (US$, billions)	Present value cost (US$, billions)	Benefit-cost ratio
By region						
Sub-Saharan Africa[a]	66.8	15.8	4.2	26.3	13.7	1.90
South Asia[a]	121.4	8.0	15.1	50.6	7.0	7.2
East Asia and Pacific[a]	125.0	7.9	15.8	52.4	6.9	7.6
By country income group						
Low-income countries[a]	17.9	10.4	1.7	4.1	9.0	0.5
Lower-middle-income countries[a]	232.4	18.4	12.6	98.2	16.0	6.2
Upper-middle-income countries[a]	103.4	4.8	21.6	44.0	4.2	10.60
Pooled	**417.4**	**39.7**	**10.5**	**172.8**	**34.4**	**5.0**
Median			4.0			1.60

a. Sample countries only.

under the more conservative scenario with a 5 percent discount rate, the benefit-cost ratio remains very comfortably above 1, indicating that preventing stunting is a sound economic investment.

Discussion

The analyses make a number of important contributions to the existing literature. First, they provide estimates for the costs of reaching the global targets for stunting. They find that significant investments in both the high-impact interventions costed here and in underlying determinants of stunting are required in order to achieve the target.

Cost estimates are consistent with the extant literature (see table 3.6). Horton et al. (2010) combine hygiene promotion and community-level WASH behavior change interventions with breastfeeding promotion and complementary feeding education. This is probably why their total costs are higher than those estimated by Bhutta et al. (2013) and by our study. Also, the Horton et al. study includes the cost of iron supplementation in pregnancy rather than multiple micronutrient supplementation, which is the probably the reason that their estimates of the cost of this intervention are lower.

Unlike the two previous studies, which estimate the cost of scaling up from current coverage to 90 percent in one year, this study models more realistic scale-up over 10 years and incorporates the under-five population change dynamics. Bhutta et al. (2013) assumed these interventions would lead to a 20 percent reduction in stunting. In contrast, this study directly models the stunting decline in each country separately. For this reason, this model provides a more explicit

Reaching the Global Target for Stunting

Table 3.6 Comparison across Three Studies of Unit Costs and Annual Financing Needs for Nutrition Interventions

Intervention	Unit costs Horton et al. 2010	Unit costs Bhutta et al. 2013	Unit costs This report	Annual financing needs (US$, millions) Horton et al. 2010	Annual financing needs (US$, millions) Bhutta et al. 2013	Annual financing needs (US$, millions) This report
For pregnant women and mothers of infants						
Antenatal micronutrient supplementation	2.00	6.15	2.80	85	479	309
Infant and young child nutrition counseling	7.50	19.59	6.62	2,900	922	904
Balanced energy-protein supplementation for pregnant women	—	25.00	24.07	—	1,041	936
For infants and young children						
Vitamin A supplementation for children	1.20	2.85	0.32	130	106	96
Prophylactic zinc supplementation for children	—	4.20–5.90	3.89	—	1,182	1,893
Public provision of complementary food for children	40.00–80.00	50.00	42.93	3,600	1,359	1,722

Note: Intermittent presumptive treatment of malaria in pregnancy in malaria-endemic regions is not included in these above-mentioned studies because financing for this intervention is assumed to come from other health budgets; — = not available.

analysis of the declines in stunting prevalence over 10 years, rather than assuming a given level of decline.

Another difference from previous studies is that the estimates presented here show higher costs for Sub-Saharan Africa than for South Asia. This is mainly because, although the number of stunted children is greater in South Asia, the costs of addressing stunting are greater in Sub-Saharan Africa because of high unit costs, particularly costly food supplements. The estimated target populations are larger in Sub-Saharan Africa for two of the three most costly interventions: the public provision of complementary foods for young children and balanced energy-protein supplementation for pregnant women (see table 3.7).

The unit costs of nutrition interventions are assumed to be fixed over the coming decade. Future analyses should assess new delivery models that could reduce unit costs and help nutrition technologies and services become more efficient; this should be done through a combination of research and development, economies of scale, and changes in service delivery models. Some of the interventions costed here are ready for immediate scale-up, but there are binding constraints for others (see chapter 7 for a detailed discussion of binding constraints). For example, rates for vitamin A supplementation for children are already relatively high and could be scaled up to full coverage relatively easily.

There are some important limitations to the analyses presented above. The cost estimates focus on the impact of nutrition-specific interventions and

Table 3.7 Population Covered and Unit Costs to Meet the Stunting Target in the Full Sample, Sub-Saharan Africa, and South Asia

Intervention	Full sample — Population covered over 10 years (millions)	Full sample — Population-weighted average unit cost (US$)	Sub-Saharan Africa — Population covered over 10 years (millions)	Sub-Saharan Africa — Population-weighted average unit cost (US$)	South Asia — Population covered over 10 years (millions)	South Asia — Population-weighted average unit cost (US$)
For pregnant women and mothers of infants						
Antenatal micronutrient supplementation	698	2.80	222	3.49	255	1.82
Infant and young child nutrition counseling	874	6.62	280	5.96	330	4.78
Balanced energy-protein supplementation for pregnant women	245	24.07	136	25.00	81	16.93
Intermittent presumptive treatment of malaria in pregnancy in malaria-endemic regions	155	2.27	155	2.27	—	—
For infants and young children						
Vitamin A supplementation for children	1,916	0.32	391	0.62	782	0.09
Prophylactic zinc supplementation for children	3,092	3.89	899	4.61	1,135	2.40
Public provision of complementary food for children	252	42.93	132	53.65	95	29.03

Note: — = not available.

do not include nutrition-sensitive interventions—those delivered through sectors such as the agriculture, education, and WASH sectors that have the potential to have an impact on nutrition outcomes. The cost of improving women's health and education and the cost of food availability and diversity could not be estimated here because there are no specific and well-defined intervention packages to improve those outcomes. Although assumptions, informed by the literature, were made regarding how increasing female-to-male life expectancy by 0.1 may affect stunting prevalence, without a well-defined package of interventions it was not possible to estimate how much increasing female-to-male life expectancy by 0.1 would cost.

WASH interventions are an exception to this rule. Estimates of the impact of these interventions on diarrhea incidence are available and their indirect impact on child nutrition outcomes, including stunting, can be modeled. Therefore the LiST tool was used to model the impact of WASH interventions on stunting prevalence. The costs of scaling up WASH interventions have been estimated elsewhere (Hutton 2015). Those estimates are not included here, because—while indispensable for achieving the stunting target—expanding the coverage of the WASH interventions will be financed by the water and sanitation sector. It needs to be noted that the benefit-cost analyses presented above also do not include the impact of changes in the underlying determinants of undernutrition on stunting prevalence. Only costs and impacts of nutrition-specific interventions are included. The estimates generated in this report assume a relatively rapid scale-up of the interventions. Although this is ambitious, countries such as Peru and Senegal (see box 9.1 and box 9.2) have shown that it is feasible.

Notes

1. Despite some promising studies on small-quantity lipid-based nutrient supplements (Adu-Afarwuah et al. 2015; Ashorn et al. 2015), it is not clear which populations would benefit most from these supplements, nor are there global recommendations on its use. Furthermore, no large-scale production or distribution is yet available, leaving many cost and implementation issues unresolved. A World Bank–supported study on these lipid supplements is currently ongoing in Madagascar.
2. The intervention *antenatal micronutrient supplementation* is sometimes referred to by different names in the literature. Alternative names include *maternal micronutrient supplementation, multiple micronutrient supplementation in pregnancy, multiple-micronutrient supplementation for women during pregnancy*, and the acronyms *MMN, MNS*, and *MMS*.
3. For these analyses, all malaria-endemic countries are in the Sub-Saharan Africa region.
4. At the time the analysis was conducted, the poverty line set by the World Bank was $1.90. For more details, see http://www.worldbank.org/en/topic/poverty/brief/global-poverty-line-faq.
5. The model incorporates a country-specific population growth of children under five years of age.
6. In this analysis, the two components of the promotion of good infant and young child nutrition and hygiene practices—complementary feeding education and breastfeeding promotion—are evaluated separately and then together. The low cost per case of stunting averted is driven largely by complementary feeding education.

References

Adair, L. S., C. H. Fall, C. Osmond, A. D. Stein, R. Martorell, M. Ramirez-Zea, H. S. Sachdev, D. L. Dahly, I. Bas, S. A. Norris, and L. Micklesfield. 2013. "Associations of Linear Growth and Relative Weight Gain during Early Life with Adult Health and Human Capital in Countries of Low and Middle Income: Findings from Five Birth Cohort Studies." *The Lancet* 382 (9891): 525–34.

Adu-Afarwuah, S., A. Lartey, H. Okronipa, P. Ashorn, M. Zeilani, J. M. Peerson, M. Arimond, S. Vosti, and K. G. Dewey. 2015. "Lipid-Based Nutrient Supplement Increases the Birth Size of Infants of Primiparous Women in Ghana." *The American Journal of Clinical Nutrition* 101 (4): 835–46.

Ashorn, P., L. Alho, U. Ashorn, Y. B. Cheung, K. G. Dewey, U. Harjunmaa, A. Lartey, M. Nkhoma, N. Phiri, J. Phuka, S. A. Vosti, M. Zeilani, and K. Maleta. 2015. "The Impact of Lipid-Based Nutrient Supplement Provision to Pregnant Women on Newborn Size in Rural Malawi: A Randomized Controlled Trial." *The American Journal of Clinical Nutrition* 101 (2): 387–97. doi:10.3945/ajcn.114.088617.

Behrman, J. R., M. C. Calderon, S. H. Preston, J. Hoddinott, R. Martorell, and A. D. Stein. 2009. "Nutritional Supplementation in Girls Influences the Growth of their Children: Prospective Study in Guatemala." *The American Journal of Clinical Nutrition* 90 (5): 1372–79.

Bhutta, Z. A., T. Ahmed, R. E. Black, S. Cousens, K. Dewey, E. Glugliani, B. A. Haider, B. Kirkwood, S. S. Morris, H. P. S. Sachdeve, and M. Shekar. 2008. "What Works? Interventions for Maternal and Child Undernutrition and Survival." *The Lancet* 371 (9610): 417–40.

Bhutta, Z. A., J. K. Das, A. Rizvi, M. F. Gaffey, N. Walker, S. Horton, P. Webb, A. Lartey, and R. E. Black. 2013. "Evidence-Based Interventions for Improvement of Maternal and Child Nutrition: What Can Be Done and at What Cost?" *The Lancet* 382 (9890): 452–77.

Black, R. E., C. G. Victora, S. P. Walker, Z. A. Bhutta, P. Christian, M. de Onis, M. Ezzati, S. Grantham-Mcgregor, J. Katz, R. Martorell, R. Uauy, and the Maternal and Child Nutrition Study Group. 2013. "Maternal and Child Undernutrition and Overweight in Low-Income and Middle-Income Countries." *The Lancet* 382: 427–51.

Carneiro, P. M., and J. J. Heckman. 2003. "Human Capital Policy." IZA Discussion Paper 821 Institute for the Study of Labor (IZA), Bonn. http://papers.ssrn.com/sol3/papers.cfm?abstract_id=434544.

Daniels, M. C., and L. S. Adair. 2004. "Growth in Young Filipino Children Predicts Schooling Trajectories Through High School." *The Journal of Nutrition* 134 (6): 1439–46.

Eisele, T. P., D. Larsen, and R. W. Steketee. 2010. "Protective Efficacy of Interventions for Preventing Malaria Mortality in Children in Plasmodium Falciparum Endemic Areas." *International Journal of Epidemiology* 39 (1): i88–i101.

Fink, G., E. Peet, G. Danaei, K. Andrews, D. C. McCoy, C. R. Sudfeld, M. C. Smith Fawzi, M. Ezzati, and W. W. Fawzi. 2016. "Schooling and Wage Income Losses Due to Early-Childhood Growth Faltering in Developing Countries: National, Regional, and Global Estimates." *The American Journal of Clinical Nutrition* 104 (1): 104–12.

Garner, P., and A. M. Gülmezoglu. 2006. "Drugs for Preventing Malaria in Pregnant Women." *Cochrane Database of Systematic Reviews* 4 (CD000169).

Haider, B. A., and Z. A. Bhutta. 2015. "Multiple-Micronutrient Supplementation for Women during Pregnancy." *Cochrane Database of Systematic Reviews* 11 (November): CD004905.

Haider, B. A., M. Y. Yakoob, and Z. A. Bhutta. 2011. "Effect of Multiple Micronutrient Supplementation during Pregnancy on Maternal and Birth Outcomes." *BMC Public Health* 11 (Suppl 3): S19.

Hoddinott, J., H. Alderman, J. R. Behrman, L. Haddad, and S. Horton. 2013. "The Economic Rationale for Investing in Stunting Reduction." *Maternal and Child Nutrition* 9 (2): 69–82. doi:10.1111/mcn.12080.

Hoddinott, J., J. Maluccio, J. R. Behrman, R. Martorell, P. Melgar, A. R. Quisumbing, M. Ramirez-Zea, R. D. Stein, and K. M. Yount. 2011. "The Consequences of Early Childhood Growth Failure over the Life Course." IFPRI Discussion Paper 01073, International Food Policy Research Institute, Washington, DC.

Horton, S., M. Shekar, C. McDonald, A. Mahal, and J. Krystene Brooks. 2010. *Scaling Up Nutrition: What Will It Cost?* Directions in Development Series. Washington, DC: World Bank.

Horton, S. and R. Steckel. 2013. "Malnutrition: Global Economic Losses Attributable to Malnutrition 1900–2000 and Projections to 2050." In *The Economics of Human*

Challenges, edited by B. Lomborg, 247–72. Cambridge, U.K.: Cambridge University Press.

Huebner, G., N. Boothby, J. L. Aber, G. L. Darmstadt, A. Diaz, A. S. Masten, H. Yoshikawa, I. Redlener, A. Emmel, M. Pitt, L. Arnold, B. Barber, B. Berman, R. Blum, M. Canavera, J. Eckerle, N. A. Fox, J. L. Gibbons, S. W. Hargarten, C. Landers, C. A. Nelson III, S. D. Pollak, V. Rauh, M. Samson, F. Ssewamala, N. St. Clair, L. Stark, R. Waldman, M. Wessells, S. L. Wilson, and C. H. Zeanah. 2016. "Beyond Survival: The Case for Investing in Young Children Globally." Discussion Paper, National Academy of Medicine, Washington, DC.

Hutton, G. 2015. "Benefits and Costs of the Water and Sanitation Targets for the Post-2015 Development Agenda." Water and Sanitation Assessment Paper. Copenhagen Consensus Center Working Paper. http://www.copenhagenconsensus.com/sites/default/files/water_sanitation_assessment_-_hutton.pdf.

Imdad, A., and Z. A. Bhutta. 2011. "Effect of Preventive Zinc Supplementation on Linear Growth in Children under 5 Years of Age in Developing Countries: A Meta-Analysis of Studies for Input to the Lives Saved Tool." *BMC Public Health* 11 (Suppl 3): S22.

———. 2012. "Maternal Nutrition and Birth Outcomes: Effect of Balanced Protein-Energy Supplementation." *Paediatric and Perinatal Epidemiology* 26: 178–90.

Imdad, A., K. Herzer, E. Mayo-Wilson, M. Y. Yakoob, and Z. A. Bhutta. 2010. "Vitamin A Supplementation for Preventing Morbidity and Mortality in Children from 6 Months to 5 Years of Age." *Cochrane Database of Systematic Reviews* 12: CD008524.

Imdad, A., M. Y. Yakoob, and Z. A. Bhutta. 2011. "Impact of Maternal Education about Complementary Feeding and Provision of Complementary Foods on Child Growth in Developing Countries." *BMC Public Health* 11 (3): S25.

Imdad, A., M. Y. Yakoob, C. R. Sudfeld, B. A. Haider, R. E. Black, and Z. A. Bhutta. 2011. "Impact of Vitamin A Supplementation on Infant and Childhood Mortality." *BMC Public Health* 11 (3): S20.

Kar, B. R., S. L. Rao, and B. A. Chandramouli. 2008. "Cognitive Development in Children with Chronic Protein Energy Malnutrition." *Behavioral and Brain Functions* 4 (1): 1.

Lamberti, L. M., C. L. Fischer Walker, A. Noiman, C. Victora, and R. E. Black. 2011. "Breastfeeding and the Risk for Diarrhea Morbidity and Mortality." *BMC Public Health* 11 (Suppl 3): S515.

Lassi, Z. S., G. S. Zahid, J. K. Das, and Z. A. Bhutta. 2013. "Impact of Education and Complementary Feeding on Growth and Morbidity of Children Less than 2 Years of Age in Developing Countries: A Systematic Review." *BMC Public Health* 13 (3): S13.

Lin, D., R. Lutter, and C. Ruhm. 2016. "What Are the Effects of Cognitive Performance on Labor Market Outcomes?" University of Virginia, July. http://batten.virginia.edu/sites/default/files/research/attachments/The%20Effects%20of%20Cognitive%20Performance%20on%20Labor%20Market%20Outcomes_final2.pdf.

LiST (Lives Saved Tool). 2015. Baltimore, MD: Johns Hopkins Bloomberg School of Public Health (accessed December 31, 2015). http://livessavedtool.org/

Lu, W. P., M. S. Lu, Z. H. Li, and C. X. Zhang. 2014. "Effects of Multimicronutrient Supplementation during Pregnancy on Postnatal Growth of Children under 5 Years of Age: A Meta-Analysis of Randomized Controlled Trials." *PLoS One* 9 (2): e88496.

Martorell, R., B. L. Horta, L. S. Adair, A. D. Stein, L. Richter, C. H. D. Fall, S. K. Bhargava, S. K. Dey Biswas, L. Perez, F. C. Barros, C. G. Victora, and Consortium on Health Orientated Research in Transitional Societies Group. 2010. "Weight Gain in the First Two Years of Life Is an Important Predictor of Schooling Outcomes in Pooled Analyses from Five Birth Cohorts from Low- and Middle-Income Countries." *The Journal of Nutrition* 140: 348–54.

Mendez, M. A., and L. S. Adair. 1999. "Severity and Timing of Stunting in the First Two Years of Life Affect Performance on Cognitive Tests in Late Childhood." *The Journal of Nutrition* 129 (8): 1555–62.

Ota, E., H. Hori, R. Mori, R. Tobe Gai, and D. Farrar. 2015. "Antenatal Dietary Education and Supplementation to Increase Energy and Protein Intake (Review)." *The Cochrane Library*.

Peña-Rosas, J. P., L. M. De-Regil, M. N. Garcia-Casal, and T. Dowswell. 2015. "Daily Oral Iron Supplementation during Pregnancy." *Cochrane Database of Systematic Reviews* 12: CD004736.

Prado, E. L., K. Maleta, P. Ashorn, U. Ashorn, S. A. Vosti, J. Sadalaki, and K. G. Dewey. 2016. "Effects of Maternal and Child Lipid-Based Nutrient Supplements on Infant Development: A Randomized Trial in Malawi." *The American Journal of Clinical Nutrition* 103 (3): 784–93.

Prendergast, A. J., and J. H. Humphrey. 2014. "The Stunting Syndrome in Developing Countries." *Paediatrics and International Child Health* 34 (4): 250–65.

Radeva-Petrova, D., K. Kayentao, F. O. ter Kuile, D. Sinclair, and P. Garner. 2014. "Drugs for Preventing Malaria in Pregnant Women in Endemic Areas: Any Drug Regimen versus Placebo or No Treatment." *Cochrane Database of Systematic Reviews* 10: CD000169.

Ruel, M. T., H. Alderman, and Maternal and Child Nutrition Study Group. 2013. "Nutrition-Sensitive Interventions and Programmes: How Can They Help to Accelerate Progress in Improving Maternal and Child Nutrition?" *The Lancet* 382 (9891): 536–51.

Sinha, B., R. Chowdury, M. J. Sankar, J. Martines, S. Taneja, S. Mazumder, N. Rollins, R. Bahl, and N. Bhandari. 2015. "Interventions to Improve Breastfeeding Outcomes: A Systematic Review and Meta-Analysis." *Acta Pediatrica* 104 (467): 114–34.

Smith, L. C., and L. Haddad. 2015. "Reducing Child Undernutrition: Past Drivers and Priorities for the Post-MDG Era." *World Development* 68: 180–204.

Thomas, D., and J. Strauss. 1997. "Health and Wages: Evidence on Men and Women in Urban Brazil." *Journal of Econometrics* 77: 159–85.

Udani, P. M. 1992. "Protein Energy Malnutrition (PEM), Brain and Various Facets of Child Development." *The Indian Journal of Pediatrics* 59 (2): 165–86.

UN DESA (United Nations, Department of Economic and Social Affairs), Population Division. 2015a. "World Population Prospects: The 2015 Revision, Key Findings and Advance Tables." Working Paper ESA/P/WP.241.

———. 2015b. *World Population Prospects: The 2015 Revision*. Custom data acquired via http://esa.un.org/unpd/wpp/DataQuery/.

UNICEF, WHO, and World Bank (United Nations Children's Fund, World Health Organization, and World Bank). 2015. *Joint Child Malnutrition Estimates*. Global Database on Child Growth and Malnutrition, http://www.who.int/nutgrowthdb/estimates2014/en/.

Victora, C. G., A. Wagstaff, J. A. Schellenberg, D. Gwatkin, M. Claeson, and J. P. Habicht. 2003. "Applying an Equity Lens to Child Health and Mortality: More of the Same Is Not Enough." *The Lancet* 362 (9379): 233–41.

WHO (World Health Organization). 2011. *Guideline: Vitamin A Supplementation in Infants and Children 6–59 Months of Age.* Geneva: WHO.

———. 2012. "Updated WHO Policy Recommendation (October 2012): Intermittent Preventive Treatment of Malaria in Pregnancy Using Sulfadoxine-Pyrimethamine (IPTp-SP)." http://www.who.int/malaria/iptp_sp_updated_policy_recommendation_en_102012.pdf.

———. 2014. *Comprehensive Implementation Plan on Maternal, Infant, and Young Child Nutrition.* Geneva: WHO. http://apps.who.int/iris/bitstream/10665/113048/1/WHO_NMH_NHD_14.1_eng.pdf?ua=1.

———. 2016. *Nutrition Topics, Moderate Malnutrition.* http://www.who.int/nutrition/topics/moderate_malnutrition/en/.

World Bank. 2006. *Repositioning Nutrition as Central to Development: A Strategy for Large-Scale Action.* Washington, DC: World Bank.

———. 2009. *Knowledge in Development Note: Measuring Global Poverty.* Washington, DC: World Bank. http://econ.worldbank.org/WBSITE/EXTERNAL/EXTDEC/EXTRESEARCH/0,,contentMDK:22452035~pagePK:64165401~piPK:64165026~theSitePK:469382,00.html#comparisons_over_time.

Yakoob, M. Y., E. Theodoratou, A. Jabeen, A. Imdad, T. P. Eisele, J. Ferguson, A. Jhass, I. Rudan, H. Campbell, R. E. Black, and Z. A. Bhutta. 2011. "Preventive Zinc Supplementation in Developing Countries: Impact on Mortality and Morbidity Due to Diarrhea, Pneumonia and Malaria." *BMC Public Health* 11 (3): S23.

CHAPTER 4

Reaching the Global Target for Anemia

Dylan Walters, Jakub Kakietek, Julia Dayton Eberwein, and Meera Shekar

Key Messages

- Anemia is a condition where red blood cells in the body are not able to deliver oxygen to tissues. This leads to a higher risk of infections and impaired cognitive function and physical work capacity. Maternal anemia is associated with intrauterine growth restriction. The three particularly vulnerable groups are pregnant women (age 15–49 years), nonpregnant women (age 15–49), and preschool children (age 6–59 months).
- Interventions to prevent anemia in pregnant and nonpregnant women include antenatal micronutrient supplementation, intermittent presumptive treatment of malaria in pregnancy in malaria-endemic regions, iron and folic acid supplementation for nonpregnant women of reproductive age, and staple food fortification.
- Achieving the global target of reducing anemia in women of reproductive age would require $12.9 billion over 10 years. This includes scaling up micronutrient interventions for nonpregnant women to unprecedented levels, and thus will require strong political will and effective delivery platforms.
- At full scale-up, investment in these four key interventions will prevent 265 million cases of anemia in women in 2025 compared to 2015 and reduce anemia prevalence to 15.4 percent among all pregnant and nonpregnant women of reproductive age, averting nearly 600,000 child deaths. Preventive treatment for malaria in pregnant women, in particular, will prevent 7,000–14,000 maternal deaths.
- The net return on this investment in low- and middle-income countries is $110.1 billion over 10 years for women and over the productive lives of child beneficiaries with a pooled benefit-cost ratio of 12.1.

Anemia is a widespread public health problem with vast human, social, and economic consequences. In 2012, the World Health Assembly called for a 50 percent reduction of anemia among women of reproductive age (15–49 years), including both nonpregnant and pregnant women (WHO and 1,000 Days 2014).[1] This chapter reports on the costs of scaling up a set of key interventions necessary to reach the anemia target, the impact of reaching the target, and potential returns on investments.

Anemia and Its Effects

Anemia is defined as a low concentration of hemoglobin in the blood or a low red blood cell (also called erythrocyte) count. This condition inhibits the delivery of oxygen to the body's tissues. Anyone can be affected by anemia, although children and women of reproductive age in low- and middle-income countries are at highest risk.

Anemia can result in adverse health and developmental effects, including maternal and perinatal mortality, intrauterine growth restriction, and low birthweight of newborns. The morbidity associated with anemia in women of reproductive age can lead to lower work productivity as a result of impaired cognitive functioning and higher risk of infections and reduced physical work capacities (WHO 2004, Stevens et al. 2013; WHO 2015b; WHO and 1,000 Days 2014).

In 2011 the global prevalence of anemia was estimated to be 29 percent for nonpregnant women and 38 percent for pregnant women—over half a billion women in total. Among these women, it is estimated that 19 million nonpregnant and 750,000 pregnant women suffer from severe anemia (see table 4.2). Even though the prevalence of anemia in women has declined by 12 percent since 1995, it remains a moderate to severe public health problem in 142 of 182 World Health Organization (WHO) member states (Stevens et al. 2013; WHO 2015b; WHO and 1,000 Days 2014).

Causes of Anemia

The determinants of anemia (see figure 4.1) cover the spectrum of political, social, and economic factors as well climate change and food diversity (Balarajan et al. 2011). Poorer and less-educated women are more likely to be anemic, which, in turn, can be a strong predictor of child anemia status. The WHO estimates that, because iron deficiency is the most common direct cause of anemia, half of the world's anemia burden in women could be eliminated with iron supplementation (WHO 2015b). It is estimated that the prevalence of iron deficiency anemia alone is 19 percent in pregnant women and 18 percent in children under five years of age around the world (Black et al. 2013). The remaining cases are attributable to a number of other nutritional causes (for example, folate, vitamin B12, and vitamin A deficiencies) and non-nutritional causes (for example, hookworm, sickle-cell, thalassemia, malaria, chronic infection, schistosomiasis, genetic conditions, and so on) (Kassebaum et al. 2014; Stevens et al. 2013).

Interventions That Effectively Prevent Anemia

The 2013 *Lancet* Series on Maternal and Child Nutrition costed and recommended the scale-up of one intervention—multiple micronutrient supplementation—to prevent anemia in pregnancy, but did not address the issue of anemia in the broader nonpregnant population (Bhutta et al. 2013). In order to achieve the

Reaching the Global Target for Anemia

Figure 4.1 Conceptual Model of Determinants of Anemia

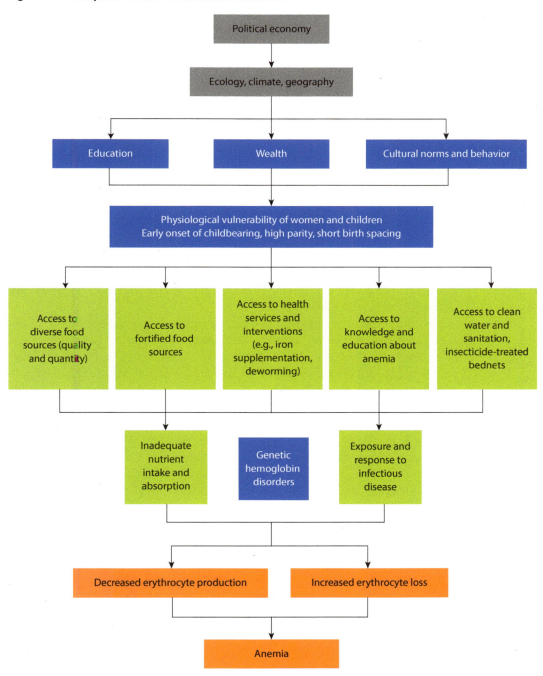

Source: Balarajan et al. 2011, p. 2125, © Elsevier. Reproduced with permission from Elsevier; further permission required for reuse.

new global target for anemia, a multisectoral approach for both pregnant women and the larger nonpregnant population of women is needed, plus efforts to address other underlying determinants of anemia, such as poverty, a lack of education, lack of dietary diversity, and gender equity.

Micronutrient Supplementation

It is estimated that approximately half of anemia in high-burden countries is the result of iron deficiency, but figures may vary by context. A Cochrane review of daily iron supplementation during pregnancy estimates a 70 percent reduction in anemia among pregnant women (Peña-Rosas et al. 2012). Antenatal multiple micronutrient supplements, such as the United Nations Children's Fund (UNICEF) Multiple Micronutrient Preparation (UNIMAP) supplement that contains 14 micronutrients, may provide additional benefits to neonatal outcomes and early childhood stunting, although there is no difference in its effectiveness for reducing maternal anemia compared to iron and folic acid supplementation (Haider and Bhutta 2015). Therefore, despite the two to three times higher costs, prioritizing the scale-up of antenatal multiple micronutrient supplementation may deliver the best long-term benefits for both mother and child.

For nonpregnant women, an intermittent (weekly) dosage of iron and folic acid supplementation is estimated to lead to a 27 percent reduction of anemia (Fernández-Gaxiola and De-Regil 2011; WHO 2011a). In areas of high prevalence (greater than 40 percent), the WHO recommends daily iron supplementation for this group (WHO 2016). Table 4.1 shows recommended dosages for nonpregnant and pregnant women based on country anemia prevalence.

Three other emerging supplementation interventions have been considered to address anemia, but these are not yet recommended by WHO for full scale-up. Micronutrient powders were found to have effects similar to those of multiple micronutrient supplementation (WHO 2011b) and WHO guidelines for scaling up supplements are forthcoming. Small quantity lipid-based nutrient supplements also had effects similar to iron and folic acid supplementation in some

Table 4.1 Recommended Iron and Folic Acid Dosages for Nonpregnant and Pregnant Women

Target population	Country anemia prevalence (%)	Iron and folic acid dosage
Nonpregnant women age 15–49	>40	Daily 30–60 mg elemental iron[1]
	>20	Weekly 60 mg iron + 2.8 mg folic acid[2]
Pregnant women	>40	Daily 60 mg iron + 0.4 mg folic acid[3]
	<40	Daily 30–60 mg elemental iron + 0.4 mg folic acid[3]
Non-anemic pregnant women	<20	Weekly 120 mg elemental iron + 2.8 mg folic acid[4]
Women diagnosed with anemia in clinical setting	All settings	Daily 120 mg elemental iron and 0.4 mg folic acid[2]

Sources: 1. WHO 2016; 2. WHO 2011a; 3. WHO 2012a; 4. WHO 2012b.
Note: mg = milligrams.

studies, but evidence of effectiveness is not yet conclusive (Choudhury et al. 2012; Suchdev, Peña-Rosas, and De-Regil 2015). Furthermore, evidence of the effect of vitamin A supplementation on anemia in adolescents and pregnant women remains mixed (Michelazzo et al. 2013). Because these interventions have not yielded significant results, there are no WHO guidelines for scaling these up as yet.

Food-Based Interventions

Food-based approaches—mainly through the fortification of staple grains and cereals and, less commonly, salt, sauces, and milk products—have also shown to be effective in reducing anemia in women (Gera, Sachdev, and Boy 2012). However, less is known about the impact of these interventions at scale. Fortification of wheat flour with iron and other micronutrients—which include zinc, folic acid, and B vitamins—is mandatory in 81 countries, some of which also require fortification of maize flour. Although Pachon et al. (2015) found limited effectiveness of flour fortification reducing prevalence of anemia in women, another review found that countries that fortify wheat flour at WHO guideline levels, after controlling for the level of development as measured by the Human Development Index and for malaria prevalence, yield a 2.4 percent reduction in the odds of anemia in nonpregnant women per year compared with countries that do not fortify (Barkley, Wheeler, and Pachon 2015). Therefore fortification can prove beneficial for large-scale reduction in anemia in general populations, and particularly among nonpregnant women.

Interventions to improve iron intake through greater dietary diversity of food produced on the homestead, biofortification, and increasing meal frequency may have potential for future impact but are difficult to measure and have limited evidence of impact at scale to date (Cercamondi et al. 2013; Olney et al. 2009).

Treatment of Diseases and Infections

In areas of moderate-to-high risk of malaria transmission, particularly Sub-Saharan Africa, WHO guidelines recommend that all pregnant women receive intermittent presumptive treatment in pregnancy with sulfadoxine-pyrimethamine at each scheduled antenatal care visit starting as early in the second trimester as possible, but coverage remains low (WHO 2014). Intermittent presumptive treatment of malaria in pregnancy has shown to reduce the risk of moderate-to-severe anemia by 40 percent and the risk of any anemia by about 17 percent among women in their first or second pregnancy (Radeva-Petrova et al. 2014). Evidence suggests that the use of insecticide-treated bed nets to prevent malaria during pregnancy reduces anemia by 5–12 percent, but these results are not statistically significant (Gamble, Ekwaru, and ter Kuile 2006). Overall, preventing anemia by reducing malaria transmission can be an effective intervention for pregnant women. Although hookworm infection and human immunodeficiency virus (HIV) are associated with anemia, deworming and antiretroviral therapy have not been shown to reduce anemia.[2]

Analytic Approaches Specific to the Anemia Target

This section lays out the methods used in the analyses that are specific to estimating the financing needs, impact, and benefit-cost ratios of reaching the anemia target. For more detail on methodology, see chapter 2.

Measurement of Anemia in Women

Anemia in women refers to anemia in women of reproductive age, which includes all nonpregnant women 15–49 years of age and all pregnant women.

Anemia in women, for the purposes of the World Health Assembly target, is measured by the prevalence of any form of anemia spanning from mild to severe forms (WHO 2015a; WHO and 1,000 Days 2014) in the above-mentioned target groups (table 4.2). The baseline prevalence data used here is from the WHO Global Targets Tracking Tool (WHO 2015) as accessed in September 2015. The original source is Stevens et al. 2013. Data on anemia, or low concentrations of hemoglobin, are collected through the Demographic and Health Surveys (DHS), Malaria Indicator Surveys (MIS), Reproductive Health Surveys (RHS), national micronutrient surveys or Multiple Indicator Cluster Surveys (MICS), or other similar national surveys and modeled to estimate the prevalence of women below the cutoff of 110 grams of hemoglobin per liter of blood for pregnant women and 120 grams per liter for nonpregnant women. Anemia prevalence as of 2011 was 38 percent in pregnant women and 29 percent in nonpregnant women, translating to 32 million pregnant women and 496 million nonpregnant women, respectively (Stevens et al. 2013).

In the country sample used in the analyses, prevalence of anemia among women ranges from 14.4 percent in Mexico to 57.5 percent in Senegal, with 12 of 26 countries above 40 percent (high prevalence) and 5 countries below 20 percent prevalence (high absolute burden).

Interventions Included in the Analyses

In order to achieve the World Health Assembly target for anemia in women, the target population benefitting from anemia prevention and control interventions will need to be significantly expanded from the 125 million pregnant women to also reach 1.5 billion nonpregnant women of reproductive age. Achieving this ambitious target will require approaches across multiple sectors. The analyses estimate the costs and impact of scaling up a minimum core set of

Table 4.2 Anemia Severity Thresholds in Women
Grams of hemoglobin/liter blood

Anemia severity threshold	Nonpregnant women (g/L)	Pregnant women (g/L)
Mild	110–119	100–109
Moderate	80–109	70–99
Severe	<80	<70

Source: WHO 2011c.
Note: g/L = grams per liter.

interventions that (1) are applicable to all countries, (2) have a strong evidence base for effectiveness in preventing anemia, and (3) together can plausibly achieve the proposed target.

Applying these criteria in consultation with the Technical Advisory Group (see appendix A), the analyses estimate the financing needs for scaling up four core anemia prevention interventions: (1) antenatal micronutrient supplementation, (2) intermittent presumptive treatment of malaria in pregnancy in malaria-endemic regions, (3) iron and folic acid supplementation in nonpregnant women 15–49 years of age, and (4) staple food fortification (wheat flour, maize flour, and rice) with iron for the general population at WHO guideline levels (see table 4.3). Because targeting the fortification of staple foods to a subgroup of women would not be feasible, nor is it recommended, and because anemia affects men as well, the target beneficiaries for staple food fortification are the entire general population (males and females of all ages).

Antenatal micronutrient supplementation is included in the analyses for pregnant women instead of iron and folic acid supplementation—despite its higher costs—because of its effectiveness in improving birth outcomes and thereby preventing childhood stunting. In addition, this allows the analysis for the anemia target to align with the stunting target and to avoid any underestimation. New WHO guidelines on antenatal micronutrient supplementation are expected in late 2016, after which this strategy can go to scale.[3]

Table 4.3 Interventions to Reach the Anemia Target

Intervention	Target population	Description and delivery methods	Evidence of effectiveness
For pregnant women			
Antenatal micronutrient supplementation[a]	Pregnant women	This is broadly defined as a micronutrient supplementation that contains iron and at least two or more micronutrients. The cost is calculated for supplementation containing 15 micronutrients/vitamins, including iron and folic acid, for 180 days per pregnancy. Supplementation is delivered through antenatal care programs.	A review by Peña-Rosas et al. (2012) finds that daily iron supplements in pregnancy lead to a 70 percent reduction in maternal anemia [RR 0.30, 95% CI 0.19–0.46]. Although antenatal multiple micronutrient supplementation is not more effective at reducing anemia than iron and folic acid supplementation alone, it is recommended because of its effectiveness in improving birth outcomes (it prevents low birthweight and newborns who are small for gestational age) and thereby preventing childhood stunting (see table 3.1 in chapter 3).

box continues next page

Table 4.3 Interventions to Reach the Anemia Target *(continued)*

Intervention	Target population	Description and delivery methods	Evidence of effectiveness
Intermittent presumptive treatment of malaria in pregnancy in malaria-endemic regions	Pregnant women in malaria-endemic regions	This intervention provides at least two doses of sulfadoxine-pyrimethamine during pregnancy. Treatment is delivered through antenatal care.	Radeva-Petrova et al. (2014) estimate that intermittent presumptive treatment of malaria in pregnancy results in a 17 percent reduction in the risk of any anemia [RR 0.83, 95% CI 0.74–0.93].
For all women of reproductive age			
Iron and folic acid supplementation for nonpregnant women	Nonpregnant women age 15–49 years	Delivery of weekly iron and folic acid supplement in school-based programs for girls age 15–19 enrolled in school, and delivery via community health workers, health facility outpatient visits, and/or via private marketplace for all others.	A review by Fernández-Gaxiola and De-Regil (2011) finds that weekly iron and folic acid supplementation results in a 27 percent reduction in anemia [RR 0.73, 95% CI 0.56–0.95].
For the general population			
Staple food fortification	General population	Fortification of wheat flour, maize flour, and rice with iron at WHO guideline levels and delivered through the marketplace.	A review of wheat flour fortification programs by Barkley, Wheeler, and Pachon (2015) finds that fortification at WHO guideline levels is associated with a 2.4 percent reduction in the odds of anemia in nonpregnant women per year [prevalence odds ratio 0.976, 95% CI 0.975–0.978]. A similar impact of fortification of maize and rice is assumed.

Note: CI = confidence interval; RR = relative risk.
a. World Health Organization (WHO) guidelines are expected in late 2016.

Daily iron and folic acid supplementation for nonpregnant women is recommended by the WHO for countries where the prevalence of anemia is greater than 40 percent. For the large population of nonpregnant women, weekly iron and folic acid supplementation is included in the analyses because of the greater feasibility of delivering a weekly supplement than a daily supplement. In this population, the analysis assumes supplementation is delivered to adolescent girls age 15–19 through school programs and to other nonpregnant girls and women through community health workers, outpatient visits, and the private marketplace (see table 4.4).

This report focuses on costing a package of primarily preventive nutrition-specific interventions that have proven efficacy in averting anemia (table 4.3). Though not included in this package, it is also important for the health system to provide for the treatment for anemia where feasible; this may require medical consultations, testing, and diagnosis of the cause in addition to

Table 4.4 Assumed Delivery Platforms for Iron and Folic Acid Supplementation for Women, by Secondary School Enrollment and Poverty Status

Delivery platform Poverty status	Women age 15–19 enrolled in school (%) School-based delivery	Women age 15–49 not enrolled in school (%)		
		Community health worker delivery	Hospital/nurse delivery	Private retailer delivery
Below the poverty line	100	70	30	0
Above the poverty line	100	49	21	30

micronutrient supplementation. This may be particularly important for women with severe anemia, which has a prevalence of only 1.8 percent in nonpregnant women and 2.0 percent in pregnant women globally (Stevens et al. 2013).

Sample Selection

The analysis for the anemia target is based on a sample of 26 countries, which includes 20 countries with the highest absolute burden and an additional 6 countries with the highest prevalence (see table 2.2 for the list of countries). The threshold for highest prevalence is a prevalence rate of anemia in women of reproductive age greater than 50 percent. Altogether, the sample accounts for 82.8 percent of the global burden of anemia in women of reproductive age.[4]

Estimating Costs

The total additional costs of achieving the anemia target is the sum of the annual costs of scaling up the four selected core interventions from baseline coverage levels in 2015 to full coverage over a 10-year timeframe for the sample of countries identified in chapter 2 (see table 2.2).

Unit costs for these interventions are derived from either the program or the ingredients approaches, depending on data availability. The cost of the iron and folic acid supplement per woman per year ($0.12) is obtained from the OneHealth Tool manual (Futures Institute 2013), to which a 10 percent transportation cost is added. In addition, the costs of four different delivery platforms for nonpregnant women are included because there is no existing platform from which to extrapolate (table 4.4). The cost of delivery through school-based programs for girls age 15–19 enrolled in secondary school (World Bank 2016) includes an additional program cost of $0.33 for the Sub-Saharan Africa and South Asia regions and $0.50 for other regions (WHO 2011c).[5] Up to 30 percent of women living above the poverty line are assumed to potentially be able to purchase iron and folic acid supplements through private retailers similar to coverage levels achieved with micronutrient powder distribution in some cases (Bahl et al. 2013), although this could vary widely across contexts.

Of the remaining women and girls above and below the poverty line, 70 percent are assumed to be able to access iron and folic acid supplements through consultations with a community health worker and 30 percent through a consultation in a hospital setting with a nurse. The distribution of iron and folic acid supplements to a woman is estimated to require two consultations of five minutes each with a health worker per year. Human resources for health costs are estimated by multiplying the time allocation for all annual consultations by salary estimates for community health workers, which range from $80 to $917 per month (Casey et al. 2011; Dahn et al. 2015; Maternal and Child Health Integrated Program 2011), and nurse salaries, which range from $3,047 to $40,265 per annum in sample countries (WHO 2005). Five countries in the sample have a prevalence of anemia in women below the WHO threshold of 20 percent for this intervention, but were selected because of their high absolute burden of anemia. However, a maximum attainable coverage of 75 percent is assumed for countries with a prevalence of between 15 and 19 percent (that is, China, Brazil, and Ethiopia) and 50 percent for countries with a prevalence below 15 percent (that is, Mexico and Vietnam). Bahl et al. (2013) find that, on average, multiple micronutrient supplements are sold with an 83 percent markup. Therefore this analysis assumes that private retailers would mark up the cost of iron and folic acid supplements to the same degree.

Estimating the costs of staple food fortification is challenging because there are large gaps in data regarding food consumption and fortification coverage as well as a wide variability of fortification costs between settings (Fiedler and Puett 2015; Fiedler, Sanghvi, and Saunders 2008). Primary sources of cost and coverage data are from the Global Alliance for Improved Nutrition (GAIN) costing model (Ghauri et al. 2016) and the Food Fortification Initiative (FFI) coverage data (Pachon 2016). The per capita fortification unit costs are lowered to 0 percent, 25 percent, and 50 percent if the available data suggest that there is, respectively, no, low, or moderate demand for consumption for each particular type of food staple in each country—this is an attempt to take into account dietary differences across populations. Baseline coverage of fortified foods is assumed to be 50 percent in countries that have legislated mandatory fortification of wheat flour, maize flour, and rice to reflect the fact that small and medium-sized mills and food producers may be excluded from legislation. The estimated total cost is the product of the unit cost for each food in each country and the gradual scale-up of fortification to the whole country between baseline coverage in 2015 and full potential coverage.

Following the GAIN costing model, domestic governments and donors would each be responsible for approximately 5 percent of the total costs—mainly for start-up programs and social marketing costs—and the remaining 90 percent would be borne by the private sector to be recouped through consumer sales of fortified products. The costs of fortifying all other foods, such as vegetable oil, dairy products, and other vegetables or grains, are not included, nor are the costs of biofortification explicitly included because they may be redundant with other fortification vehicles. Costing of two interventions—antenatal micronutrient supplementation and intermittent presumptive treatment of malaria in pregnancy in malaria-endemic regions—uses a methodology similar to the stunting target (see chapter 3).

Estimating Impact

For the impact analysis, a model in Microsoft Excel was developed to parallel the pathways for interventions that affect anemia in women in the Lives Saved Tool (LiST) (Bhutta et al. 2013; Walker, Tam, and Friberg 2013; Winfrey, McKinnon, and Stover 2011). The specific pathways and effect sizes used in this model are shown in figure 4.2. Preventative interventions for the nonpregnant female population are included in this model, but not other modeling tools. Effect sizes of interventions are taken from recent systematic reviews (see table 4.3).

The Excel model computes the number of cases of anemia in women averted in each sample country over the 10-year scale-up of interventions compared with the baseline. A limitation of all these models is the inability to differentiate between mild, moderate, and severe cases of anemia (see table 4.2). The number of child and maternal deaths averted attributed to the scale-up of interventions that affect anemia is estimated using LiST.[6] Because it is not possible to distinguish between the effects of iron and folic acid supplementation and those of food fortification on mortality in the model, it is assumed that the child deaths averted are attributable to the combined impact of the two interventions. The analyses did not estimate potential reductions in low birthweight and small for gestational age of children born to anemic mothers.

In addition, a historical trend for declining anemia rates is assumed to extend over the next 10 years. The modeled 1.1 percent decline per year in anemia rates is based on the WHO Global Targets Tracking Tool dataset (WHO 2015a). This trend may capture the effects of underlying determinants of anemia—such as food diversity, levels of women's education, and previous delivery of interventions at lower coverage levels. The cost per case-year of anemia averted and the cost per death averted by these interventions are also estimated in order to assess the allocative efficiency of each intervention and the full package.

Figure 4.2 Underlying Model Used to Estimate the Impact of Interventions on Anemia in Women

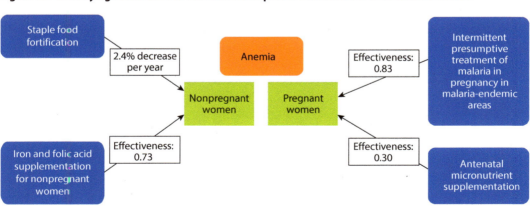

Note: Effectiveness is the proportionate reduction in each outcome that results from the intervention. It is used in conjunction with an affected fraction value to estimate the impact of an intervention on each outcome. See table 4.3 for sources.

An Investment Framework for Nutrition • http://dx.doi.org/10.1596/978-1-4648-1010-7

Benefit-Cost Analyses

The benefit-cost analysis of investing in the selected anemia interventions uses a methodology similar to that for the stunting target (see chapter 3). Monetary benefits are estimated for three economic outcomes attributed to reductions in the prevalence of anemia in women: (1) female earnings gained as a result of increased productivity, (2) earnings gained as a result of maternal deaths averted, and (3) earnings gained as a result of child mortality averted. The outputs from the Excel model for projected anemia prevalence reductions and the LiST results for the number of maternal and child deaths averted over the 2016–25 period are inserted as inputs into the benefit-cost analysis. This approach is used by Horton and Ross (2003, 2007) and Casey et al. (2011) for estimating the earnings gained by women as a result of increased productivity in terms of gross domestic product (GDP) per capita, in which a 50 percent labor share of GDP is assumed. The earnings gained are estimated as the product of the number of cases of anemia averted because of interventions and the higher wages in manual occupations because of higher productivity without anemia (wages are 5 percent higher for light labor, 17 percent higher for heavy manual labor, and 4 percent for other work). The female labor force participation rate is also factored in using the International Labour Organization's ILOSTAT database so as not to overestimate the number of employed women (ILO 2015). Productivity-related earnings gained in adults are assumed to be incurred in the same year as the intervention is delivered (Horton and Ross 2003).

Estimating the earnings gained related to mortality averted uses the same methodology as in the stunting target analysis, which assumes that earning gains would be incurred for children over their working lives from age 18 until mean life expectancy in each country or 65 years of age, whichever is lower. For earnings gains due to maternal mortality averted as a result of the intermittent presumptive treatment of malaria in pregnancy in malaria-endemic regions, earnings gained between the mean maternal age in each country until the mean life expectancy or 65 years of age, whichever is lower, is estimated (World Bank 2016). A 3 percent GDP growth rate is assumed across countries, which is lower than the historical average of low- and middle-income countries. The analysis varies the discount rates of benefits and costs to 3 percent and 5 percent for comparison, as done in Horton and Hoddinott (2014).

This benefit-cost analysis does not include all potential benefits, including savings from reduced health care costs for the diagnosis and treatment of anemia, other indirect consequences of anemia in women, and benefits of reduced anemia in children and men attributed to the scale-up of staple food fortification. In that sense, the total benefits described are underestimates.

Sensitivity Analyses

As mentioned above, there are gaps in data required for the analyses, particularly related to projections for feasible scale-up scenarios of interventions, the effectiveness of fortification, and unit costs for emerging delivery platforms. One-way sensitivity analyses are presented for the key drivers of costs, impacts,

Reaching the Global Target for Anemia

and benefit-cost ratios by altering several variables for each analysis. Sensitivity analyses are presented for the total 10-year costs of anemia interventions with the following variable changes: (1) removing public sector human resource for health delivery costs for iron and folic acid supplementation, (2) adjusting the target coverage of iron and folic acid supplementation in the five countries with a prevalence of anemia below the 20 percent WHO guideline threshold to coverage ranging from 0 percent to 100 percent (signifying fully including or excluding in those countries),[7] and (3) lowering the maximum scale-up coverage achievable for all interventions from 90 percent to a more feasible 50 percent or 75 percent. The impact sensitivity analysis shows the change in impact expected by varying the same last two variables as in the cost sensitivity plus the effectiveness of food fortification equal to no effect (0 percent reduction of anemia per year) and the effectiveness of the other three interventions to the lower and upper bounds of the 95 percent confidence interval estimates stated in the literature.

Results

This section presents the results of the analyses of the interventions described above, including costs, impacts, and benefit-cost results.

Unit Costs

The unit costs employed in the analyses for the interventions targeting pregnant women are the same as those used for the stunting target in chapter 3. The costing literature for interventions for anemia prevention in nonpregnant women is less well established, and micronutrient costs are known to vary widely between contexts (Fiedler, Sanghvi, and Saunders 2008; Fiedler and Semakula 2014). See table 4.5 for a list of the minimum, maximum, and

Table 4.5 Minimum, Maximum, and Mean Unit Costs of Interventions to Meet the Anemia Target (Annual)
US$

Intervention	Minimum	Maximum	Mean unit cost
Antenatal micronutrient supplementation	1.80	7.55	2.99
Intermittent presumptive treatment of malaria in pregnancy in malaria-endemic regions	2.06	2.06	2.06
Iron and folic acid supplementation for nonpregnant women			
School-based program delivery	0.46	0.63	0.55
Community health delivery	0.21	1.78	0.73
Hospital/nurse delivery	0.54	5.54	1.78
Private retailer delivery	0.24	0.24	0.24
Staple food fortification			
Wheat flour	0.08	0.29	0.18
Maize flour	0.09	0.29	0.13
Rice	0.08	1.41	0.74

Note: The mean unit costs are population-weighted means.

An Investment Framework for Nutrition • http://dx.doi.org/10.1596/978-1-4648-1010-7

population-weighted mean unit cost by intervention used across the sample countries. Gaps in cost data are filled by proxy values from a similar country in the same region or income group.

Estimated Total Financing Needs

The total additional costs of scaling up the selected core set of interventions necessary to meet the World Health Assembly anemia target in low- and middle-income countries is approximately $12.9 billion from domestic government resources and official development assistance (ODA) from 2016 to 2025. Under this scale-up scenario, the total annual additional costs would escalate from baseline to $1.7 billion by 2021 (see figure 4.3), and would then increase slightly over the maintenance phase because of the population growth in women of reproductive age in low- and middle-income countries. The majority of domestic government and ODA financing needs are for iron and folic acid supplementation for nonpregnant women ($6.7 billion) and smaller investments for staple food fortification for the general population ($2.4 billion), for antenatal micronutrient supplementation ($2.0 billion), and for intermittent presumptive treatment of malaria in pregnancy in malaria-endemic regions ($337 million).

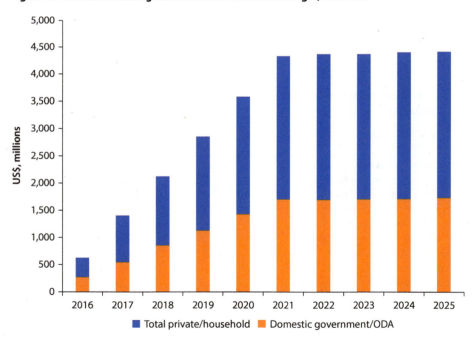

Figure 4.3 Annual Financing Needs to Meet the Anemia Target, 2016–25

Note: ODA = official development assistance.

Table 4.6 Ten-Year Total Financing Needs to Meet the Anemia Target

Intervention	Total 10-year intervention costs (US$, millions)	Share of total 10-year cost (%)
Antenatal micronutrient supplementation	2,017	18
Intermittent presumptive treatment of malaria in pregnancy in malaria-endemic regions	337	3
Iron and folic acid supplementation for nonpregnant women	6,705	58
Staple food fortification (wheat flour, maize flour, and rice)	2,443	21
Subtotal	*11,502*	*100*
Program (capacity strengthening, monitoring and evaluation, and policy development)	1,380	n.a.
Total public costs	12,882	n.a.

Note: n.a. = not applicable.

In addition, there are further household costs in the amount of $505 million for the purchase of iron and folic acid supplementation by a share of women above the poverty line and $19.1 billion for the expected incremental additional cost of fortified foods (compared with unfortified foods) purchased by households (table 4.6).

East Asia and the Pacific region requires a $5.24 billion share of the total financing needs, whereas Sub-Saharan Africa ($2.50 billion) and South Asia ($2.45 billion) each require smaller shares of the total 10-year public sector/ODA cost (figure 4.4).

The total cost for East Asia and the Pacific is greater than it is for South Asia and Sub-Saharan Africa in this model primarily because of the higher quantity of fortified rice expected to be consumed proportional to other less costly fortified foods in other regions as well as higher delivery costs for iron and folic acid supplementation than in the South Asia and African regions. By income group, low-income countries account for 13 percent of the total costs, lower-middle-income countries for 40 percent, and upper-middle-income countries for 47 percent (figure 4.5).

Sensitivity Analyses of Estimates of Financing Needs

The total costs for reaching the anemia target are sensitive to changes in several key variables. One of the uncertainties pertaining to this analysis is the unprecedented scale-up of iron and folic acid supplementation for nonpregnant women, which is needed to meet the target. The sensitivity analysis tornado diagram (figure 4.6) shows that, if public health system personnel costs are removed (which would be possible only if this intervention could be bundled with an already existing intervention for this population group), the total 10-year financing needs would decrease by $7 billion. Another factor that has a large effect on total financing needs is the scale-up of iron and folic acid supplementation for

Figure 4.4 Ten-Year Total Financing Needs to Meet the Anemia Target, by Region

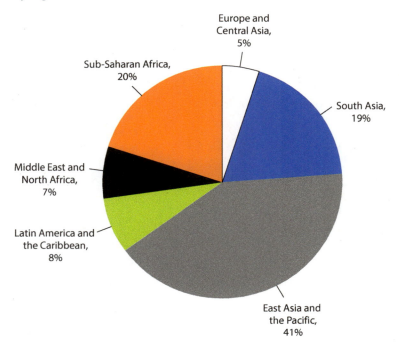

Figure 4.5 Ten-Year Total Financing Needs to Meet the Anemia Target, by Country Income Group

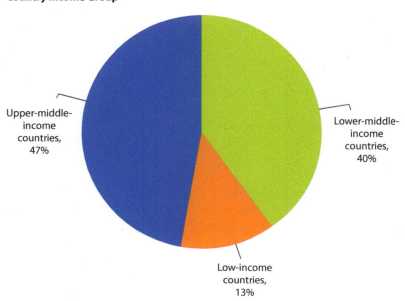

Figure 4.6 Sensitivity Analysis for 10-Year Total Financing Needs to Meet the Anemia Target

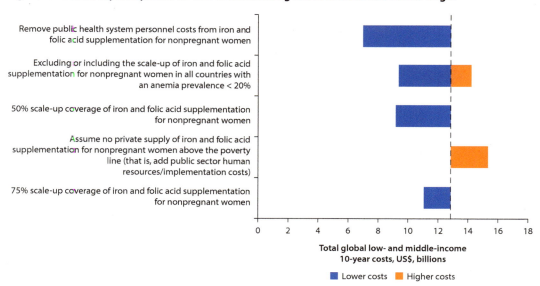

nonpregnant women in the five countries that have less than a 20 percent prevalence of anemia. Initially either 50 percent or 75 percent of the female populations in these countries have been included as potential target beneficiaries. Excluding the scale-up in countries with less than 20 percent national prevalence would reduce the global costs by about $3 billion over 10 years, but there would be a trade-off in terms of prevalence reductions. Lowering the maximum attainable coverage level for all interventions to 75 percent or 50 percent would be more realistic and would lower the total 10-year costs by $4 billion and $2 billion, respectively. Replacing the private sector delivery of iron and folic acid supplementation for nonpregnant women living above the poverty line with public sector delivery would add about $2 billion in human resource costs for delivery over 10 years.

Estimated Impacts of the Scale-Up

The model suggests that it is possible to achieve the World Health Assembly target for anemia by 2025, albeit this may be ambitious. This investment in anemia prevention interventions is projected to result in 265 million fewer anemic women in the year 2025 compared with the baseline in 2015 (see figure 4.7). If achieved, the prevalence of anemia is projected to decrease to 15.4 percent in 2025, resulting in 799,000 child deaths averted in the next 10 years. This includes the impact of the four nutrition interventions plus the continuation of the 1.1 percent per year annual rate of reduction (that is, the historical trend) across all low- and middle-income countries, based on the WHO Global Targets Tracking Tool dataset (WHO 2015a). In addition, the scale-up of intermittent

Figure 4.7 Costs and Impacts of a 10-Year Scale-Up of Interventions to Meet the Anemia Target

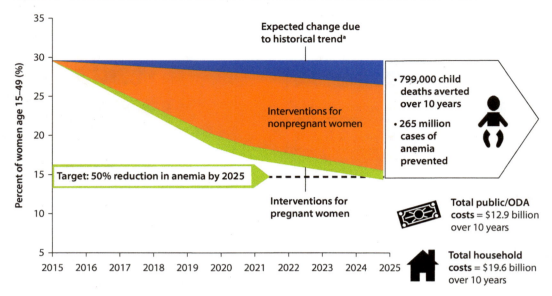

Note: ODA = official development assistance.
a. This trend represents an extension of average annual rate of reduction of anemia rate without scale-up.

presumptive treatment of malaria in pregnant women in malaria-endemic regions would prevent between 7,000 and 14,000 maternal deaths over the next 10 years. The five countries with the highest total child deaths averted are India, Nigeria, Pakistan, China, and Bangladesh,[8] which together account for 63 percent of estimated child deaths averted across all low- and middle-income countries.

In terms of allocative efficiency, both micronutrient interventions demonstrate a relatively low cost per case-year for anemia compared with the cost for intermittent presumptive treatment of malaria in pregnancy in malaria-endemic regions. Not surprisingly, the two interventions targeting pregnant women—antenatal micronutrient supplementation and intermittent presumptive treatment of malaria in pregnancy in malaria-endemic regions—demonstrate lower cost per death averted than the interventions for nonpregnant women and the population at large (table 4.7). The effects of iron and folic acid supplementation and staple food fortification on child mortality are not modeled separately because they have overlapping causal pathways for anemia and mortality and are modeled jointly in LiST.

Sensitivity Analyses of the Impact of the Scale-Up

This global projection for achieving the World Health Assembly target for the reduction in anemia prevalence over the next 10 years depends on major assumptions about the collective ability to secure financing and implement interventions on an unprecedented scale. The sensitivity analyses for impacts (see figure 4.8) demonstrate that reducing the attainable level of scale-up coverage or varying the effectiveness of staple food fortification of other micronutrient interventions results in underachieving the target by 5–10 percentage points. Furthermore, if the assumption on the extension of the historic trend in declining anemia rates does not continue, then the prevalence will underachieve by an additional 0–10 percentage points.

Table 4.7 Total Cost, Cost per Case-Year of Anemia Averted, and Costs per Death Averted

Intervention	Total 10-year costs (US$, billions)	Cost per case-year of anemia averted (US$)	Costs per child death averted (US$)
Antenatal micronutrient supplementation	2.26	11	6,740
Intermittent presumptive treatment of malaria in pregnancy in malaria-endemic regions	0.38	62	4,531
Iron and folic acid supplementation for nonpregnant women	7.51	10	26,914[a]
Staple food fortification	2.74	7	
Full package	**12.88**	**9**	**16,121**

Note: Because of rounding, the total 10-year costs do not equal the sum of the cost of each intervention.
a. This figure is the combined cost per death averted estimated to result from iron and folic acid supplementation for nonpregnant women and the cost of staple food fortification in the preconceptual stage, because it was not possible to independently estimate the impact on mortality of these interventions in the model.

Figure 4.8 Sensitivity Analyses of the Impact of Interventions to Meet the Anemia Target

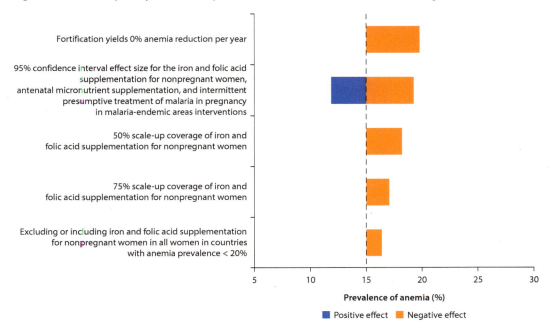

Note: This package is estimated to reach 15.4 percent prevalence; the sensitivity analyses show potential deviations from this estimate.

Table 4.8 Benefit-Cost Ratios of Scaling Up Interventions to Meet the Anemia Target, 3 and 5 Percent Discount Rates

	3% discount rate			5% discount rate		
Group	Present value benefit (US$, billions)	Present value cost (US$, billions)	Benefit-cost ratio	Present value benefit (US$, billions)	Present value cost (US$, billions)	Benefit-cost ratio
By region						
Sub-Saharan Africa[a]	16.1	1.2	13.1	9.4	1.1	8.6
South Asia[a]	25.9	1.9	14.0	14.2	1.6	8.7
East Asia and the Pacific[a]	33.0	3.0	10.9	21.2	2.7	7.9
By country income group						
Low-income countries[a]	2.6	0.6	4.2	1.5	0.6	2.6
Lower-middle-income countries[a]	47.9	3.2	15.2	27.0	2.8	9.7
Upper-middle-income countries[a]	40.1	3.7	10.9	26.0	3.3	7.9
Pooled	**110.1**	**7.6**	**12.1**	**66.1**	**8.1**	**8.2**
Median[a]			10.6			7.4

a. Sample countries only.

Benefit-Cost Analyses

The benefit-cost analysis of investing in the modeled package of interventions to prevent anemia in women suggests that there would most likely be a positive return on investment for low- and middle-income countries in the sample. Assuming a 3 percent GDP growth rate across countries and 3 percent discount of costs and benefits projects a total net benefit from the investment in anemia prevention of $110.1 billion over 10 years for women and over the productive lives of child beneficiaries and a pooled benefit-cost ratio of 12.1 (the median benefit-cost ratio in sample is 10.6). When pooled by income group, the result is a benefit-cost ratio of 4.2 for low-income countries, 15.2 for lower-middle-income countries, and 10.9 for upper-middle-income countries, respectively (table 4.8). By region, this translates into a benefit-cost ratio of 13.1 for Sub-Saharan Africa, 14.0 for South Asia, and 10.9 East Asia and the Pacific.

Using 5 percent discount rates for comparison, the benefit-cost ratios decrease slightly across the sample. This more conservative model projects a total net benefit of over $66 billion and a pooled 8.2 benefit-cost ratio across countries (median benefit-cost ratio in sample is 7.4). In general, the benefit-cost analyses suggest that there would be a positive return on investment and substantial productivity gains to be generated from preventing anemia in women.

Discussion

Achieving the anemia target will improve the lives of millions of women and their newborns and may contribute toward a more productive economy. However, achieving this ambitious goal will be a challenge because the current trend in the decline of prevalence rates is vastly insufficient to reach the target. A major investment is needed to rapidly scale up evidence-based interventions that reduce the burden of anemia among women.

Expanding micronutrient programs from the current focus on children and pregnant women to all the 1.5 billion nonpregnant women in low- and middle-income countries requires a leap in supply chain logistics and increased availability and access to health services. Reaching the target also depends on large-scale expansion of food fortification. Staple food fortification has been shown to be highly effective and—with further advances in research and implementation at scale—could well be part of the solution. For example, iodized salt is one of the most effective interventions for reducing disabilities including cognitive losses due to iodine deficiency. It is mandated in several countries throughout the world, but in most regions, coverage has reached only 50–70 percent of households (Mannar 2014). It is not, however, incorporated into this analysis because iodine deficiency is not included in the global targets.

The analyses are limited by the quality of the data and the validity of assumptions made in their place. The cost analysis could be vastly improved with more rigorous unit cost data and food consumption coverage data. Additional ex-post evaluations and a review of case studies on real-world scale-up scenarios as well as an analysis of both barriers and enablers to scale-up would also be helpful so that the models can more accurately reflect reality.

Anemia in women is easily preventable through low-cost interventions that provide positive returns on investment and reduce its significant mortality costs. Reducing anemia in women may also contribute to reducing gender wage gaps and help some women escape poverty. Governments, donors, and communities should together seize the opportunity to increase investment in anemia prevention and control.

Notes

1. Although anemia is a concern in both women of reproductive age (15–49 years of age) and young children (6–59 months of age), the anemia target as set by the World Health Assembly refers only to anemia in women of reproductive age—that is, both pregnant and nonpregnant women aged 15–49. Throughout this report we use the term *anemia in women* to refer to anemia in women of reproductive age.
2. Hookworm infection is associated with the prevalence of anemia in both pregnant and nonpregnant women (Smith and Brooker 2010), but a review of deworming interventions, such as antihelminthics, shows that they do not significantly impact hemoglobin levels or anemia prevalence (Salam et al. 2015). Anemia is also a strong predictor of disease progression and death among people infected with HIV, including those who have initiated antiretroviral therapy. Generally, antiretroviral therapy improves hemoglobin status but it does not always resolve anemia and, in some contexts, leads to a higher risk of anemia (Johannessen et al. 2011; Takuva et al. 2013; Widen et al. 2015).
3. As of the writing of this report, the WHO website indicated that a guideline containing recommendations relevant to this intervention is planned for release in 2016. See http://www.who.int/elena/titles/micronutrients_pregnancy/en/.

4. For the purposes of this report, the term *anemia in women of reproductive age* has been shortened to *anemia in women*.
5. A program unit cost, in addition to the cost of the micronutrient supplement, is included in order to develop and sustain the infrastructure with the education system and schools for the effective delivery to adolescent girls.
6. A beta version of LiST (version 5.41 beta 13) is used for the analyses.
7. The five countries with anemia prevalence below 20 percent are Brazil, China, Ethiopia, Mexico, and Vietnam (Stevens et al. 2013).
8. The estimated number of child deaths averted is 286,854 in India; 83,612 in Nigeria; 65,762 in Pakistan; 36,825 in China; and 33,989 in Bangladesh.

References

Bahl, K., E. Toro, C. Qureshi, and P. Shaw. 2013. *Nutrition for a Better Tomorrow: Scaling Up Delivery of Micronutrient Powders for Infants and Young Children*. Washington, DC: Results for Development Institute. http://www.resultsfordevelopment.org/nutrition-for-a-better-tomorrow.

Balarajan, Y., U. Ramakrishnan, E. Ozaltin, A. H. Shankar, and S. V. Subramanian. 2011. "Anaemia in Low-Income and Middle-Income Countries." *The Lancet* 378: 2123–35.

Barkley, J. S., K. S. Wheeler, and H. Pachon. 2015. "Anaemia Prevalence May Be Reduced among Countries That Fortify Flour." *The British Journal of Nutrition* 114: 265–73.

Bhutta, Z. A, J. K. Das, A. Rizvi, M. F. Gaffey, N. Walker, S. Horton, P. Webb, A. Lartey, and R. E. Black. 2013. "Evidence-Based Interventions for Improvement of Maternal and Child Nutrition: What Can Be Done and at What Cost?" *The Lancet* 382 (9890): 452–77.

Black, R. E., C. G. Victora, S. P. Walker, Z. A. Bhutta, P. Christian, M. de Onis, M. Ezzati, S. Grantham-Mcgregor, J. Katz, R. Martorell, R. Uauy, and the Maternal and Child Nutrition Study Group. 2013. "Maternal and Child Undernutrition and Overweight in Low-Income and Middle-Income Countries." *The Lancet* 382: 427–51.

Casey, G. J., D. Sartori, S. E. Horton, T. Q. Phuc, L. B. Phu, D. T. Thach, T. C. Dai, G. Fattore, A. Montresor, and B.-A. Biggs. 2011. "Weekly Iron-Folic Acid Supplementation with Regular Deworming Is Cost-Effective in Preventing Anaemia in Women of Reproductive Age in Vietnam." *PLoS One* 6: e23723.

Cercamondi, C. I., I. M. Egli, E. Mitchikpe, F. Tousou, C. Zeder, J. D. Hounhouigan, and R. F. Hurrell. 2013. "Total Iron Absorption by Young Women from Iron-Biofortified Pearl Millet Composite Meals Is Double That from Regular Millet Meals but Less than That from Post-Harvest Iron-Fortified Millet Meals." *The Journal of Nutrition* 143: 1376–82.

Choudhury, N., A. Aimone, S. M. Hyder, and S. H. Zlotkin. 2012. "Relative Efficacy of Micronutrient Powders versus Iron-Folic Acid Tablets in Controlling Anemia in Women in the Second Trimester of Pregnancy." *Food and Nutrition Bulletin* 33: 142–49.

Dahn, B., A. Woldemariam, H. Perry, A. Maeda, D. von Glahn, R. Panjabi, N. Merchant, K. Vosburg, D. Palazuelos, C. Lu, J. Simon, J. Pfaffmann, D. Brown, A. Hearst, P. Heydt, and C. Qureshi. 2015. *Strengthening Primary Health Care through Community Health Workers: Investment Case and Financing Recommendations*. http://www.who.int/hrh/news/2015/chw_financing/en/.

Fernández-Gaxiola, A. C., and L. M. De-Regil. 2011. "Intermittent Iron Supplementation for Reducing Anaemia and Its Associated Impairments in Menstruating Women." *Cochrane Database of Systematic Reviews* December (12).

Fiedler, J. L., and C. Puett. 2015. "Micronutrient Program Costs: Sources of Variations and Noncomparabilities." *Food and Nutrition Bulletin* 36: 43–56.

Fiedler, J. L., T. G. Sanghvi, and M. K. Saunders. 2008. "A Review of the Micronutrient Intervention Cost Literature: Program Design and Policy Lessons." *The International Journal of Health Planning and Management* 23: 373–97.

Fiedler, J. L., and R. Semakula. 2014. "An Analysis of the Costs of Uganda's Child Days Plus: Do Low Costs Reveal an Efficient Program or an Underfinanced One?" *Food and Nutrition Bulletin* 35: 92–104.

Futures Institute. 2013. *OneHealth Model: Intervention Treatment Assumptions.* Glastonbury: Futures Institute. http://avenirhealth.org/Download/Spectrum/Manuals/Intervention percent20Assumptions percent202013percent209 percent2028.pdf.

Gamble, C., J. P. Ekwaru, and F. O. ter Kuile. 2006. "Insecticide-Treated Nets for Preventing Malaria in Pregnancy." *The Cochrane Database of Systematic Reviews* (2): CD003755.

Gera, T., H. S. Sachdev, and E. Boy. 2012. "Effect of Iron-Fortified Foods on Hematologic and Biological Outcomes: Systematic Review of Randomized Controlled Trials." *The American Journal of Clinical Nutrition* 96: 309–24.

Ghauri, K., S. Horton, R. Spohrer, and G. Garrett. 2016. "Food Fortification Cost Model." Unpublished material, Global Alliance for Improved Nutrition, Washington, DC.

Haider, B. A., and Z. A. Bhutta. 2015. "Multiple-Micronutrient Supplementation for Women during Pregnancy." *Cochrane Database of Systematic Reviews* 11 (November): CD004905.

Horton, S., and J. Hoddinott. 2014. "Benefits and Costs of the Food and Nutrition Targets for the Post-2015 Development Agenda: Post-2015 Consensus." Food Security and Nutrition Perspective paper. Copenhagen Consensus Center.

Horton, S., and J. Ross. 2003. "The Economics of Iron Deficiency." *Food Policy* 28: 51–75.

———. 2007. "The Economics of Iron Deficiency: Corrigendum." *Food Policy* 32: 141–43.

ILO (International Labour Organization). 2015. ILOSTAT (database), ILO, Geneva (accessed May 2, 2015), http://www.ilo.org/ilostat/faces/home/statisticaldata?_afrLoop=39430847112133#percent40percent3F_afrLooppercent3D39430847112133 percent26_adf.ctrlstatepercent3Dbakdhzsnf_4.

Johannessen, A., E. Naman, S. G. Gundersen, and J. N. Bruun. 2011. "Antiretroviral Treatment Reverses HIV-Associated Anemia in Rural Tanzania." *BMC Infectious Diseases* 11: 190-2334-11-190.

Kassebaum, N. J., R. Jasrasaria, M. Naghavi, S. K. Wulf, N. Johns, R. Lozano, M. Regan, D. Weatherall, D. P. Chou, T. P. Eisele, S. R. Flaxman, R. L. Pullan, S. J. Brooker, and C. J. Murray. 2014. "A Systematic Analysis of Global Anemia Burden from 1990 to 2010." *Blood* 123 (5): 615–24.

Mannar, M. G. V. 2014. "Making Salt Iodization Truly Universal by 2020." *IDD Newsletter*, May. http://www.ign.org/newsletter/idd_may14_usi_by_2020.pdf.

Maternal and Child Health Integrated Program. 2011. *Community-Based Distribution for Routine Iron/Folic Acid Supplementation in Pregnancy.* Washington, DC: MCHIP. http://www.mchip.net/node/632.

Michelazzo, F. B., J. M. Oliveira, J. Stefanello, L. A. Luzia, and P. H. Rondo. 2013. "The Influence of Vitamin A Supplementation on Iron Status." *Nutrients* 5: 4399–413.

Olney, D. K., A. Talukder, L. L. Iannotti, M. T. Ruel, and V. Quinn. 2009. "Assessing Impact and Impact Pathways of a Homestead Food Production Program on Household and Child Nutrition in Cambodia." *Food and Nutrition Bulletin* 30: 355–69.

Pachon, H. 2016. *Food Fortification Coverage Data*. Unpublished data, Food Fortification Initiative, Atlanta, GA.

Pachon, H., R. Spohrer, Z. Mei, and M. K. Serdula. 2015. "Evidence of the Effectiveness of Flour Fortification Programs on Iron Status and Anemia: A Systematic Review." *Nutrition Reviews* 73: 780–95.

Peña-Rosas, J. P., L. M. De-Regil, T. Dowswell, and F. E. Viteri. 2012. "Daily Oral Iron Supplementation during Pregnancy." *Cochrane Database of Systematic Reviews* 12 (December): CD004736.

Radeva-Petrova, D., K. Kayentao, F. O. ter Kuile, D. Sinclair, and P. Garner. 2014. "Drugs for Preventing Malaria in Pregnant Women in Endemic Areas: Any Drug Regimen versus Placebo or No Treatment." *Cochrane Database of Systematic Reviews* 10: CD000169.

Salam, R. A., B. A. Haider, Q. Humayun, and Z. A. Bhutta. 2015. "Effect of Administration of Antihelminthics for Soil-Transmitted Helminths during Pregnancy." *The Cochrane Database of Systematic Reviews* 6: CD005547.

Smith, J. L., and S. Brooker. 2010. "Impact of Hookworm Infection and Deworming on Anaemia in Nonpregnant Populations: A Systematic Review." *Tropical Medicine & International Health* 15: 776–95.

Stevens, G. A., M. M. Finucane, L. M. De-Regil, C. J. Paciorek, S. R. Flaxman, F. Branca, J. P. Peña-Rosas, Z. A. Bhutta, and M. Ezzati. 2013. "Global, Regional, and National Trends in Haemoglobin Concentration and Prevalence of Total and Severe Anaemia in Children and Pregnant and Nonpregnant Women for 1995–2011: A Systematic Analysis of Population-Representative Data." *The Lancet Global Health* 1 (1): e16–e25.

Suchdev, P. S., J. P. Peña-Rosas, and L. M. De-Regil. 2015. "Multiple Micronutrient Powders for Home (Point-of-Use) Fortification of Foods in Pregnant Women." *The Cochrane Database of Systematic Reviews* 6: CD011158.

Takuva, S., M. Maskew, A. T. Brennan, I. Sanne, A. P. MacPhail, and M. P. Fox. 2013. "Anemia among HIV-Infected Patients Initiating Antiretroviral Therapy in South Africa: Improvement in Hemoglobin Regardless of Degree of Immunosuppression and the Initiating ART Regimen." *Journal of Tropical Medicine* 162950.

Walker, N., Y. Tam, and I. K. Friberg. 2013. "Overview of the Lives Saved Tool (LiST)." *BMC Public Health* 13 (Suppl 3): S1-2458-13-S3-S1. Epub 2013 Sep 17.

WHO (World Health Organization). 2004. *Global Burden of Disease 2004 Update: Disability Weights for Diseases and Conditions*. Geneva: WHO. http://www.who.int/healthinfo/global_burden_disease/GBD2004_DisabilityWeights.pdf?ua=1.

———. 2005. *Choosing Interventions That Are Cost-Effective* (WHOCHOICE) (accessed 2015), http://www.who.int/choice/costs/prog_costs/en/.

———. 2011a. *Guideline: Intermittent Iron and Folic Acid Supplementation in Menstruating Women*. Geneva: WHO. http://apps.who.int/iris/bitstream/10665/44649/1/9789241502023_eng.pdf?ua=1&ua=1.

———. 2011b. *Guideline: Use of Multiple Micronutrient Powders for Home Fortification of Foods Consumed by Pregnant Women.* Geneva: WHO. http://apps.who.int/iris/bitstream/10665/44650/1/9789241502030_eng.pdf?ua=1&ua=1.

———. 2011c. *Weekly Iron and Folic Acid Supplementation Programmes for Women of Reproductive Age: An Analysis of Best Programme Practices.* Geneva: WHO. http://www.wpro.who.int/publications/PUB_9789290615231/en/.

———. 2012a. *Guideline: Daily Iron and Folic Acid Supplementation in Pregnant Women.* Geneva: WHO. http://apps.who.int/iris/bitstream/10665/44650/1/9789241502030_eng.pdf?ua=1&ua=1.

———. 2012b. *Guideline: Intermittent Iron and Folic Acid Supplementation in Non-Anaemic Pregnant Women.* Geneva: WHO.

———. 2014. *WHO Policy Brief for the Implementation of Intermittent Preventive Treatment of Malaria in Pregnancy Using Sulfadoxine-Pyrimethamine (IPTp-SP).* Geneva: WHO. http://www.who.int/malaria/publications/atoz/policy_brief_iptp_sp_policy_recommendation/en/.

———. 2015a. Global Targets Tracking Tool (accessed September 15, 2015), https://extranet.who.int/sree/Reports?op=vs&path=percent2FWHO_HQ_Reports/G16/PROD/EXT/Targets_Menu&VSPARAM_varLanguage=E&VSPARAM_varISOCODE=ALB.

———. 2015b. *The Global Prevalence of Anaemia in 2011.* Geneva: WHO. http://www.who.int/nutrition/publications/micronutrients/global_prevalence_anaemia_2011/er/.

———. 2016. *Guideline: Daily Iron Supplementation in Adult Women and Adolescent Girls.* Geneva: WHO. http://apps.who.int/iris/bitstream/10665/204761/1/9789241510196_eng.pdf?ua=1&ua=1.

WHO and 1,000 Days. 2014. *WHA Global Nutrition Targets 2025: Anaemia Policy Brief.* Geneva: WHO. http://www.who.int/nutrition/topics/globaltargets_anaemia_policybrief.pdf.

Widen, E. M., M. E. Bentley, C. S. Chasela, D. Kayira, V. L. Flax, A. P. Kourtis, S. R. Ellington, Z. Kacheche, G. Tegha, D. J. Jamieson, C. M. van der Horst, L. H. Allen, S. Shahab-Ferdows, L. S. Adaio, and BAN Study Team. 2015. "Antiretroviral Treatment Is Associated with Iron Deficiency in HIV-Infected Malawian Women That Is Mitigated with Supplementation, but Is Not Associated with Infant Iron Deficiency During 24 Weeks of Exclusive Breastfeeding." *Journal of Acquired Immune Deficiency Syndromes* 69 (3): 319–28.

Winfrey, W., R. McKinnon, and J. Stover. 2011. "Methods Used in the Lives Saved Tool (LiST)." *BMC Public Health* 11 (Suppl 3): S32-2458-11-S3-S32.

World Bank. 2016. World Development Indicators (database), World Bank, Washington, DC (accessed March 1, 2016), http://data.worldbank.org/data-catalog/world-development-indicators.

CHAPTER 5

Reaching the Global Target for Breastfeeding

Dylan Walters, Julia Dayton Eberwein, Lucy Sullivan, and Meera Shekar

Key Messages

- Optimal breastfeeding promotes child growth and cognitive and socio-emotional development, prevents childhood illness and death, and protects against maternal morbidity, including breast cancers. It also protects against diseases in adulthood and enhances future incomes and labor-market productivity of children in adulthood.
- The World Health Assembly set the target of increasing exclusive breastfeeding for infants up to six months of age from 37 percent in 2012 to 50 percent by 2025.
- Creating an enabling culture and environment in support of breastfeeding requires interventions to provide education and counseling to mothers, widespread media campaigns to promote optimal breastfeeding practices, as well as the development of appropriate policies and legislation to protect exclusive breastfeeding.
- The estimated global financing required to scale up a core set of interventions across all low- and middle-income countries to achieve the World Health Assembly target for exclusive breastfeeding by 2025 is $5.7 billion, or approximately $4.70 for every newborn.
- The costs of not making this investment would be at least 520,000 child deaths and 105 million children not exclusively breastfed, plus additional morbidity from childhood diseases and cognitive losses.
- Every $1 invested is estimated to generate $35 in economic returns, making a breastfeeding strategy one of the best investments a country can make.
- The extension of maternity leave cash benefits from current status to six months in duration, which may increase breastfeeding rates and generate other social, health, and developmental benefits, is estimated to cost an additional $24.1 billion over 10 years, although these resources will need to come from other sectors.
- Although achieving this target requires substantial effort, it appears less ambitious than the other global nutrition targets. The sensitivity analyses presented in this chapter show that there may be scope to go beyond the current target by 2025 or 2030.

The World Health Assembly set a global nutrition target to "increase the rate of exclusive breastfeeding in the first six months to 50 percent" globally by 2025 (WHO and UNICEF 2014). This chapter reports on the estimated global financing needs of key breastfeeding interventions needed to reach this target and presents the estimated impacts and returns on investment of those interventions. These results are intended to inform the prioritization of investments by governments, official development assistance, and other stakeholders.

Optimal Breastfeeding and Its Benefits

Exclusive breastfeeding is defined as the practice of giving an infant only breast milk for the first six months of life, with no other food, other liquids, or even water (UNICEF 2011). *Optimal breastfeeding* practices also include the early initiation of breastfeeding immediately after birth and continued breastfeeding until two years of age and beyond. Optimal breastfeeding could have the single largest potential impact on child mortality of any preventive intervention (Bhutta et al. 2013).

The evidence of the health, nutritional, cognitive, and long-term economic benefits of breastfeeding is clear. Breastfeeding has protective effects for newborns and young children that prevent common diseases such as diarrhea and pneumonia, which are the major causes of child mortality (Victora et al. 2016). Breastfeeding may also reduce the risk of childhood obesity and diabetes and, for nursing mothers, reduce the risk of breast cancer later in life. Exclusive breastfeeding for the first six months is also a natural contraceptive that can be helpful in increasing birth spacing (Victora et al. 2016). Recent evidence shows that breastfeeding is also associated with higher intelligence quotients (IQs) (Horta, Loret de Mola, and Victora 2015) and, in the longer term, with enhanced labor market and economic outcomes (Lutter 2016; Rollins et al. 2016).

The State of Breastfeeding Worldwide

Globally, only 43 percent of infants younger than six months are exclusively breastfed (UNICEF 2016). In low- and middle-income countries, this means that over 68 million children born this year will not be exclusively breastfed. The *Global Nutrition Report* suggests that 47 countries are off-course for reaching the breastfeeding target, and a further 110 have missing data for this indicator (IFPRI 2016). However, rates of exclusive breastfeeding in some regions—South Asia and Eastern and Southern Africa for example—have increased since the year 2000 and now surpass the 50 percent target (UNICEF 2016). The rates in other regions are below the target but are progressing slowly, with the exception of the East Asia and Pacific region, which has remained at around 30 percent over the last 15 years. Although beyond the scope of this report, many high-income countries also have very low rates of exclusive breastfeeding, and comparable data for many high-income countries are lacking.

The recent *Lancet* breastfeeding series estimates that optimal breastfeeding could help prevent 823,000 child deaths per year and 20,000 maternal deaths from breast cancer per year (Rollins et al. 2016; Victora et al. 2016). In addition, the current low breastfeeding rates globally are estimated to result in economic losses of about $302 billion annually, or 0.49 percent of world gross national income (Victora et al. 2016).

The determinants of breastfeeding are complex. There are numerous social, cultural, economic, and commercial forces that act as barriers to breastfeeding or promote inadequate breastfeeding, as outlined in figure 5.1 (Rollins et al. 2016). The pressures to not breastfeed also increase as a country transitions to a higher income level.

Although there have been modest gains in exclusive breastfeeding rates globally in recent years, the trends are not expected to continue without investment in comprehensive breastfeeding strategies. Current levels of investment in breastfeeding, though largely undocumented, are perceived to be insufficient to increase rates beyond where they are now (Holla-Bhar et al. 2015; Piwoz and Huffman 2015).

Given the undeniable benefits of breastfeeding and proven returns on investment in terms of economic and human development gains, greater investment is needed toward this highly cost-effective strategy.

Figure 5.1 Conceptual Framework for an Enabling Environment That Supports Breastfeeding

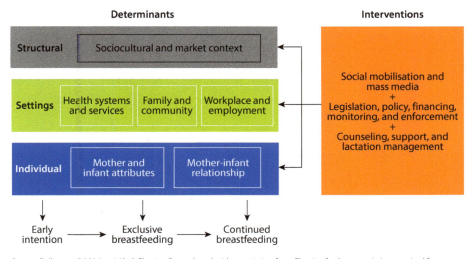

Source: Rollins et al. 2016, p. 162, © Elsevier. Reproduced with permission from Elsevier; further permission required for reuse.

Interventions That Effectively Promote Breastfeeding

Having a comprehensive breastfeeding strategy at the national level is the most effective way to influence the powerful social, economic, and cultural forces affecting a mother's decision to breastfeed (Rollins et al. 2016) (see figure 5.1).

A comprehensive breastfeeding strategy is composed of several types of interventions; the exact mix of interventions may vary from country to country, depending on the local context. For the purposes of these analyses, two interventions for pregnant women and mothers of young children (infant and young child nutrition counseling and maternity leave cash benefits),[1] as well as two interventions directed at the entire society (pro-breastfeeding social policies and national breastfeeding promotion campaigns) (table 5.1), are assumed to

Table 5.1 Interventions to Meet the Breastfeeding Target

Intervention	Target population	Description	Evidence of effectiveness
For mothers of infants			
Infant and young child nutrition counseling	Mothers of children age 0–11 months	This intervention comprises individual or group-based counseling sessions to promote exclusive breastfeeding delivered in the community and/or health facility, depending on country context.	Reanalysis by Sinha et al. (2015) for LiST shows that receiving breastfeeding promotion increased exclusive breastfeeding in children age 0–5 months [OR 2.5 in health system, OR 2.61 in home/community setting].
Maternity leave benefits	Mothers of children age 0–11 months	This consists of an extension of maternity leave cash benefits from the level and duration of benefits provided at baseline to six months at 67 percent wage level from public payer in line with International Labour Organization recommendations.	Sinha et al. (2015) show that maternity leave is associated with a 52 percent increase in exclusive breastfeeding [RR 1.52, 95% CI 1.03–2.03], but this is not specific to the effect of the extension of maternity leave cash benefits or to certain durations or levels of cash transfers. This intervention is included in the costing analysis but not the impact model.
For the general population			
Pro-breastfeeding social policies	General population	This intervention consists of policies, legislation, and monitoring and enforcement of policies related to the WHO's International Code on Marketing of Breastmilk Substitutes, the WHO Ten Steps of Successful Breastfeeding integration into hospital accreditation, and maternity protection/leave.	This intervention is included in the costing analysis but not the impact model.
National breastfeeding promotion campaigns	General population	This intervention uses mass advertising and campaigns to promote breastfeeding.	Sinha et al. (2015) show that strategies with media intervention integrated with counseling and community mobilization may have a significant effect on increasing exclusive breastfeeding rates [RR 1.17, 95% CI 1.01–1.14]. This intervention is included in the costing analysis but not the impact model.

Note: CI = confidence interval; LiST = Lives Saved Tool; OR = odds ratio; RR = relative risk; WHO = World Health Organization.

make up a minimum core of the comprehensive strategy applicable to most contexts, which can be adapted and added to as need be.

Counseling for Mothers and Caregivers on Good Infant and Young Child Nutrition and Hygiene Practices

This intervention includes individual or group-based counseling sessions delivered in the community and/or health facility to promote exclusive breastfeeding, depending on country context. Breastfeeding counseling or education delivered at the community level may be required in countries with weak health systems and lack of access to health facilities. A review by Haroon et al. (2013) demonstrates that breastfeeding counseling results in a 90 percent increase in rates of exclusive breastfeeding in infants age 0–5 months. Sinha et al. (2015) also find that counseling delivered in a health facility or in the community increases the likelihood of breastfeeding when compared with not receiving any counseling.

Pro-Breastfeeding Social Policies

Pro-breastfeeding social policies are designed to create an enabling environment for breastfeeding and motivate maternal and household decision making toward optimal child care and feeding practices. Among countries with an exclusive breastfeeding rate below 30 percent, those that rate high on a composite indicator for pro-breastfeeding social policies are estimated to have seen improvements in exclusive breastfeeding by 1 percent per year, or five times higher than countries with a low rating on this indicator (Rollins et al. 2016). Estimating the effect sizes for each individual policy intervention is challenging given their varying timing, degree of implementation, and number of cofounders. In particular, the adoption and enforcement of national legislation in line with the World Health Organization (WHO) International Code on Marketing of Breastmilk Substitutes is considered necessary to address aggressive marketing of breast milk substitutes (Baker et al. 2016).[2]

Access to maternity leave is associated with higher rates of breastfeeding (Sinha et al. 2015) and even lower infant mortality in some countries (Nandi et al. 2016). For new mothers who are working, one study found that national policies guaranteeing breastfeeding breaks in the workplace were associated with an increase in the rate of exclusive breastfeeding of infants younger than six months of age by 8.9 percentage points (Rollins et al. 2016). Although most low- and middle-income countries have some form of maternity leave and protection policies in position, only a few have adequate enforcement of laws or a sustainable financing scheme in place.

The Baby Friendly Hospital Initiative, established in 1991 by WHO and the United Nations Children's Fund (UNICEF) as a broad program designed to strengthen the culture of breastfeeding in hospitals (Labbok 2012), may also be a policy option for certain countries. The integration of WHO's Ten Steps of Successful Breastfeeding (WHO 1998) into existing hospital accreditation systems is an important policy approach in that direction. The specific orientation of pro-breastfeeding social policies in each country will vary because of country context, but the core policies that foster a culture that supports breastfeeding need resources for development, legislation, monitoring, and enforcement.

Extension of Maternity Leave Benefits

Maternity leave cash benefits refer to a cash transfer to the woman, from public funds or private employers, for a stipulated duration and level of compensation, which varies widely by country. Cash benefits reduce the opportunity cost for mothers of taking maternity leave for caregiving of newborns and infants. Sinha et al. (2015) show that maternity leave is associated with a 52 percent increase in exclusive breastfeeding, but this is not specific to the effect of the extension of maternity leave cash benefits or to certain durations or levels of cash transfers. Maternity leave for new mothers probably also results in broader social, developmental, and health benefits for working mothers and their newborns. Furthermore, the high rates of informal sector work in low- and middle-income countries adds to the low coverage of maternity leave cash benefits and, therefore, limits the population reach of these benefits. However, these benefits will be more and more important for working mothers as wealthier and transitioning economies develop (Rollins et al. 2016). More research is needed on the effect of maternity leave cash benefits and workplace interventions on breastfeeding.

National Breastfeeding Promotion Campaigns

Evidence suggests that mass media campaigns to promote breastfeeding are important elements in increasing national breastfeeding rates. Sinha et al. (2015) show that strategies with media intervention integrated with counseling and community mobilization may have a significant effect on increasing exclusive breastfeeding rates. As an example of what is possible, the integrated Alive & Thrive program in Vietnam (see box 9.3 in chapter 9)—which includes a mass media campaign at scale in addition to infant and young child nutrition counseling and advocacy for pro-breastfeeding social policies—demonstrated a total 28.3 percentage point increase in exclusive breastfeeding for the first six months compared to control sites over the period 2010–14 (Walters et al. 2016). There are positive signs that investing in large-scale media promotion and social marketing are important for counteracting the influence of marketing for breastmilk substitutes and developing a culture that supports optimal breastfeeding.

Analytic Approaches Specific to the Breastfeeding Target

The methods for estimating costs, impacts and benefit-cost ratios are presented in chapter 2; this section reviews important definitions, sample selection, and data specific to the breastfeeding target.

Measuring Exclusive Breastfeeding

In 2012, the indicator selected to measure progress with regard to *exclusive breastfeeding* was the prevalence of exclusive breastfeeding for all infants in the first six months of age (WHO and UNICEF 2014). The primary source of breastfeeding practice data for this analysis, the Demographic and Health Surveys (DHS) and Multiple Indicator Cluster Surveys (MICS) household surveys, asks mothers if they have breastfed their infants within the last 24 hours. Exclusivity of breastfeeding is determined by mothers reporting that infants did not receive any liquids or foods while breastfeeding. The data on national exclusive breastfeeding for these analyses are drawn from the WHO/UNICEF Global Targets Tracking Tool (September 2015 version) (WHO 2015). India's exclusive breastfeeding rate of 65 percent, reported in the 2013–14 Rapid Survey of Children (RSOC), is included in this analysis because the previous survey reported was a decade ago (Government of India and UNICEF 2015).

Sample Selection
The estimates in this chapter are based on a sample of 27 countries (20 with the highest absolute burden and 7 with exclusive breastfeeding prevalence lower than 10 percent). These 27 countries account for 78 percent of the burden of non-exclusively breastfed infants (up to six months of age) (see table 2.2 for the list of countries.) A multiplier of 1.28 was then used to extrapolate the sample cost to all low- and middle-income countries.

Interventions Included in the Analyses
As discussed above, the most effective way to increase rates of exclusive breastfeeding requires implementing a comprehensive strategy that includes, at minimum, pro-breastfeeding social policies, a national breastfeeding promotion campaign, and infant and young child nutrition counseling for expectant and new mothers. These interventions are included because they (1) are applicable to all countries, (2) address multiple levels of complex factors affecting breastfeeding, and (3) together can plausibly achieve the estimated impact on the rate of exclusive breastfeeding. In the long term, it is also important to reduce the perceived opportunity costs of breastfeeding through either maternity leave and cash benefits or workplace supports. The analyses estimate the global costs of extending maternity leave cash benefits for working mothers in the formal sector, but these costs are not included in the package of nutrition-specific interventions because it is an intervention that aims to achieve multiple social, economic, and health outcomes and will need to be financed from other sectors. See table 5.1 for further descriptions and effect size estimates used in the impact analyses. While all these interventions may have an independent effect on exclusive breastfeeding, only the effect of nutrition counseling is included in the impact model, whereas the costs include the cost of scaling up all four interventions. Therefore the overall benefit-cost ratios are an underestimate.

Estimating Unit Costs
Because of a lack of cost data on policy and media interventions at scale, the annual national unit costs of the pro-breastfeeding social policies and national breastfeeding promotion campaigns are based on the experience of the

Alive &Thrive program (Alive and Thrive 2013, 2014; Walters et al. 2016). The following assumptions are made: there are combined national costs for the pro-breastfeeding social policies and national breastfeeding promotion campaigns interventions of $1.0 million, $3.0 million, $5.0 million, and $10 million in countries with a population of less than 10 million, 10–50 million, 50–250 million, and more than 250 million, respectively. Twenty percent of the national costs are earmarked for the pro-breastfeeding social policies and 80 percent for the national breastfeeding promotion campaigns. It is assumed that economies of scale could be achieved for these two interventions in larger countries. Unit costs for infant and young child nutrition counseling come from a review of literature on cost data (see appendix C). Because the target definition is specific to exclusive breastfeeding from birth to six months, and not optimal breastfeeding until age two, costs include only one year of infant and young child nutrition counseling intervention delivery per mother and child pair.[3] The unit costs for the extension of maternity leave cash benefits include the costs of extending cash benefits from current duration to six months paid from public sources at a rate of 67 percent of minimum wage level in each country (ILO 2015).

Estimating Existing Levels of Coverage

For breastfeeding counseling, the analyses rely on the Lives Saved Tool (LiST) default rate for breastfeeding promotion coverage in each country, which is equivalent to the exclusive breastfeeding rate of infants age 1–5 months. Although this measure has weaknesses, mainly because there is wide variation in what constitutes "counseling" and coverage varies accordingly,[4] it is considered the best available measure at this time. Similar analyses in the future would benefit from standardized data on counseling coverage. Existing coverage of pro-breastfeeding is estimated on the basis of qualitative evidence of full or partial implementation of the International Code of Breastmilk Substitutes (WHO, UNICEF, and IBFAN 2016) and maternity leave policies (ILO 2015). Coverage of maternity leave cash benefits is estimated as the product of female labor force participation rate and the International Labour Organization (ILO) coverage in practice estimates for each country.[5]

Estimating Total Costs

The costing methodology is similar to all other targets included in the analyses. The total additional financing needs of achieving the target is the sum of the annual additional costs of scaling up the core interventions from baseline coverage level to full coverage, assuming the same linear scale-up from current to full coverage in the first five years plus a five-year maintenance phase are used. The number of beneficiaries (that is, mother-child pairs) for infant and young child nutrition counseling and maternity leave is calculated by subtracting the number of twin pairs at birth from the population of children at birth (WHO 2015).

Estimating Impacts

For the impact analyses, a Microsoft Excel model was developed to parallel the approach used by LiST (Bhutta et al. 2013; Walker, Tam, and Friberg 2013; Winfrey, McKinnon, and Stover 2011). Although multiple interventions are costed for the breastfeeding target, in the final analysis only one intervention—infant and young child nutrition counseling—is included in the impact model. The other policy and media-oriented interventions are recommended interventions, but there are too few effectiveness studies completed to confidently include their effects in the impact model. The formulae and odds ratios from the reanalysis of pooled estimates conducted by Sinha et al. (2015) for the LiST update (version 5.41 beta 13) are used in the model for estimating the impact of infant and young child nutrition counseling on exclusive breastfeeding prevalence (see table 5.1). The reanalysis suggests that children whose mothers receive breastfeeding promotion intervention delivered in the health system, home/community setting, and both health and community settings have odds ratios of 2.5, 2.61, and 5.1, respectively, for being exclusively breastfed compared to children whose mothers do not receive the intervention. It is assumed that the effect size for delivery in the health system is most suitable for upper-middle-income countries and that delivery in home/community setting is suitable for low-income and lower-middle-income countries. In order to be conservative in the impact projections, the higher effect size option associated with the combined delivery of breastfeeding promotion in both health system and home/community setting is not used in the model for the analyses. In LiST, breastfeeding promotion has an indirect effect on preventing neonatal and infant mortality through diarrhea and acute respiratory infections (that is, pneumonia). Therefore the breastfeeding counseling coverage projections from the Microsoft Excel model are inserted into LiST to estimate the number of child deaths averted that is attributable to breastfeeding promotion.

Benefit-Cost Analyses

The benefit-cost analyses of investing in breastfeeding include two main types of monetary benefits attributed to increases in exclusive breastfeeding prevalence: (1) earnings gains related to all-cause child mortality averted and (2) earnings gains related to cognitive losses averted in children. For the estimation of cognitive losses, these analyses employ an approach similar to the method used in Rollins et al. 2016 and Walters et al. 2016. However, these analyses estimate the potential earnings gains due to cognitive losses averted in children over their entire adult working lives from age 18 until they reach their average life expectancy or 65 years of age, whichever is earlier, rather than potential earnings in a one-year steady-state period. Key factors for this calculation are that ever being breastfed results in a 2.62 point IQ increase compared to not being breastfed (Horta, Loret de Mola, and Victora 2015), and 1 standard deviation increase in IQ leads to a 17 percent increase in wage earnings (Hanushek and Woessmann 2008). Potential benefits not included are the savings from reduced health care costs for the treatment of diarrhea and pneumonia attributed to inadequate breastfeeding, indirect costs borne by families related to the treatment of attributed childhood illnesses, costs of purchasing infant formula, and the mortality costs attributed to the higher risk of breast cancer in the mothers of nonbreastfed children. The benefit-cost analyses are, therefore, conservative estimates.

Sensitivity Analyses

The analyses employ one-way sensitivity analyses for the key drivers of cost, impact, and benefit-cost ratio results. For the cost sensitivity analysis, the assumption about the baseline coverage of breastfeeding counseling varies in line with other plausible proxies. For the impact sensitivity analysis, the overall exclusive breastfeeding rate projection in 2025 is presented, with the following changes in variables: (1) a less conservative delivery setting option in LiST for the effect size of breastfeeding promotion (combined delivery in health system and home/community setting) is included; (2) India's exclusive breastfeeding result from the 2013–14 RSOC is excluded; (3) an effect of gross domestic product (GDP) growth across low- and middle-income countries (based on historical trends) is included, resulting in an average annual reduction in the rate of exclusive breastfeeding of 0.34 percentage points per year in children 0–5 months of age (Victora et al. 2016);[6] and (4) the average historical trend of increase in exclusive breastfeeding rates equivalent to +0.40 percentage points per year across low- and middle-income countries is extended into future projections (WHO 2015).

Results

This section presents the results of the analyses described above, including both costs and impacts.

Breastfeeding Prevalence

The WHO Global Targets Tracking Tool database reports the global exclusive breastfeeding prevalence as 38 percent (WHO 2015), similar to the findings in the *Lancet* Breastfeeding Series (Victora et al. 2016). Because of India's size and influence over global nutrition indicators, the inclusion of India's exclusive breastfeeding rate from the 2013–14 RSOC increases the lower-middle-income country rate—from 38 percent in 2012 to 43 percent in 2015. *Therefore India single-handedly achieves 40 percent of the global World Health Assembly target for breastfeeding.* This result for India is included in the baseline prevalence of exclusive breastfeeding for the analyses.

Unit Costs

The population-weighted mean unit cost estimate for good infant and young child nutrition counseling is $7.32 per year per mother and child pair, but country-level unit costs range from $0.7 per year in Guatemala to $13.35 for Middle East and North Africa countries. The range of all unit costs for interventions included is shown in table 5.2. The unit costs of extending maternity leave cash benefits to six months vary greatly because of differences in country-level policies and wages.

Table 5.2 Minimum, Maximum, and Mean Unit Costs to Meet the Breastfeeding Target (Annual)
U.S.$

Intervention	Minimum	Maximum	Mean unit cost
Cost is per person per year			
Infant and young child nutrition counseling	0.70	13.35	7.32
Extension of maternity leave cash benefits from current duration to six months	0.00	1,401.96	273.64
Cost is per country per year			
Pro-breastfeeding social policies	100,000	1,000,000	n.a.
National breastfeeding promotion campaigns	2,000,000	8,000,000	n.a.

Note: The mean unit costs are population-weighted means; n.a. = not applicable.

Table 5.3 Total Financing Needs to Meet the Breastfeeding Target

Intervention	Total 10-year costs 2016–25 (US$, millions)	Share of total 10-year costs (%)
Infant and young child nutrition counseling	4,159	80
Pro-breastfeeding social policies	111	2
National breastfeeding promotion campaigns	906	18
Subtotal	**5,176**	**100**
Program (capacity strengthening and monitoring and evaluation)	570	n.a.
Total costs	**5,746**	**n.a.**

Note: Maternity leave cash benefits are excluded from the package costs; n.a. = not applicable.

Estimated Total Financing Needs

The total additional costs of scaling up the selected core set of interventions necessary to meet the breastfeeding target in low- and middle-income countries is $5.7 billion over 10 years (see table 5.3). This translates to approximately $4.70 per newborn. The majority of costs are for infant and young child nutrition counseling ($4.2 billion) and smaller amounts for pro-breastfeeding social policies ($111 million) and national breastfeeding promotion campaigns ($906 million). The annual additional costs would increase from $136 million in 2016 to $763 million by 2021 as programs scale up to full coverage over five years (see figure 5.2).

The total financing needs for the extension of maternity leave cash benefits from current status to six months in duration is estimated to be $24.1 billion over 10 years across low- and middle-income countries. Because maternity leave cash benefits are important for other social, labor, gender, and development objectives—not only breastfeeding—these costs are excluded from the nutrition-specific interventions package listed above.

The East Asia and Pacific region requires a 38 percent share of the total costs ($2.3 billion), the Sub-Saharan Africa region requires one-quarter ($1.5 billion), South Asia ($0.7 billion), and other regions require smaller total scale-up costs

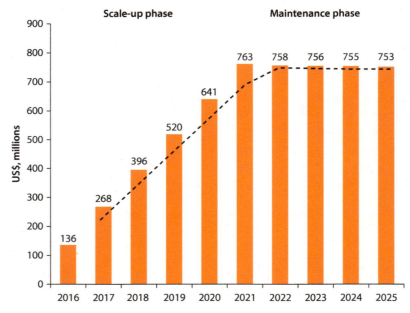

Figure 5.2 Annual Financing Needs to Meet the Breastfeeding Target

Note: Maternity leave cash benefits are excluded from the package costs.

(figure 5.3). By income group (see figure 5.4), the total costs are shared equally between lower-middle-income countries and upper-middle-income countries (45 and 46 percent, respectively); low-income countries require a much smaller share of the total (9 percent).

Sensitivity Analyses for Cost Estimates

Adding a second year of infant and young child nutrition counseling, as per guidelines and in line with the costing of the stunting target, increases costs to a total of $8.7 billion. Coverage rates for infant and young child nutrition counseling may be the largest source of uncertainty in this model. The sensitivity analysis tornado diagram (see figure 5.5) shows that assuming a more conservative coverage rate—such as exclusive breastfeeding at 4–5 months as reported by DHS and MICS, or simply assuming no coverage at all (0 percent coverage)—would bring the total target financing needs over 10 years to $6.3 billion or $7.3 billion, respectively. The minimum coverage level required to reach the target is 53 percent, but the reduced cost would come with the trade-off of a substantial reduction in the number of child deaths and diseases averted.

Reaching the Global Target for Breastfeeding

Figure 5.3 Ten-Year Total Financing Needs to Meet the Breastfeeding Target, by Region

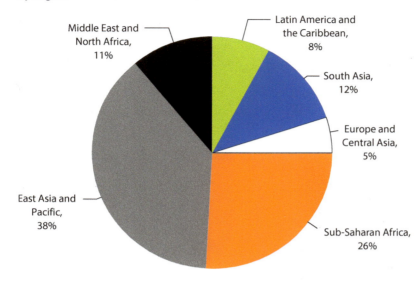

Figure 5.4 Ten-Year Total Financing Needs to Meet the Breastfeeding Target, by Country Income Group

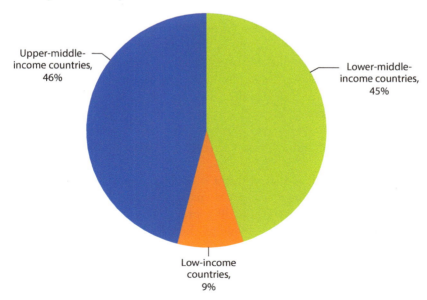

An Investment Framework for Nutrition • http://dx.doi.org/10.1596/978-1-4648-1010-7

Figure 5.5 Sensitivity Analyses for 10-Year Total Financing Needs to Meet the Breastfeeding Target

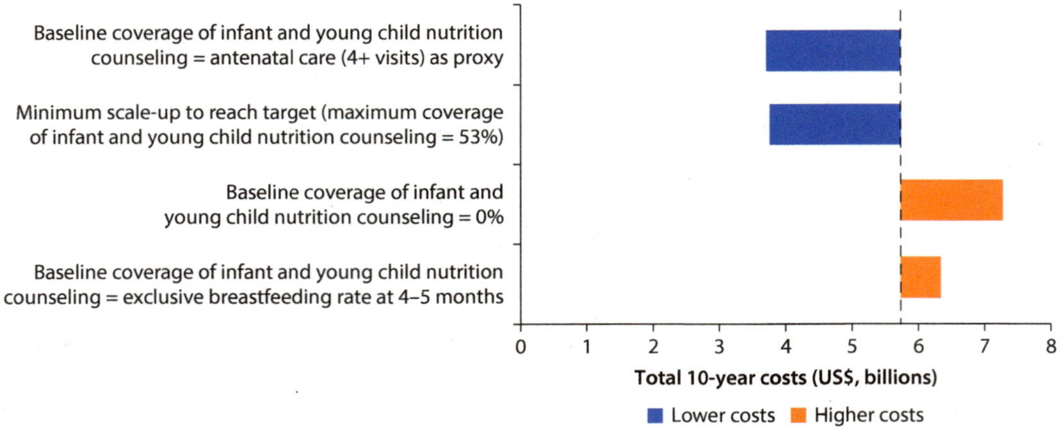

[Bar chart showing Total 10-year costs (US$, billions) on x-axis from 0 to 8, with four categories:
- Baseline coverage of infant and young child nutrition counseling = antenatal care (4+ visits) as proxy: Lower costs bar
- Minimum scale-up to reach target (maximum coverage of infant and young child nutrition counseling = 53%): Lower costs bar
- Baseline coverage of infant and young child nutrition counseling = 0%: Higher costs bar (~7.3)
- Baseline coverage of infant and young child nutrition counseling = exclusive breastfeeding rate at 4–5 months: Higher costs bar (~6.3)

Legend: Lower costs (blue), Higher costs (orange)]

Expected Impacts of the Scale-Up

This investment in the breastfeeding intervention package is estimated to result in an additional 105 million children being exclusively breastfed globally over the next 10 years and an increase in the exclusive breastfeeding rate to 54 percent (see figure 5.6).[7] Achieving this level of exclusive breastfeeding in low- and middle-income countries will result in a cumulative total of 520,000 child deaths averted over the next 10 years. In addition, millions of cases of diarrhea and pneumonia will have been prevented, and more children will reach their potential in terms of cognitive development. The five countries with the highest total child deaths averted are India, Pakistan, Nigeria, the Democratic Republic of Congo, and Ethiopia, which together account for 57 percent of estimated child deaths averted across all low- and middle-income countries. Though not calculated in the analyses, this increase in exclusive breastfeeding rates will also lead to substantially fewer women dying of breast cancer as a result of the protective effects that breastfeeding extends to the mother.

It should be noted that the current modeling approach used by LiST and in the Excel model may be problematic for particular countries with extremely low-exclusive breastfeeding prevalence in the 0 to 10 percent range. Because the formulae determining the effect size of breastfeeding counseling are dependent on the problematic default indicator for coverage (that is, 1–5 month exclusive breastfeeding prevalence), countries with extremely low exclusive breastfeeding rates can achieve only a limited increase in breastfeeding rates in these models. For example, in the LiST model, Djibouti can achieve a rise in exclusive breastfeeding rates from 1 percent in 2015 to only 3.1 percent in 2025 despite scale-up to 90 percent coverage of counseling

Figure 5.6 Projected Exclusive Breastfeeding Prevalence and Child Deaths Averted with Scale-Up of Interventions to Meet the Breastfeeding Target

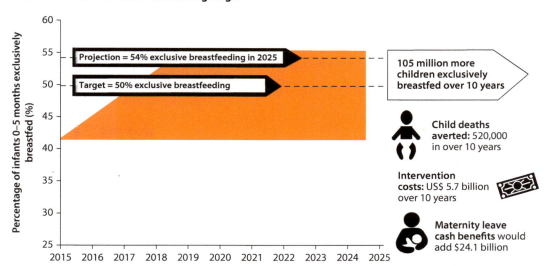

over 10 years. This is a limitation in the current LiST modeling of breastfeeding promotion that will affect the country-level projections for countries with low baseline rates. However, this limitation will have minimal impact on the global results of this analysis because most countries in the sample were chosen on the basis of high absolute burden.

Sensitivity Analyses of the Impacts of the Scale-Up

With the confluence of factors affecting breastfeeding behaviors across different country contexts, it is challenging to make accurate predictions into the future. The sensitivity analyses show the change in exclusive breastfeeding projection if the effect size for breastfeeding promotion in LiST is set to the combined effect of counseling in both health system and home/community settings. Excluding the 2013–14 India RSOC exclusive breastfeeding result from baseline exclusive breastfeeding prevalence reduces the global projection for 2025 from 54 percent to 50 percent. It also demonstrates the potential change in the exclusive breastfeeding rate projection in 2025 by considering the inclusion of an effect of GDP on future exclusive breastfeeding rates and extending the historical trend in exclusive breastfeeding (see figure 5.7). In both cases, the target would still be achieved.

Although achieving this target requires substantial effort, it appears less ambitious than the other global nutrition targets. These analyses show that there may be scope to go beyond the current breastfeeding target by 2025 or 2030.

Figure 5.7 Sensitivity Analyses of the Estimated Impact of Interventions on Exclusive Breastfeeding Rates

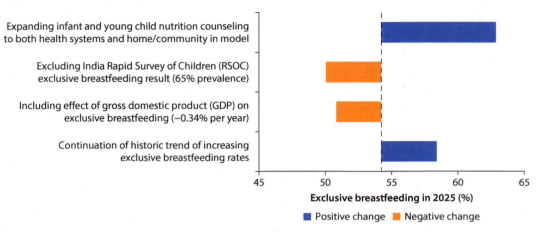

Table 5.4 Benefit-Cost Ratios of Scaling Up Interventions to Meet the Breastfeeding Target, 3 and 5 Percent Discount Rates

	3% discount rate			5% discount rate		
Group	Present value of benefits (US$, billions)	Present value of costs (US$, billions)	Benefit-cost ratio	Present value of benefits (US$, billions)	Present value of costs (US$, billions)	Benefit-cost ratio
By region						
Sub-Saharan Africa[a]	20.0	1.1	18.2	8.6	1.0	8.9
South Asia[a]	36.1	0.9	37.0	14.5	0.9	16.8
East Asia and the Pacific[a]	108.2	3.2	33.8	43.3	2.8	15.2
By country income group						
Low-income countries[a]	3.5	0.6	6.3	1.3	0.5	2.5
Lower-middle-income countries[a]	81.7	3.0	27.7	33.3	2.6	12.8
Upper-middle-income countries[a]	147.2	3.2	46.3	59.5	2.8	21.1
Pooled	**297.6**	**8.6**	**34.7**	**120.3**	**7.6**	**15.8**
Median[a]	n.a.	n.a.	17.5	n.a.	n.a.	7.6

Note: n.a. = not applicable.
a. Sample countries only.

Benefit-Cost Analyses

Investing in a comprehensive breastfeeding promotion and support package is an excellent investment for countries. Assuming a conservative 3 percent GDP growth rate and a 3 percent discount rate for costs and benefits yields an estimated net benefit of $298 billion over the productive lives of child beneficiaries, a pooled benefit-cost ratio of 34.7, and a median benefit-cost ratio of 17.5 (see table 5.4). By region, this translates into a benefit-cost ratio of 18.2 for Sub-Saharan Africa, 37.0 for South Asia, and 33.8 for East Asia and Pacific. By income group, this translates into a benefit- cost ratio of 6.3 for low-income countries, 27.7 for lower-middle income countries, and 46.3 for upper-middle income countries.

When assuming a more conservative 5 percent discount rate, the median benefit-cost ratio decreases to 7.6 and the pooled rate to 15.8.

Discussion

Humans have known and science has shown that breastfeeding provides unparalleled nutritional and immunological benefits for infants and young children. The analyses demonstrate that, although there may be notable costs to investing in breastfeeding promotion, protection, and support, reaching the global target for breastfeeding can be achieved and would result in saving a large number of children's lives and also in substantial reductions in maternal morbidity. In fact, there is potential to surpass the current target for breastfeeding and there may be scope to revise this target to be more ambitious.

The return on the investment across countries is positive and strong: estimates show that the investment would generate a net present value of $298 billion in benefits over the productive lives of child beneficiaries, a pooled benefit-cost ratio of 34.7, and median benefit-cost ratios of 17.5 (15.8 and 7.6, respectively, under more conservative discounting assumptions). Recent research shows that lifetime labor earnings gains for a breastfed child would amount to approximately $20,000 in the United States (Lutter 2016). Although projected earnings gains estimated in the analyses are lower than those in the United States given the lower-income status of countries in the sample, this new finding further reiterates the need for the promotion of exclusive breastfeeding.

The accuracy with which future behavior patterns can be predicted is only as good as the tools and data available and the assumptions made. These analyses were conducted with the best available data, but there is an urgent need for improved data on intervention coverage, costs, and effectiveness (for certain interventions). Interventions and policy levers such as maternity leave cash benefits currently generate high costs and cover only the formal labor sector. Because large numbers of women, especially in developing countries, work in the informal sector, reaching these women is essential for achieving greater impact. Better measurement of the coverage of infant and young child nutrition counseling, from pregnancy through age two, is urgently needed. It is expected that a recently added DHS survey question addressing breastfeeding counseling will help with the estimation of coverage of any counseling, but will not be sufficient to assess intervention coverage of comprehensive counseling for new mothers all the way through to age two.

There is also an urgent need for implementers and researchers to collect and publish cost data so that future costing studies can be based on stronger data. Impact modeling software also must adapt to include a variety of breastfeeding interventions and to make stronger projections for the highest-burden countries. Further advances in experimental and quasi-experimental methods are also needed to better understand the impact of interventions such as policies, media, and maternity leave, among others. Decades of underfinancing support for nursing mothers have resulted in creating a culture, particularly among higher-income and emerging economies, that stigmatizes breastfeeding and downplays the trade-offs of not breastfeeding. Now the case for investing in a breastfeeding renaissance in the 21st century is clear. The analyses show that scaling up a core set of interventions that enable optimal breastfeeding can have a major impact on preventing child deaths and generating strong returns on investment over time for societies, labor markets, and their economies.

Notes

1. In the analyses, *maternity leave cash benefits* refers to the actual cash transfer to the woman, not the policy that required it. Any policies or guidelines on maternity leave benefits are included within the pro-breastfeeding social policies intervention.
2. To date, 39 countries have fully legislated the International Code on Marketing of Breastmilk Substitutes while another 96 have some legal measures in place, although many continue to lack resources for monitoring implementation and enforcement against violations of the Code (WHO, UNICEF, and IBFAN 2016).
3. This is different from what was costed to achieve the stunting target, which included two years of promotion of good infant and young child nutrition and hygiene (see chapter 3).
4. For some, "counseling" may be a short interaction between a pregnant woman and a health care professional as part of antenatal care. At the other end of the spectrum, "counseling" may entail up to 15 nutritional consultations from pregnancy through the infant's second year of life.
5. The ILO estimates the *coverage in practice* of maternity leave cash benefits for women in each country; this is defined as the number of people who have the right to receive benefits but are not necessarily currently beneficiaries.
6. The *Lancet* Breastfeeding Series suggests a strong inverse correlation between GDP and breastfeeding rates and estimates that for "each doubling in the gross domestic product per head, breastfeeding prevalence at 12 months decreased by ten percentage points" (Victora et al. 2016, 477). For this study, this effect size was modified to suit by the sensitivity analysis pertaining to exclusive breastfeeding rates and the low- and middle-income countries subject to this analysis. Assuming the 10-year historical (2004–14) GDP per capita growth rate in low- and middle-income countries of 5.5 percent (World Bank 2015) will continue, this is expected to yield only a 70 percent increase by 2025, not double. Furthermore, as estimated by Victora et al. (2016), the correlation between GDP per capita and exclusive breastfeeding is approximately half as strong (that is, –0.41) as at 12 months (that is, –0.84). Therefore the authors' calculations for an effect of GDP growth on exclusive breastfeeding in the context of the WHA target costing are: –10% * 70% * (–0.41/–0.84)/10 years = –0.34 percentage points per year.
7. Importantly, this projection depends heavily on India's 2013–14 Rapid Survey of Children result of 65 percent exclusive breastfeeding rate, which—because of India's population size—affects the global figures greatly. See the discussion in the section "Sensitivity Analyses of the Impacts of the Scale-Up".

References

Alive and Thrive. 2013. *Vietnam Costing Study: Implementation Expenditure and Costs.* Hanoi: Alive & Thrive.

———. 2014. *Country Brief: Alive & Thrive Program Approach and Results in Vietnam. June 2009 to December 2014*. Hanoi: Alive and Thrive. http://aliveandthrive.org/resources/country-brief-alive-thrives-program-approach-andresults-in-viet-nam-june-2009-to-december-2014/.

Baker, P., J. Smith, L. Salmon, S. Friel, G. Kent, A. Iellamo, J. P. Dadhich, and M. J. Renfrew. 2016. "Global Trends and Patterns of Commercial Milk-Based Formula Sales: Is an Unprecedented Infant and Young Child Feeding Transition Underway?" *Public Health Nutrition* 19 (14): 2540–50.

Bhutta, Z. A., J. K. Das, A. Rizvi, M. F. Gaffey, N. Walker, S. Horton, P. Webb, A. Lartey, and R. E. Black. 2013. "Evidence-Based Interventions for Improvement of Maternal and Child Nutrition: What Can Be Done and at What Cost?" *The Lancet* 382 (9890): 452–77.

Cai, X., T. Wardlaw, and D. W. Brown. 2012. "Global Trends in Exclusive Breastfeeding." *International Breastfeeding Journal* 7: 12.

Government of India and UNICEF (United Nations Children's Fund). 2015. *Rapid Survey on Children (RSOC) 2013–14: National Report*. Ministry of Women and Child Development, New Delhi. http://wcd.nic.in/sites/default/files/RSOC%20National%20Report%202013-14%20Final.pdf.

Hanushek, E., and L. Woessmann. 2008. "The Role of Cognitive Skills in Economic Development." *Journal of Economic Literature* 46: 607–68.

Haroon, S., J. K. Das, R. A. Salam, A. Imdad, and Z. A. Bhutta. 2013. "Breastfeeding Promotion Interventions and Breastfeeding Practices: A Systematic Review." *BMC Public Health* 13 (Suppl 3): S20.

Holla-Bhar, R., A. Iellamo, A. Gupta, J. P. Smith, and J. P. Dadhich. 2015. "Investing in Breastfeeding: The World Breastfeeding Costing Initiative." *International Breastfeeding Journal* 10: 8.

Horta, B. L., C. Loret de Mola, and C. G. Victora. 2015. "Breastfeeding and Intelligence: A Systematic Review and Meta-Analysis." *ActaPaediatrica* 104: 14–19.

IFPRI (International Food Policy Research Institute). 2016. *Global Nutrition Report 2016: From Promise to Impact: Ending Malnutrition by 2030*, Washington, DC: IFPRI. http://ebrary.ifpri.org/utils/getfile/collection/p15738coll2/id/130354/filename/130565.pdf.

ILO (International Labour Organization). 2015. ILOSTAT (database), ILO, Geneva (accessed May 2, 2015), http://www.ilo.org/ilostat/faces/oracle/webcenter/portalapp/pagehierarchy/Page137.jspx?_afrLoop=522111198762802&clean=true#!%40%40%3F_afrLoop%3D522111198762802%26clean%3Dtrue%26_adf.ctrl-state%3Dtsep308c4_159.

Labbok, M. H. 2012. "Global Baby-Friendly Hospital Initiative Monitoring Data: Update and Discussion." *Breastfeeding Medicine: The Official Journal of the Academy of Breastfeeding Medicine* 7: 210–22.

Lutter, R. 2016. "Cognitive Performance, Labor Market Outcomes, and Estimates of Economic Value of Cognitive Effects of Breastfeeding." Unpublished manuscript, University of Virginia, Charlottesville, VA.

Nandi, A., M. Hajizadeh, S. Harper, A. Koski, E. C. Strumpf, and J. Heymann. 2016. "Increased Duration of Paid Maternity Leave Lowers Infant Mortality in Low- and Middle-Income Countries: A Quasi-Experimental Study." *PLoS Medicine* 13: e1001985.

Piwoz, E. G., and S. L. Huffman. 2015. "The Impact of Marketing of Breast-Milk Substitutes on WHO-Recommended Breastfeeding Practices." *Food and Nutrition Bulletin* 36 (4): 373–86.

Rollins, N. C., N. Bhandari, N. Hajeebhoy, S. Horton, C. K. Lutter, J. C. Martines, E. G. Piwoz, L. M. Richter, and C. G. Victora. 2016. "Why Invest, and What It Will Take to Improve Breastfeeding Practices?" *The Lancet* 387 (10017): 491–504.

Sinha, B., R. Chowdury, M. J. Sankar, J. Martines, S. Taneja, S. Mazumder, N. Rollins, R. Bahl, and N. Bhandari. 2015. "Interventions to Improve Breastfeeding Outcomes: A Systematic Review and Meta-Analysis." *Acta Pediatrica* 104 (467): 114–34.

UNICEF (United Nations Children's Fund). 2011. *Infant and Young Child Feeding: Programming Guide*. http://www.unicef.org/nutrition/files/Final_IYCF_programming_guide_2011.pdf.

———. 2016. *From the First Hour of Life: Making the Case for Improved Infant and Young Child Feeding Everywhere*. New York: UNICEF. https://data.unicef.org/resources/first-hour-life-new-report-breastfeeding-practices/.

Victora, C., R. Bahl, A. Barros, G. V. A. França, S. Horton, J. Krasevec, S. Murch, M. J. Sankar, N. Walker, and N. C. Rollins. 2016. "Breastfeeding in the 21st Century: Epidemiology, Mechanisms and Lifelong Effect." *The Lancet* 387 (10017): 475–490.

Walker, N., Y. Tam, and I. K. Friberg. 2013. "Overview of the Lives Saved Tool (LiST)." *BMC Public Health* 13 (Suppl 3): S1.

Walters, D., S. Horton, A. Y. Siregar, P. Pitriyan, N. Hajeebhoy, R. Mathisen, L. T. Phan, and C. Rudert. 2016. "The Cost of Not Breastfeeding in Southeast Asia." *Health Policy and Planning* 31 (8): 1107–16.

WHO (World Health Organization). 1998. *Evidence for the Ten Steps to Successful Breastfeeding*. Geneva: WHO.

———. 2015. Global Targets Tracking Tool (accessed September 15, 2015), https://extranet.who.int/sree/Reports?op=vs&path=%2FWHO_HQ_Reports/G16/PROD/EXT/Targets_Menu&VSPARAM_varLanguage=E&VSPARAM_varISOCODE=ALB.

WHO and UNICEF (World Health Organization and United Nations Children's Fund). 2014. *Global Nutrition Targets 2025: Breastfeeding Policy Brief*. http://apps.who.int/iris/bitstream/10665/149022/1/WHO_NMH_NHD_14.7_eng.pdf?ua=1.

WHO, UNICEF, and IBFAN (World Health Organization, United Nations Children's Fund, and International Baby Food Action Network). 2016. *Marketing of Breast-milk Substitutes: National Implementation of the International Code*. Status Report 2016. Geneva: WHO. http://apps.who.int/iris/bitstream/10665/206008/1/9789241565325_eng.pdf?ua=1&ua=1.

Winfrey, W., R. McKinnon, and J. Stover. 2011. "Methods Used in the Lives Saved Tool (LiST)." *BMC Public Health* 11 (Suppl 3): S32.

World Bank. 2015. World Development Indicators (database), World Bank, Washington, DC (accessed 2015), http://data.worldbank.org/data-catalog/world-development-indicators.

CHAPTER 6

Scaling Up the Treatment of Severe Wasting

Jakub Kakietek, Michelle Mehta, and Meera Shekar

Key Messages

- Given the current state of evidence on the prevention of wasting, it is impossible to estimate the costs of reaching the global wasting target. Rapidly developing the evidence base and policy and intervention guidelines is imperative if the world is to meet this target.
- Unlike prior chapters, the analyses included in this chapter focus on estimating the costs of treating severe acute malnutrition and mitigating its impacts. It does not include the costs or impacts of treating moderate acute malnutrition because the evidence base and World Health Organization (WHO) guidelines for treatment are lacking.
- Scaling up the treatment of severe acute malnutrition for 91 million children in low- and middle-income countries will require about $9.1 billion over 10 years. This averages to about $110 per child in Africa and $90 per child in South Asia.
- During that time frame, the scale-up would prevent at least 860,000 deaths in children under age five.
- A conservative estimate is that the scale-up of treatment of severe acute malnutrition for children would result in at least $25 billion in annual increases in economic productivity over the productive lifetimes of children who benefitted from the program. Every $1 invested in treatment would result in about $4 in economic returns (discounted at 3 percent annually).
- These are conservative estimates based only on mortality reductions. It is possible that wasting treatment has other benefits for child development (for example, reducing cognitive losses and physical disability). Such additional benefits have, however, yet to be quantified.
- More research is needed on the pathways leading to the incidence of wasting; on understanding the cyclical nature of wasting (for example, whether and how frequently a given child experiences multiple bouts of wasting during a given year) and subsequent consequences and vulnerability created by repeated episodes; and the relationship between wasting and stunting and the short-, medium-, and long-term impacts of wasting on children's physical and cognitive development. Without a rapid investment in knowledge, it is not possible to build an effective global investment case for preventing wasting.

Wasting and Its Effects

Wasting, also known as *acute malnutrition*, is a reduction or loss of body weight in relation to height. WHO classifies wasting as severe or moderate, according to the WHO growth standard for weight-for-height.[1] *Severe acute malnutrition* is defined as severe wasting and/or mid-upper arm circumference (MUAC) less than 115 millimeters and/or bilateral pitting edema. *Moderate acute malnutrition* is defined as moderate wasting and/or MUAC greater than or equal to 115 millimeters and less than 125 millimeters (WHO 2014). The variations in the classification of wasting pose challenges in identifying children for treatment. Although neither weight-for-height nor MUAC are shown to be good predictors of mortality, on balance, the MUAC has shown better predictive power (ENN et al. 2012). Because of this, clinical assessment of complications such as bilateral pitting edema are essential for distinguishing severe cases needing inpatient treatment versus uncomplicated cases that can be treated at community levels. Children suffering from severe acute malnutrition have a mortality risk 11 times higher than children who are not malnourished. The WHO estimates that wasting accounts for about 2 million deaths among children under age five globally—5 percent of all deaths in that age group (McDonald et al. 2013).

As of 2015, 50 million children globally were wasted (UNICEF, WHO, and World Bank 2015), one-third of whom were severely wasted. Of the total number of wasted children, about 34 million live in South Asia and about 14 million live in Sub-Saharan Africa. India, Djibouti, South Sudan, and Sri Lanka face the greatest burden of wasting, with over 15 percent prevalence in each country, although the etiology and causes of wasting may be different across regions. Particularly in South Asia, wasting is often seen in children well below six months of age, pointing to more chronic and societal etiologies such as poor maternal nutrition, poor infant feeding practices, and lower class/caste status contributing to wasting rates (Menon 2012). A growing burden is also developing in the Middle East and North Africa, with countries such as the Republic of Yemen seeing wasting rates of over 16 percent (UNICEF, WHO, and World Bank 2015). In total, 14 countries globally have wasting rates above the public health emergency range (greater than 10 percent prevalence). Unlike stunting, trends in wasting probably underestimate the true burden of wasting because this is a measure of acute or short-term incidences in malnutrition, which can occur during peak times of famine, crises, low harvest periods, or bouts of illness. Therefore, during survey times, which may be outside of seasonal peaks in wasting, a relatively large prevalence of incidence cases may be missed. Nonetheless, wasting prevalence has remained steady at 8 percent globally with a recent minimal decline to 7.5 percent (UNICEF, WHO, and World Bank 2015).

The 2012 World Health Assembly target is to reduce and maintain childhood wasting to less than 5 percent. Like the stunting target, the World Health Assembly target for wasting has been incorporated into Sustainable

Development Goal 2 and its target 2.2. This target focuses on reducing the prevalence of wasting and, consequently, on preventing and treating wasting. In order to reach the target, effective strategies are needed to treat current cases and to prevent future cases of wasting. However, to date, evidence on how to prevent wasting is limited and inconclusive. Coffey (2016) identifies five systematic reviews and a meta-analysis examining the impact of nutrition-specific interventions on weight-for-height z-scores. The interventions include food supplementation and micronutrient supplementation (including lipid nutrient supplements, hot meals, and fortified milks, combined with nutrition, health, and hygiene education) for children under five, and weight-for-height is analyzed only as a secondary outcome of interest. Food supplementation shows no impact on weight-for-height. One meta-analysis shows a statistically significant but very small impact of zinc supplementation on weight-for-height (Ramakrishnan, Nguyen, and Martorell 2009). Evidence is also inadequate for the impact of nutrition-sensitive interventions on wasting. A Cochrane review of the literature on water, sanitation and hygiene (WASH) interventions finds no evidence of the impact of WASH on wasting (Dangour et al. 2013). The lack of documented impact is at least partly due to the poor quality of the studies reviewed and the fact that weight-for-height is included only as a secondary outcome (see Coffey 2016 for a more in-depth discussion). One study of cash transfer programs combined with food supplementation shows significant and substantial reduction (84 percent) in the risk of wasting for children in a group that received unconditional cash transfers and food supplementation compared with children who received only food supplementation (Langendorf et al. 2014). However, more evidence is needed to establish a robust evidence base of the impact of similar social protection programs.

In sum, the extant literature has not focused on understanding the pathways leading to the incidence of wasting and the effectiveness of interventions to prevent it from occurring in different contexts. It is possible that a better understanding of the determinants of acute malnutrition could be gained by reanalyzing the data collected as part of the existing studies. However, to date, this has not been a priority for researchers. Most of the attention has been given to recovery and relapse. Therefore one of the conclusions from these analyses is to recommend that more research be undertaken to document the evidence base for preventing wasting.

On the other hand, the treatment of severe acute malnutrition in children has a strong and well-established evidence base (see Lenters et al. 2013 for a review). For this reason the analyses included in this chapter focus on estimating the costs of treating severe acute malnutrition and mitigating its impacts.[2] In the context of the global target for wasting, these analyses provide an estimate of the costs of *not* reaching the wasting target. In the absence of effective prevention strategies, the world will need to invest in an expansion of treatment programs in order to avoid deaths among children suffering from severe acute malnutrition.

Treatment of Severe Acute Malnutrition in Children

WHO recommends outpatient treatment of children with uncomplicated severe acute malnutrition (85–90 percent of cases) using ready-to-use therapeutic food and a seven-day preventive course of antibiotics (WHO 2013). This treatment has been shown to reduce mortality and lead to recovery in about 80 percent of cases (Hossain et al. 2009; Khanum, Ashworth, and Huttly 1994, 1998; Lenters et al. 2013).

Although the treatment of severe acute malnutrition has been proven to be highly effective, the scale-up of these interventions is limited: only about 15 percent of children with severe acute malnutrition have access to treatment (WHO 2014). One of the reasons for low access to treatment is its relatively high cost (see, for example, Bhutta et al. 2013; Horton et al. 2010). A number of studies examine different strategies for reducing costs and improving cost-effectiveness of severe acute malnutrition treatment interventions. Several authors compare outpatient and inpatient-based treatment regimens (Bachmann 2009, 2010; Greco et al. 2006; Puett et al. 2013; Sandige et al. 2004). Some authors compare the costs and cost-effectiveness of using locally produced ready-to-use therapeutic food products (Greco et al. 2006; Singh et al. 2010).

This chapter presents an analysis of the investments needed to expand the current coverage of this intervention to reach 90 percent of children suffering from severe acute malnutrition in low- and middle-income countries by 2025 and the impact of such scale-up on child mortality. A benefit-cost analysis is also included here, along with a comparison of the investment costs and the estimated economic benefits resulting from the treatment of severe acute malnutrition in children.

These analyses do not include the management of moderate acute malnutrition. Treatment of severe acute malnutrition is a well-defined intervention with supporting WHO guidelines (see WHO 2013). In contrast, the management of moderate acute malnutrition is much less well defined. No guidelines exist for the treatment of moderate acute malnutrition.[3] As a result, different countries and different agencies use very different approaches. These variations range from blanket provision of fortified or unfortified staples including corn-soy blends and other specialty cereal-based products (such as SuperCereal), which targets populations at large to prevent acute malnutrition and to treat existing cases of moderate acute malnutrition in children, to programs that provide lipid-based nutrition supplements to target populations. In the absence of global guidelines or standards, the entry and exit criteria for benefitting from such feeding and supplementation programs vary widely. Furthermore, the literature on the impact of the treatment of moderate acute malnutrition is limited (see Lenters et al. 2013). In light of this, the treatment of moderate acute malnutrition is not included in these analyses.

Analytic Approaches Specific to the Wasting Target

The methods used in these analyses are described in chapter 2. A few key methodological considerations specific to the coverage expansion of the treatment of severe acute malnutrition for children are summarized below.

Measuring the Incidence of Wasting

The target population for the treatment of severe acute malnutrition is defined as children 6–59 months of age suffering from severe wasting, determined by measurement of weight-for-height or MUAC, or clinical assessment of bilateral pitting edema. Routinely collected data on the nutrition status of children—for example, through Demographic and Health Surveys (DHS) or Multiple Indicator Cluster Surveys (MICS)—include information on the prevalence of severe wasting in a given year. However, annual prevalence very likely underestimates the number of children who require treatment for two reasons. First, severe wasting is an acute condition, the prevalence of which likely varies within a year. In the lean season, or during periods of drought or other natural (or manmade) disasters, the percentage of children with acute malnutrition can increase rapidly. Second, it is possible, and even likely, that a single child can experience multiple episodes of acute malnutrition in a given year. At present, longitudinal data are limited to surveillance systems used in emergency situations, particularly in Ethiopia, Niger, and Sudan, where data on cases of severe acute malnutrition are captured over time in highly food insecure areas (Tuffrey 2016). This does not fully allow for estimating the incidence of severe acute malnutrition in a way that would capture seasonal variations and multiple episodes of acute malnutrition outside of emergency situations. For this analysis, the United Nations Children's Fund (UNICEF) programmatic guidance is used (UNICEF 2015). Following the methodology presented in that guidance, the annual incidence of severe acute malnutrition is approximated by multiplying the annual prevalence by a factor of 1.6. The annual population in need of severe acute malnutrition treatment is calculated as:

(Number of children 6–59 months) * (Prevalence of severe wasting) * (1.6)

Measuring Existing Treatment Coverage

No country-level estimates of the coverage of the treatment of severe acute malnutrition for children currently exist. To develop baseline coverage, these analyses rely on data from the Coverage Monitoring Network on the percentage of children suffering from severe wasting at subnational levels (for example, districts) for a number of countries.[4] This database uses information collected from organizations implementing programs in specific subnational geographic locations. For countries where coverage data were available from only one region, these data are used to represent coverage at the national level. For countries where data from multiple regions were available, a population-weighted average is used as a proxy for the national level. It should be noted that this approach probably overestimates the current treatment coverage. For countries without available data, the current coverage of treatment is assumed to be zero. Baseline coverage data used in the analyses are presented in appendix B.

Sample Selection

The estimates of financing needs are based on a sample of 24 countries (20 countries with the highest absolute burden and 4 countries with wasting prevalence higher than 15 percent), together accounting for 82.9 percent of the burden of wasted children. The list of countries included in each sample for each target is shown in table 2.2.

Unit Costs and Assumptions about Changes over Time

Unit costs are obtained through a literature review from 2000 onward, a scan of gray literature, and websites of organizations providing treatment of severe acute malnutrition (UNICEF, Save the Children, Action Contre la Faim, and others). If no unit cost data were available for a given intervention in a given country, the average (mean) unit cost for other countries in that region is used. If there were no unit cost data for any country in a given region, the average from the countries with available unit costs is used. All costs are converted to U.S. dollars and inflated to 2015 values. A list of unit costs used as well as unit cost data sources is included in appendix C.

Treatment of severe acute malnutrition for children has higher unit costs than other nutrition interventions. This is partly because of the intensive curative nature of the intervention, which, even if delivered in the outpatient setting, requires a significant amount of time to be spent with health care providers (this includes initial triage, anthropometric measurement and diagnosis, assessment for complications, drug and ready-to-use therapeutic food dispensing, nutrition counseling for mothers and/or caregivers, and weekly follow-up visits). In addition, ready-to-use therapeutic food is an expensive commodity as compared to those used in other nutrition interventions. Currently, dried skimmed milk is estimated to account for between 40 and 50 percent of the ready-to-use therapeutic food input costs and over one-third of the total ready-to-use therapeutic food manufacturing cost (Manary 2006; Santini et al. 2013). It is assumed that, in the next 10 years, a more cost-effective formulation of ready-to-use therapeutic foods will be developed to replace dried skimmed milk with an alternative source protein that is comparable to the current formulation with respect to recovery rate and time. Such an alternative formulation could potentially lead to a 33 percent reduction in ready-to-use therapeutic food price per kilogram. The estimated monetary value of the reduction is based on the average price charged by 17 global and local suppliers that sold ready-to-use therapeutic food to UNICEF in 2015. The average global price of a carton (15 kilograms) of ready-to-use therapeutic food was $51.57 (in 2015 US$; UNICEF Supply Division 2015 data). The assumed 33 percent decline in the product cost is equivalent to a $17.02 cost reduction per case treated. Those cost reductions are assumed to be realized by 2020.

A further 20 percent reduction in the cost of delivery of treatment of severe acute malnutrition for children over the 10-year period is also assumed. This is expected to result from improved protocols and better integration of the treatment of severe acute malnutrition into national health care delivery systems. Empirical literature on cost savings in nutrition programming that result from changes in delivery platforms is very limited.[5] However, the assumed cost reduction of 20 percent is consistent with the findings from Khan and Ahmed (2003),

Scaling Up the Treatment of Severe Wasting

Figure 6.1 Total Annual Financing Needs for the Treatment of Severe Acute Malnutrition under Constant and Declining Unit Cost Assumptions, 2016–25

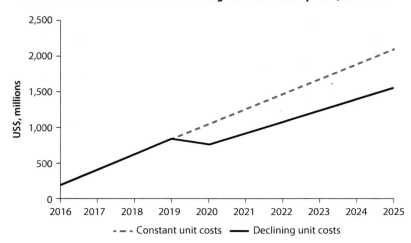

who examine the difference in cost per case of community nutrition services provided through a vertical program run by nongovernmental organizations and a government program run through the health system in Bangladesh.[6] Like the declines in prices of ready-to-use therapeutic food, those cost savings are assumed to be realized by 2020 (figure 6.1).

On the basis of the assumptions presented above, the overall costs of the scale-up of the treatment of severe acute malnutrition for children globally is estimated to be 21 percent lower than if no cost savings were realized over the same period (see figure 6.1 for estimated annual costs for 2016 to 2025 under both sets of assumptions). This result is consistent with existing projections for cost declines in the treatment of severe acute malnutrition (for example, Shoham, Dolan, and Gostelow 2013). However, this assumption—of a 21 percent decline in costs by 2020—is probably optimistic.

Assumptions about the Pace of the Scale-Up over 10 Years

A gradual, linear scale-up was assumed for each country from the current coverage level to 90 percent by 2025. This coverage expansion scenario is different from the ones for stunting, anemia, and breastfeeding. For these three targets, a five-year rapid expansion phase and a five-year maintenance phase were modeled to allow for the full accrual of the full scale-up interventions for all children under age five (see chapter 2 for details). Because severe wasting is an acute condition, with treatment affecting the beneficiaries immediately, and because the treatment of severe acute malnutrition is not included under any of the other targets, a linear scale-up was assumed here. Given the nature of the causes of severe acute malnutrition and the fact that the treatment is resource intensive and costly, and to be consistent with the extant literature (Bhutta et al. 2013; Horton et al. 2010), it was assumed that 100 percent of coverage is unrealistic even in a 10-year timeframe. Thus, coverage expansion of up to 90 percent was modeled.

Estimating Impact

The Lives Saved Tool (LiST) is used to estimate the number of deaths averted. LiST models the impact of severe acute malnutrition mortality indirectly. In the model, severe acute malnutrition increases a child's risk of dying from four specific conditions: postneonatal diarrhea, postneonatal measles, postneonatal pneumonia, and postneonatal other.[7] Figure 6.2 summarizes the LiST severe acute malnutrition impact model.

In LiST, the impact of severe acute malnutrition on child mortality depends critically on the incidence of the four key causes of mortality in a given country. Children suffering from severe acute malnutrition will be much more likely to die in a country where the incidence of diarrhea, pneumonia, measles, and other postneonatal causes (see note 7) is high than in a country where the incidence of those diseases is low. This also means that the treatment of severe acute malnutrition will have a different impact in different countries depending on the incidence of these diseases. For example, if severe acute malnutrition increases the risk of dying from diarrhea by three times, and if 10 percent of all children who get diarrhea die, in country A where 10 percent of children get diarrhea, one would expect that among 1,000 children suffering from severe acute malnutrition there would be about 30 excess

Figure 6.2 The Lives Saved Tool Model of the Impact of the Treatment of Severe Acute Malnutrition on Mortality in Children under Age 5 Years

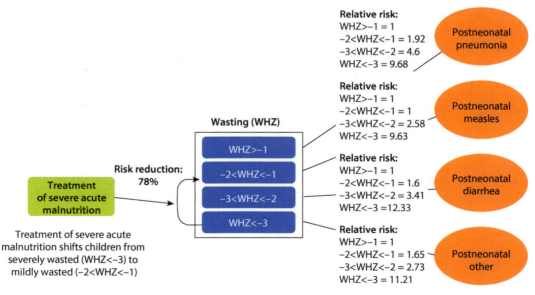

Source: Calculations from LiST.

Table 6.1 Differential Impact of Treatment of Severe Acute Malnutrition on Mortality by Underlying Prevalence of Disease Risk Factors

Country	Country A	Country B
Number of children suffering from severe acute malnutrition	1,000	1,000
Increase in risk of dying from diarrhea in children suffering from severe acute malnutrition	3	3
Risk of dying from diarrhea (%)	10	10
Diarrhea prevalence (%)	10	50
Deaths in the absence of severe acute malnutrition treatment	30	150
Percentage of children recovering from severe acute malnutrition thanks to treatment	80	80
Deaths saved thanks to severe acute malnutrition treatment	24	120

deaths from diarrhea. In contrast, in country B, where 50 percent of children get diarrhea, among the same number of children suffering from severe acute malnutrition, 150 excess deaths would be expected. Furthermore, assuming that treatment cures 80 percent of the children suffering from severe acute malnutrition, treating all 1,000 children in country A would avert 24 deaths but treating all 1,000 children in country B would avert 120 deaths—almost six times more (see table 6.1).

Using LiST, mortality is modeled in all sample countries separately; the impact is then extrapolated to all low- and middle-income countries by multiplying the number of deaths averted in the sample by 1.2 (derived by 1/0.829, where 0.829 is the proportion of children suffering from wasting in the sample countries).

Benefit-Cost Analyses

The economic benefits of the expansion of treatment coverage are estimated on the basis of mortality reductions. Each life saved as a result of the treatment is valued at one times gross domestic product (GDP) per capita per year (discounted); the assumption is that children would start working and contributing to the economy at 18 years of age and continue working until they reach their country's life expectancy or the age of 65, whichever is lower. It is possible, and indeed likely, that children experience multiple episodes of acute malnutrition before they reach age five. Understanding how often a child experiences acute malnutrition is critical for estimating the economic benefits of treating acute malnutrition based on deaths averted. To calculate benefits, the analysis assumes that each treated child will survive past age five and then, once she reaches adulthood, will contribute to the economy of the country. If an average child experiences only one episode of acute malnutrition over five years, then that child's future contributions to the economy are compared to the cost of a single treatment episode. If an average child experiences two or three episodes of acute malnutrition, the cost (of treatment) will need to be multiplied accordingly two or three times.

An Investment Framework for Nutrition • http://dx.doi.org/10.1596/978-1-4648-1010-7

Unfortunately, no longitudinal studies exist that would allow an estimation of the number of acute malnutrition episodes a child experiences on average during a given period of time. Some studies report the percentage of children who do not respond to treatment or who relapse (Isanaka et al. 2011), but those numbers capture only children in treatment and very likely severely underestimate the number of acute malnutrition episodes per year per child. Given the absence of data, an assumption is made that each child under five who was ever acutely malnourished experienced about 1.6 episodes in his or her lifetime.[8] For the base case scenario, a 3 percent discount rate is assumed for costs and benefits, along with a 3 percent annual GDP growth rate.

Results

This section presents the results of the analysis of the intervention described above for the wasting target via the treatment of severe acute malnutrition, including costs, impacts, and benefit-cost analyses.

Estimated Total Financing Needs

Scaling up the treatment of severe acute malnutrition for children in low- and middle-income countries would require about $9.1 billion over 10 years. Of this amount, about $8.1 billion would be required for direct service provision with an additional 12 percent of the direct services costs ($971 million) for capacity strengthening; for developing the necessary policies, protocol, and guidelines; and for monitoring and evaluation of treatment programs. Those investments would allow treatment for an additional 91 million of cases of severe acute malnutrition in all low- and middle-income countries over 10 years.

When considered by region, about 45 percent of the total costs would be needed to expand the coverage of the treatment of severe acute malnutrition in South Asia (figure 6.3). Within South Asia, over 80 percent is estimated for treatment expansion in India. Another 25 percent of the total financing needs are to scale up treatment in Sub-Saharan Africa. Scale-up costs are higher in South Asia than in Sub-Saharan Africa despite the fact that the estimated average unit cost of treatment is higher in Sub-Saharan Africa ($110 per child treated, compared with $90 per child treated in South Asia). This is because of the higher estimated absolute burden: 40 million cases would be treated in South Asia over 10 years compared with 11.4 million cases in Sub-Saharan Africa. About 16 percent of the total financing needs are to expand coverage in the Middle East and North Africa region, 11 percent in the East Asia and Pacific region, and the remaining 3 percent in Latin America and the Caribbean and the Europe and Central Asia region.

Low-income countries account for about 20 percent of the total financing needs, with the other 80 percent for middle-income countries (70 percent for lower-middle-income countries and 10 percent for upper-middle-income countries) (figure 6.4). India alone accounts for more than half of the financing required for lower-middle-income countries.

Scaling Up the Treatment of Severe Wasting

Figure 6.3 Ten-Year Total Financing Needs for the Treatment of Severe Acute Malnutrition, by Region

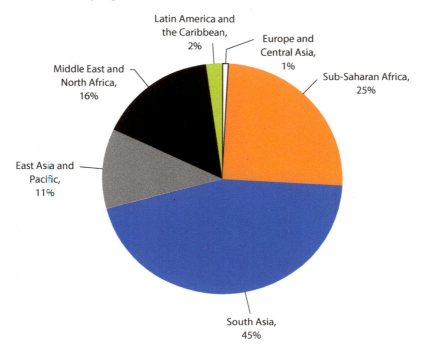

Figure 6.4 Ten-Year Total Financing Needs for the Treatment of Severe Acute Malnutrition, by Country Income Group

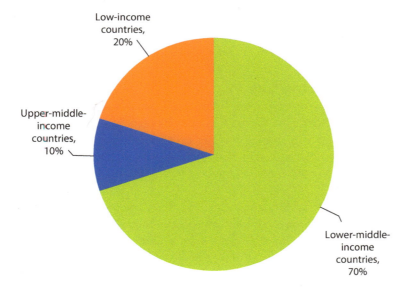

An Investment Framework for Nutrition • http://dx.doi.org/10.1596/978-1-4648-1010-7

Figure 6.5 Total Annual Financing Needs to Scale Up the Treatment of Severe Acute Malnutrition, 2016–25

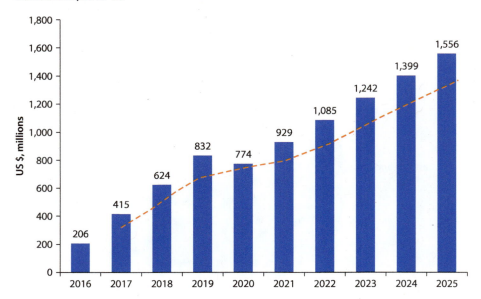

Figure 6.5 presents the annual global costs for the 10 years between 2016 and 2025. On average, an additional $910 million per year in financing is required to scale up the treatment of severe acute malnutrition for children with about $1.6 billion in the last year to reach and maintain 90 percent coverage in all low- and middle-income countries. As noted above, the assumption is that cost savings from new formulations of ready-to-use therapeutic food and improved service delivery would be realized by 2020. Those savings account for the cost reduction from 2019 to 2020, even though treatment coverage would continue to expand.

Estimated Impacts of the Scale-Up

These analyses estimate that about 91 million cases of severe acute malnutrition in children 6–59 months will be treated over 10 years as a result of the expanded treatment coverage. The average cost per case treated would be about $90. This figure incorporates the assumption about declines in the unit cost that result from reductions in ready-to-use therapeutic food prices and improvements in the efficiency of service delivery.

On the basis of LiST modeling, the scale-up of the treatment of severe acute malnutrition for children in all low- and middle-income countries over 10 years would prevent about 860,000 deaths in children under five years of age (table 6.2). About 49 percent of those deaths would be averted in Sub-Saharan Africa, 44 percent in South Asia, and the remaining 7 percent in other regions.

Benefit-Cost Analyses

Under the base case scenario (3 percent discount rate for cost and benefits and 3 percent annual GDP growth rate),[9] expanding the coverage of the treatment of severe acute malnutrition for children in all low- and middle-income countries and the resulting mortality averted would generate about $25 billion of annual increases in economic productivity over the productive lifetimes of children who benefitted from the program (table 6.3). The pooled benefit-cost ratio under the base case scenario is 3.6,[10] suggesting that every dollar invested in the treatment of severe acute malnutrition would result in about four dollars in economic returns.

These results are sensitive to changes in the assumptions. Increasing the discount rate to 5 percent changes the benefit-cost ratio to 1.5. When changing the assumption regarding the number of wasting episodes a child under age five experiences on average from 1.6 to 2.0 or 3.0, the benefit-cost ratio declines from 3.6 to 2.7 or 1.4, respectively (table 6.4).

Table 6.2 Estimated Impact over 10 Years of the Treatment of Severe Acute Malnutrition

Impact	Treatment of severe acute malnutrition
Total 10-year costs (US$, billions)	9.1 billion
Number of cases treated over 10 years	91 million
Number of deaths averted over 10 years	860,000
Cost per case of severe acute malnutrition treated (US$)	100[a]
Cost per death averted (US$)	10,500

a. The unit cost is $89, plus 12 percent program costs.

Table 6.3 Benefit-Cost Ratios of Scaling Up Treatment of Severe Acute Malnutrition, 3 and 5 Percent Discount Rates

	3% discount rate			5% discount rate		
Group	Present value benefit (US$, billions)	Present value cost (US$, billions)	Benefit-cost ratio	Present value benefit (US$, billions)	Present value cost (US$, billions)	Benefit-cost ratio
By region						
Sub-Saharan Africa	13.0	1.1	11.6	5.8	1.0	6.0
South Asia	6.7	3.2	2.1	2.0	2.8	0.7
East Asia and the Pacific	1.8	0.7	2.6	0.6	0.6	1.1
By income group						
Low-income countries	1.7	1.0	1.7	0.4	0.8	0.5
Lower-middle-income countries	19.3	4.6	4.2	7.5	4.0	1.9
Upper-middle-income countries	0.4	0.4	1.1	0.1	0.3	0.2
Pooled	25.3	7.1	3.6	9.1	5.2	1.5
Median			1.8			0.5

Note: The results in this table are for sample countries only.

Table 6.4 Benefit-Cost Ratios of Scaling Up Treatment of Severe Acute Malnutrition, by Number of Episodes per Year

Assumption	Benefit-cost ratio
Assuming 1.6 number of episodes per year and 3% discount rate	3.6
Assuming 2.0 number of episodes per year and 3% discount rate	2.7
Assuming 3.0 number of episodes per year and 3% discount rate	1.4

Discussion

Given the current state of evidence of the prevention of wasting, it is impossible to estimate the costs of reaching the global wasting target. Therefore, the first major recommendation from these analyses is to prioritize research on the prevention of wasting. It is clear that, without such evidence, reaching the global wasting target will not be possible. Because the cost of reaching the wasting target cannot be estimated, this chapter focuses on the costs of expanding the treatment of severe acute malnutrition for children, even though it is entirely possible that preventing wasting would be more cost-effective than treating it, especially given the high costs of treatment. Thus, expanding treatment can be considered to be the cost of *mitigating the impact* of wasting, rather than preventing wasting.

In the absence of preventive interventions, treatment will be necessary to save the lives of children suffering from severe acute malnutrition. Currently, only a small minority of children with severe acute malnutrition receive treatment. In fact, the coverage of outpatient treatment programs in low- and middle-income countries remains largely unknown. In order to expand treatment to 90 percent by 2025, an additional $9.1 billion dollars in new financing will be needed.

These cost estimates are lower than those reported in earlier studies for a number of reasons (table 6.5). First, baseline unit costs used here are lower than those in Horton et al. (2010) and Bhutta et al. (2013). This is largely because new unit cost data available from country studies (see, for example, Alive & Thrive and UNICEF 2013; IFPRI 2014; Shekar et al. 2014; Shekar, Mattern, Eozenou et al. 2015; Shekar, Mattern, Laviolette et al. 2015; Tekeste et al. 2012) are lower than those used in previous estimates. Second, these analyses assume some reductions in treatment unit costs over time as a result of lower prices of ready-to-use therapeutic food and improvements in the efficiency of service delivery. Finally, unlike the previous two global studies, the present analyses incorporate population growth dynamics over the next decade. Annual scale-up costs are lower because of the population declines projected in the South Asia, East Asia and Pacific, and Middle East and North Africa regions.

On the basis of the modeling using LiST, the scale-up of the treatment of severe acute malnutrition for children would prevent about 860,000 deaths over 10 years. This estimate is lower than those published previously. For example, Schofield and Ashworth (1996) estimate that, in the absence of any treatment, up to 30 percent of children suffering from severe acute

Scaling Up the Treatment of Severe Wasting

Table 6.5 Comparison of Cost Estimates of the Treatment of Severe Acute Malnutrition

	Unit costs (US$)			Global annual costs (US$, billions)		
Intervention	Horton et al. 2010	Bhutta et al. 2013	Current analysis	Horton et al. 2010	Bhutta et al. 2013	Current analysis
Treatment of severe acute malnutrition for children	$201	$149–250	$89	$2,600	$2,563	$1,109

malnutrition will die. Similarly, Bulti et al. (2015) estimate that the mortality rate for untreated severe acute malnutrition in Nigeria is about 250 per 1,000 (or about 25 percent).

Calculating baseline mortality risk resulting from severe wasting in LiST is somewhat challenging because, as mentioned above, it is modeled through specific diseases, such as pneumonia, diarrhea, and measles, and therefore depends on the incidence of those diseases in a specific country. In other words, this model takes into account the underlying causes of death in children who are severely malnourished.

In order to calculate the baseline mortality risk in LiST, the number of deaths resulting from changes in wasting prevalence in each country was calculated. However, LiST allows for calculating changes in mortality that result only from decreases in wasting prevalence (rather than from increases in prevalence). Therefore, for each country, reductions in mortality were estimated for lowering the prevalence of severe wasting by (only) one percentage point.[11] The number of cases of severe wasting and the number of deaths were then compared for the baseline prevalence and the reduced prevalence.

The difference in the number of children suffering from severe acute malnutrition between the baseline and the reduced scenario was interpreted as the additional number of children suffering from severe acute malnutrition:

Additional *SAM* cases = Number of children in *SAM* (baseline)
— Number of deaths (reduced *SAM* prevalence)

where *SAM* = severe acute malnutrition.

Similarly, the difference in the number of deaths between the baseline scenario and the scenario with reduced severe wasting prevalence was interpreted as the number of deaths resulting from the increased number of children suffering from severe acute malnutrition:

Additional *SAM* deaths = Number of deaths (baseline)
— Number of deaths (reduced *SAM* prevalence)

Put simply, the calculation offers a direct measure of how many deaths would occur if the number of wasted children increased by a specific number. The ratio of the additional deaths and additional severe acute malnutrition cases was interpreted as the underlying risk of dying from severe wasting:

SAM mortality risk = Additional *SAM* deaths/Additional *SAM* cases

These analyses show that, in the sample of the 24 countries with a high burden of wasting, the pooled risk of mortality that results from severe acute malnutrition is 1.43 percent.[12] For individual countries, the risk ranges from 0.1 percent for Sri Lanka to 6.2 percent for Chad. As expected, the mortality risk is higher in countries with higher mortality risk from diarrhea, measles, pneumonia, and other causes. Consequently, the average mortality risk is higher in Sub-Saharan Africa (3.5 percent) than in the overall sample.

If severe acute malnutrition mortality risk were adjusted to the level estimated by Bulti et al. (2015) (25 percent), expanding the coverage of severe acute malnutrition treatment would, over 10 years, prevent over 15 million deaths (see table 6.6). It would also significantly decrease the cost per death averted and increase the cost-effectiveness of severe acute malnutrition treatment. In the LiST-based model, preventing one death through treatment of severe acute malnutrition would cost about $10,000; if the baseline mortality risk is adjusted to the level reported by Bulti et al., the cost would drop to about $600. Consequently, the benefit-cost ratio could increase from 3.6 to as much as 62.6.

Estimates from Bulti et al. (2015) and from Schofield and Ashworth (1996) seem high. The study by Schofield and Ashworth is over two decades old, and it is very likely that mortality from wasting would now be lower thanks to healthier environments in which children grow up, better vaccination coverage, greater access to maternal and child health services, and so forth. Estimates from Bulti et al. were derived from data from a community-based management of acute malnutrition program in northern Nigeria, where mortality in general—and therefore wasting mortality as well—was higher than in many other countries included in this study. If we applied this rate to India, where about 8 million children in 2015 suffered from severe wasting, a 25 percent mortality risk would result in about 1.3 million deaths annually. This, in turn, would translate to a mortality rate attributable to wasting of about 10.5 per 1,000. Given that the total under five mortality rate in India in 2015 was estimated to be

Table 6.6 Mortality Estimates for Severe Acute Malnutrition

Indicator	Lives Saved Tool (LiST) estimates	Bulti et al. 2015 estimates
Severe acute malnutrition mortality risk	1.43%	25.00%
Number of severe acute malnutrition cases treated (millions)	90.7	90.7
Number of deaths averted (millions)	0.9	15.1
Total costs (US$, millions)	$9,062	$9,062
Cost per death averted (US$)	$10,516	$601

Source: Bulti et al. 2015.

48 (World Bank 2015), it seems very unlikely that wasting is an underlying cause of 21 percent of all under five deaths in India.[13] Therefore, clearly, using high mortality risk values from either the Schofield and Ashworth or Bulti studies will likely overestimate the impact of the scale-up of the severe acute malnutrition treatment. Nevertheless, the adjusted mortality estimates could be treated here as an upper-bound estimate, with the LiST-generated estimates considered a conservative lower bound.

The advantage of the LiST approach is that it models the impact of wasting by looking at mortality from infectious disease and thus takes into account the overall underlying mortality risk in different country contexts. Therefore the gains from mortality reductions in this target are higher in countries with a greater underlying disease burden. This is reflected in the analyses presented above: even though only about 25 percent of the total costs are for program expansion in Sub-Saharan Africa, about 47 percent of deaths averted are from that region. Consequently, the cost per death averted is much lower in Sub-Saharan Africa (about $6,400) than it is in South Asia or in the overall sample of high-burden countries ($12,600 and $10,500, respectively), and the benefit-cost ratio is much higher in Sub-Saharan Africa (about 11.6) than in the overall sample or in other regions (3.6 in the 24 high-burden countries, 2.1 in South Asia).

The economic benefits from expanding the treatment of severe acute malnutrition for children are estimated to be about $25 billion (discounted at 3 percent). These are conservative estimates based only on mortality reductions. It is possible that severe acute malnutrition treatment has other benefits for child development (such as reducing cognitive losses and physical disability). For example, existing studies suggest that episodes of wasting negatively affect linear growth (Black et al. 2008; Khara and Dolan 2014). However, the evidence base is not currently strong enough to allow the quantification of such additional benefits.

The analyses presented in this chapter suggest that treatment of severe acute malnutrition for children can be a cost-effective intervention, with a very high cost-effectiveness ratio, especially in countries where risk factors such as infectious diseases and poor hygiene and sanitation are rampant. However, to better understand the benefits of investing in both the treatment and prevention of acute malnutrition, more research is needed on the incidence of wasting; the number of acute malnutrition episodes children may suffer; the relationship between wasting and stunting and other child health outcomes; and the short-, medium-, and long-term impacts of acute malnutrition on children's physical and cognitive development. Furthermore, although treatment of severe acute malnutrition can be cost-effective, it is an expensive intervention (approximately $110 per child in Sub-Saharan Africa and $90 per child in South Asia per episode). Future research efforts must focus on finding strategies to prevent wasting so as to reduce the numbers of children who need treatment. Without a rapid investment in knowledge, it is not possible to build an effective global investment case for achieving the wasting target.

Notes

1. For details about WHO growth standards for weight-for-height, see http://www.who.int/childgrowth/standards/weight_for_height/en/
2. In this report, the term *wasting* is used when discussing prevalence rates or reaching the global wasting target. However, because diagnosis is measured by wasting and/or MUAC and/or bilateral pitting edema, the term *acute malnutrition* is most appropriate when referring to treatment. The costs and impact analyses in this report are based specifically on the treatment of severe acute malnutrition.
3. To date, WHO has issued only a Technical Note on the use of supplemental foods for the management of moderate acute malnutrition; see WHO 2012 at http://apps.who.int/iris/bitstream/10665/75836/1/9789241504423_eng.pdf?ua=1.
4. The Coverage Monitoring Network is a consortium of nongovernmental organizations (led by Action Against Hunger) that implement community-based management of acute malnutrition programs globally.
5. Currently, randomized controlled trials are examining differences in delivery platforms. In particular, integration of treatment of severe acute malnutrition for children into the existing community-level delivery within the health system is under way in Mali and Pakistan; preliminary results are expected at the end of 2016.
6. These cost reductions were not applied in East Asia because the unit cost used already assumed a fully integrated severe acute malnutrition delivery model (see Alive & Thrive and UNICEF 2013).
7. In the LiST model, "other" indicates a specific category of mortality.
8. The same correction factor is used as the one used by the UNICEF guidance for translating wasting prevalence into incidence (UNICEF 2015).
9. The same assumptions were used in benefit-cost analyses across all targets.
10. Note that the benefit-cost ratio is calculated by dividing discounted benefits ($25 billion) by discounted costs ($7.1 billion) using the 3 percent annual discount rate in the base case scenario.
11. Changes only in severe wasting were modeled because the focus of this chapter is the treatment of severe wasting. One percentage point was an arbitrary rate of change; it was chosen because it could be easily implemented for the purposes of this simulation.
12. The *pooled risk* is the total number of severe acute malnutrition cases from all 24 countries divided by the total number of additional severe acute malnutrition cases from all 24 countries.
13. The same exercise conducted for Nigeria would result in a wasting-related mortality of about 4.5 per 100 or about 4 percent of the total mortality in children under five (109 per 1,000 in 2015), which is much closer to the global WHO estimate of 5 percent (World Bank 2015).

References

Alive & Thrive and UNICEF (United Nations Children's Fund). 2013. "Costs of Providing Nutrition Examination & Counseling Services and Integrated Management of Severe Acute Malnutrition in Vietnam." June 2013.

Bachmann, M. O. 2009. "Cost Effectiveness of Community-Based Therapeutic Care for Children with Severe Acute Malnutrition in Zambia: Decision Tree Model." *Cost Effectiveness and Resource Allocation* 7 (1): 1–9.

———. 2010. "Cost-Effectiveness of Community-Based Treatment of Severe Acute Malnutrition in Children." *Expert Review of Pharmacoeconomics & Outcomes Research* 10 (5): 605–12.

Bhutta, Z. A, J. K. Das, A. Rizvi, M. F. Gaffey, N. Walker, S. Horton, P. Webb, A. Lartey, and R. E. Black. 2013. "Evidence-Based Interventions for Improvement of Maternal and Child Nutrition: What Can Be Done and at What Cost?" *The Lancet* 382 (9890): 452–77.

Black, R. E., L. H. Allen, Z. A. Bhutta, L. E. Caulfield, M. de Onis, M. Ezzati, C. Mathers, J. Rivera, and the Maternal and Child Undernutrition Study Group. 2008. "Maternal and Child Undernutrition: Global and Regional Exposures and Health Consequences." *The Lancet* 371 (9608): 243–60.

Bulti A., S. Chtiekwe, C. Puett, and M. Myatt. 2015. "How Many Lives Do Our CMAM Programmes Save? A Sampling-Base Approach to Estimating the Number of Deaths Averted by the Nigerian CMAM Programme." Field Exchange 50, August. http://www.ennonline.net/fex/50/Deathsavertedcmamnigeria.

Coffey. C. 2016. "A Review of Evidence on the Prevention of Acute Malnutrition: Non-Systematic Rapid Review, Draft 7." Unpublished, prepared for Department for International Development.

Dangour, A. D., L. Watson, O. Cumming, S. Boisson, Y. Che, Y. Velleman, S. Cavil, E. Allen, and R. Uauy. 2013. "Interventions to Improve Water Quality and Supply, Sanitation and Hygiene Practices, and Their Effects on the Nutritional Status of Children." *Cochrane Database Syst Rev 8*. doi: 10.1002/14651858.CD009382.pub2.

ENN, SCUK, ACF, and UNHCR (Emergency Nutrition Network, Save the Children UK, Action Against Hunger, and the UN Refugee Agency). 2012. *Mid Upper Arm Circumference and Weight-for-Height Z-Score as Indicators of Severe Acute Malnutrition: A Consultation of Operational Agencies and Academic Specialists to Understand the Evidence, Identify Knowledge Gaps and to Inform Operational Guidance.* Oxford, UK: ENN.

Greco, L., J. Balungi, K. Amono, R. Iriso, and B. Corrado. 2006. "Effect of a Low-Cost Food on the Recovery and Death Rate of Malnourished Children." *Journal of Pediatric Gastroenterology and Nutrition* 43 (4): 512–17.

Horton, S., M. Shekar, C. McDonald, A. Mahal, and J. Krystene Brooks. 2010. *Scaling Up Nutrition: What Will It Cost?* Directions in Development Series, Washington, DC: World Bank.

Hossain, M. M., M. Q. Hassan, M. H. Rahman, A. Kabir, A. H. Hannan, and A. Rahman. 2009. "Hospital Management of Severely Malnourished Children: Comparison of Locally Adapted Protocol with WHO Protocol." *Indian Pediatrics* 46: 213–17.

IFPRI (International Food Policy Research Institute). 2014. *Global Nutrition Report 2014*. Washington, DC: IFPRI.

Isanaka, A., R. F. Grais, A. Briend, and F. Checchi. 2011. "Estimates of the Duration of Untreated Acute Malnutrition in Children from Niger." *American Journal of Epidemiology* 173 (8): 932–40.

Khan, M. and S. Ahmed. 2003. "Relative Efficiency of Government and Non-Government Organizations in Implementing a Nutrition Intervention Programme: A Case Study from Bangladesh." *Public Health Nutrition* 6 (1): 19–24.

Khanum, S., A. Ashworth, and S. Huttly. 1994. "Controlled Trial of Three Approaches to the Treatment of Severe Malnutrition." *The Lancet* 344 (8939): 1728–32.

———. 1998. "Growth, Morbidity, and Mortality of Children in Dhaka after Treatment for Severe Malnutrition: A Prospective Study." *American Journal of Clinical Nutrition* 67: 940–45.

Khara, T., and C. Dolan. 2014. *Technical Briefing Paper: Associations between Wasting and Stunting, Policy, Programming and Research Implications*. Oxford: Emergency Nutrition Network. http://www.ennonline.net/waststuntreview2014.

Langendorf, C., T. Roederer, S. de Pee, D. Brown, S. Doyon, A.-A. Mamaty, L. W.-M. Touré, M. L. Manzo, and R. F. Grais. 2014. "Preventing Acute Malnutrition among Young Children in Crises: A Prospective Intervention Study in Niger." *PLOS Med* 11 (9): e1001714. doi:10.1371/journal.pmed.1001714.

Lenters, L. M., K. Wazny, P. Webb, T. Ahmed, and Z. A. Bhutta. 2013. "Treatment of Severe and Moderate Acute Malnutrition in Low- and Middle-Income Settings: A Systematic Review, Meta-Analysis and Delphi Process." *BMC Public Health* 13 (3): 1.

Lives Saved Tool (LiST). 2015. Baltimore, MD: Johns Hopkins Bloomberg School of Public Health. http://livessavedtool.org/(accessed December 31, 2015).

Manary, M. 2006. "Local Production and Provision of Ready-to-Use Therapeutic Food (RUTF) Spread for the Treatment of Severe Acute Childhood Malnutrition." *Food and Nutrition Bulletin* 27 (Suppl. 3): S83–89.

McDonald, C. M., I. Olofin, S. Flaxman, W. W. Fawzi, D. Spiegelman, L. E. Caulfield, R. E. Black, M. Ezzati, and G. Danaei. 2013. "The Effect of Multiple Anthropometric Deficits on Child Mortality: Meta-Analysis of Individual Data in 10 Prospective Studies from Developing Countries." *American Journal of Clinical Nutrition* 97 (4): 896–901. doi:10.3945/ajcn.112.047639.

Menon, P. 2012. "Childhood Undernutrition in South Asia: Perspectives from the Field of Nutrition." *CESifo Economic Studies* 58 (2): 274–95. http://cesifo.oxfordjournals.org/content/58/2/274.abstract.

Puett, C., K. Sadler, H. Alderman, J. Coates, J. Fiedler, and M. Myatt. 2013. "Cost-Effectiveness of the Community-Based Management of Acute Malnutrition by Community Health Workers Program in Southern Bangladesh." *Health Policy and Planning* 28 (4): 386–99.

Ramakrishnan, U., P. Nguyen, and R. Martorell. 2009. "Effects of Micronutrients on Growth of Children under 5 Y of Age: Meta-Analyses of Single and Multiple Nutrient Interventions." *American Journal of Clinical Nutrition* 89 (1): 191–203.

Sandige, H., M. J. Ndekha, A. Briend, P. Ashorn, and M. J. Manary. 2004. "Home-Based Treatment of Malnourished Malawian Children with Locally Produced or Imported Ready-to-Use Food." *Journal of Pediatric Gastroenterology and Nutrition* 39 (2): 141–46.

Santini, A., E. Novellino, V. Armini, and A. Ritieni. 2013. "State of the Art of Ready-to-Use Therapeutic Food: A Tool for Nutraceuticals Addition to Foodstuff." *Food Chemistry* 140 (3): 843–49.

Schofield, C., and A. Ashworth. 1996. "Why Have Mortality Rates for Severe Malnutrition Remained So High?" *Bulletin of the World Health Organization* 74: 223–29.

Shekar, M., C. McDonald, A. Subandoro, J. Dayton Eberwein, M. Mattern, and J. K. Akuoku. 2014. "Costed Plan for Scaling Up Nutrition: Nigeria." Health, Nutrition and Population (HNP) Discussion Paper, The World Bank Group, Washington, DC.

Shekar, M., M. Mattern, P. Eozenou, J. Dayton Eberwein, J. K. Akuoku, E. Di Gropello, and W. Karamba. 2015. "Scaling Up Nutrition for a More Resilient Mali: Nutrition Diagnostics and Costed Plan for Scaling Up." Health, Nutrition and Population (HNP) Discussion Paper, The World Bank Group, Washington, DC.

Shekar, M., M. Mattern, L. Laviolette, J. Dayton Eberwein, W. Karamba, and J. K. Akuoku. 2015. "Scaling Up Nutrition in the DRC: What Will It Cost?" Health, Nutrition and Population (HNP) Discussion Paper, World Bank, Washington, DC.

Shoham, J., C. Dolan, and L. Gostelow. 2013. "Managing Acute Malnutrition at Scale: A Review of Donor and Government Financing Arrangements." Humanitarian Practice Network Paper 75, Overseas Development Institute, London.

Singh, A. S., G. Kang, A. Ramachandran, R. Sarkar, P. Peter, and A. Bose. 2010. "Locally Made Ready-to-Use Therapeutic Food for Treatment of Malnutrition: A Randomized Controlled Trial." *Indian Pediatrics* 47 (8): 679–86.

Tekeste, A., M. Wondafrash, G. Azene, and K. Deribe. 2012. "Cost Effectiveness of Community-Based and In-Patient Therapeutic Feeding Programs to Treat Severe Acute Malnutrition in Ethiopia." *Cost Effectiveness and Resource Allocation* 10 (1): 1.

Tuffrey, V. 2016. *Nutrition Surveillance Systems: Their Use and Value.* London: Save the Children and Transform Nutrition.

UNICEF (United Nations Children's Fund). 2015. *Management of Severe Acute Malnutrition in Children: Working towards Results at Scale.* Geneva: UNICEF. http://www.unicef.org/eapro/UNICEF_program_guidance_on_manangement_of_SAM_2015.pdf.

UNICEF, WHO, and World Bank (United Nations Children's Fund, World Health Organization, and World Bank). 2015. *Joint Child Malnutrition Estimates.* Global Database on Child Growth and Malnutrition, http://www.who.int/nutgrowthdb/estimates2014/en/.

WHO (World Health Organization). 2012. *Technical Note: Supplementary Foods for the Management of Moderate Acute Malnutrition in Infants and Children 6–59 Months of Age.* Geneva: WHO.

———. 2013. *Guideline: Updates on the Management of Severe Acute Malnutrition in Infants and Children.* Geneva: World Health Organization. http://apps.who.int/iris/bitstream/10665/95584/1/9789241506328_eng.pdf.

———. 2014. *WHA Global Nutrition Targets 2025: Wasting Policy Brief.* http://www.who.int/nutrition/topics/globaltargets_wasting_policybrief.pdf.

World Bank. 2015. World Development Indicators (database), World Bank, Washington, DC (accessed 2015), http://data.worldbank.org/data-catalog/world-development-indicators.

CHAPTER 7

Financing Needs to Reach the Four Global Nutrition Targets: Stunting, Anemia, Breastfeeding, and Wasting

Jakub Kakietek, Meera Shekar, Julia Dayton Eberwein, and Dylan Walters

Key Messages

- Reaching the targets to reduce stunting among children and anemia in women, increase exclusive breastfeeding rates, and treat 91 million wasted children will require an investment of $70 billion over the next 10 years.
- This investment can yield tremendous returns: 3.7 million child lives saved, at least 65 million fewer stunted children, 265 million fewer women suffering from anemia in 2025, 105 million more infants exclusively breastfed up to six months of age as compared to the 2015 baseline, and 91 million children treated for wasting, in addition to other health and poverty reduction efforts.
- Every dollar invested has the potential to generate $10 in economic returns (between $4 and $35), depending on the target. Thus the returns on these investments in nutrition are high and positive, but they will vary in different country contexts. Of particular significance is the high return on investment in increasing rates of exclusive breastfeeding ($35 in economic returns for every dollar invested).
- In case of resource constraints, this chapter lays out two alternative investment packages to prioritize and catalyze progress, with the caveat that investing in a smaller set of interventions would fall short of reaching some of the global targets by 2025. Investing in a "priority package" of immediately ready to scale interventions would require an additional $23 billion over the next 10 years, or $2.3 billion per year. A slightly more ambitious package of investments, called the "catalyzing progress package" would scale up the priority package plus a more phased-in expansion of the other interventions to strengthen delivery mechanisms and support research and program implementation and invest in better technologies, requiring an additional $37 billion over the next 10 years, or $3.7 billion per year. Further investments would be needed over time to build up to scaling up the full package.

Chapter 2 described the methods used for estimating financing needs to reach each of the four global targets included in these analyses. This chapter describes how the financing needs for these four targets are aggregated and presents the total financing needs and benefits of reaching all four targets.

Method for Aggregating Financing Needs across All Four Targets

Because some interventions overlap across targets, it is not possible to aggregate costs by simply adding up the scale-up costs across the four targets. Instead, to avoid double counting, interventions that address more than one target were counted only once toward the grand total. This pertains to three interventions: antenatal micronutrient supplementation, infant and young child nutrition counseling, and intermittent presumptive treatment of malaria in pregnancy in malaria-endemic areas.[1] For these interventions, if the cost varies across different targets, the highest cost is applied toward the total. For example, the cost of scaling up infant and young child nutrition counseling for achieving the stunting target is estimated at $6.8 billion dollars: this estimate includes the two years of counseling needed to prevent stunting. This intervention is also key for increasing exclusive breastfeeding, but for that target only $4.2 billion is required because only one year of the intervention is needed.[2] Therefore, when aggregating costs, the larger of the two numbers ($6.8 billion) is included toward the grand total; table 7.1 shows the costs from each intervention/target that contributed to the grand total costs designed with a superscript c.

As described in chapter 2 on methods, program costs (for capacity strengthening, monitoring and evaluation, and policy development) are added to the costs of intervention delivery for each target (see table 7.1). The following assumptions are made for these program costs: 9 percent of the total intervention costs for capacity strengthening for program implementation, 2 percent for monitoring and evaluation, and 1 percent for policy development, following the method used by Horton et al. (2010). There is one exception: in the case of the target for breastfeeding, an additional 1 percent for policy development is not included because the development, adoption, and enforcement of pro-breastfeeding policies are already counted explicitly as an intervention.

Total Financing Needs to Achieve All Four Targets

An estimated additional $69.9 billion will be required over 10 years to achieve all four nutrition targets (table 7.1). This includes $62.4 billion for direct intervention costs and $7.5 billion in estimated costs for capacity strengthening for program implementation, monitoring and evaluation, and policy development.

Two interventions for children—prophylactic zinc supplementation and the public provision of complementary food—account for over 40 percent of the total global costs (23 percent and 20 percent, respectively). Four interventions account for a further 45 percent of the global total: the treatment of severe acute malnutrition for children, balanced energy-protein supplementation for pregnant women, infant and young child nutrition counseling, and iron and folic acid supplementation for nonpregnant women (13 percent, 11 percent, 11 percent, and 11 percent, respectively).[3] Antenatal micronutrient supplementation and staple food fortification were each estimated to account for 4 percent

Table 7.1 Ten-Year Total Financing Needs to Meet All Four Targets

Intervention	Stunting (US$, millions)	Breastfeeding (US$, millions)	Anemia (US$, millions)	Wasting (US$, millions)	Total (US$, millions)	Share of total costs (%)
Antenatal micronutrient supplementation	2,309[c]	n.a.	2,017	n.a.	2,309	3.7
Infant and young child nutrition counseling[a]	6,823[c]	4,159	n.a.	n.a.	6,823	10.9
Balanced energy-protein supplementation for pregnant women	6,949[c]	n.a.	n.a.	n.a.	6,949	11.1
Intermittent presumptive treatment of malaria in pregnancy in malaria-endemic regions	416[c]	n.a.	337	n.a.	416	0.7
Vitamin A supplementation for children	716[c]	n.a.	n.a.	n.a.	716	1.1
Prophylactic zinc supplementation for children	14,212[c]	n.a.	n.a.	n.a.	14,212	22.8
Public provision of complementary food for children	12,750[c]	n.a.	n.a.	n.a.	12,750	20.4
Treatment of severe acute malnutrition for children	n.a.	n.a.	n.a.	8,091[c]	8,091	13.0
Iron and folic acid supplementation for nonpregnant women[b]	n.a.	n.a.	6,705[c]	n.a.	6,705	10.7
Staple food fortification	n.a.	n.a.	2,443[c]	n.a.	2,443	3.9
Pro-breastfeeding social policies	n.a.	111[c]	n.a.	n.a.	111	0.2
National breastfeeding promotion campaigns	n.a.	906[c]	n.a.	n.a.	906	1.5
Subtotal	44,175	5,176	11,502	8,091	62,431	100
Capacity strengthening (assumed to be 9% of subtotal)	3,976	466	1,035	728	5,619	n.a.
Monitoring and evaluation (assumed to be 2% of subtotal)	884	104	230	162	1,249	n.a.
Policy development (assumed to be 1% of subtotal)	442	n.a.	115	81	614	n.a.
Total	49,476	5,745	12,882	9,062	69,913	n.a.

Note: n.a. = not applicable.
a. Includes two years of education for the stunting target and one year for the breastfeeding target.
b. Includes only two types of costs (drug costs and public sector distribution costs); excludes out-of-pocket costs for women above the poverty line.
c. For these interventions, there is overlap in costs associated with more than one target. To avoid double counting, only the higher value was used to calculate the grand total.

of the total,[4] and national breastfeeding promotion campaigns account for about 2 percent of the total. Finally, vitamin A supplementation for children, intermittent presumptive treatment of malaria in pregnancy in malaria-endemic regions, and pro-breastfeeding social policies each account for 1 percent or less of total costs.

The relative proportion of the global costs devoted to each target is shown in figure 7.1. However, there is overlap in some of the costs across targets. The lion's share of the costs goes toward interventions to reduce stunting ($49.5 billion), followed by costs for preventing anemia in women ($12.9 billion), then costs for treating wasting ($9.1 billion), and finally costs for promoting exclusive breastfeeding ($5.7 billion). All costs are for a 10-year period.

Sub-Saharan Africa accounts for the largest share of the costs (39 percent), followed by South Asia (24 percent) and East Asia and Pacific (24 percent) (figure 7.2). When considered by country income group, low-income countries account for about one-fourth (27 percent) of the total additional scale-up costs, lower-middle-income countries for about half of all costs (51 percent), and upper-middle-income countries account for less than a quarter (22 percent) (figure 7.3).

Figure 7.1 Ten-Year Total Financing Needs to Meet All Four Targets, Breakdown by Target

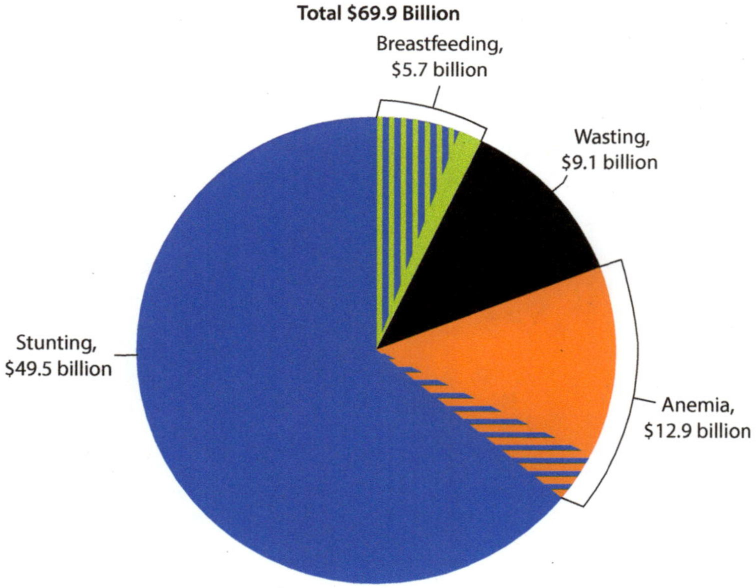

Total $69.9 Billion
- Breastfeeding, $5.7 billion
- Wasting, $9.1 billion
- Anemia, $12.9 billion
- Stunting, $49.5 billion

Note: Striped areas indicate overlapping financing needs toward interventions meeting more than one target.

Financing Needs to Reach the Four Global Nutrition Targets

Figure 7.2 Ten-Year Total Financing Needs to Meet All Four Targets, by Region

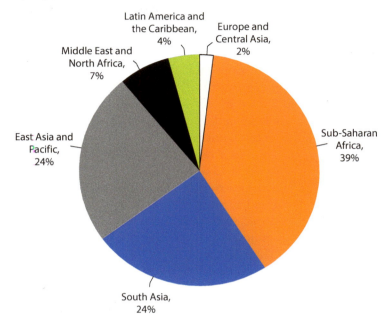

Figure 7.3 Ten-Year Total Financing Needs to Meet All Four Targets, by Country Income Group

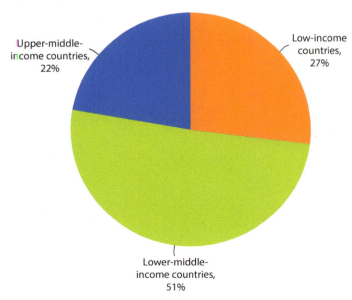

An Investment Framework for Nutrition • http://dx.doi.org/10.1596/978-1-4648-1010-7

Estimated Impacts: Method for Aggregating across Targets

Chapter 2 lays out the methodology for estimating financing needs, impacts, and benefits for each target. For each target, target-specific benefits are estimated. These take the form of reductions in the number of stunted children for the stunting target, reductions in the number of women suffering from anemia for the anemia target, and increases in the number of infants who are exclusively breastfed for the breastfeeding target (see table 7.2). For wasting, the estimate is the number of children treated for severe acute malnutrition because it is not possible to estimate a reduction in the number of children wasted (see chapter 6 for a detailed discussion on this point).

In addition, deaths averted as a result of the expansion of all interventions under the four targets are calculated using the Lives Saved Tool (LiST). Because three interventions—antenatal micronutrient supplementation, infant and young child nutrition counseling, and intermittent presumptive treatment of malaria in pregnancy in malaria-endemic regions—are included to meet more than one target (see table 7.1), an estimation of total mortality reductions is adjusted to account for this overlap. The cumulative health gains are calculated as follows: first, total deaths averted in children under age five are estimated for all the interventions included under the *stunting target:* infant and young child nutrition counseling, vitamin A supplementation for children, prophylactic zinc supplementation for children, public provision of complementary food for children, antenatal micronutrient supplementation, balanced energy-protein supplementation for pregnant women, and intermittent presumptive treatment of malaria in pregnancy in malaria-endemic regions. On the basis of the LiST model, scaling up these interventions would avert about 2.8 million deaths in children under five in low- and middle-income countries (see chapter 3 for details).

Table 7.2 Estimated Impacts of Meeting All Four Targets, 2025, Compared with 2015 Baseline

Outcome/target	Stunting	Anemia	Breastfeeding	Wasting	Total
Cases of stunting prevented in 2025	30,000,000[a]	n.a.	n.a.	n.a.	30,000,000
Number of child deaths averted	2,800,000[a]	800,000 (380,000)[a]	520,000	860,000 (554,000)[a]	3,700,000
Cases of anemia in women prevented in 2025	n.a.	265,000,000[a]	n.a.	n.a.	265,000,000
Additional babies exclusively breastfed	n.a.	n.a.	105,000,000[a]	n.a.	105,000,000
Number of children treated for severe wasting	n.a.	n.a.	n.a.	91,000,000[a]	91,000,000

Note: Numbers in parentheses indicate additional deaths averted on top of those averted for the stunting target, contributing to the grand total; n.a. = not applicable.
a. Value that contributes to the grand total.

For the *breastfeeding target*, the impact of only one intervention—infant and young child nutrition counseling—is modeled. Reductions in child mortality resulting from the scale-up of this intervention are included in the estimates for the stunting target. Similarly, for the *anemia target*, mortality in children under age five averted as a result of the scale-up of intermittent presumptive treatment of malaria in pregnancy in malaria-endemic regions and antenatal micronutrient supplementation is already included in the mortality reductions estimated for the stunting target. An additional 380,000 child deaths averted because of iron and folic acid supplementation (delivered in the preconceptual period through the fortification of staples) are estimated and added to the impact estimates for stunting interventions.

Finally, for the *wasting target*, mortality reductions resulting from the scale-up of the treatment of severe acute malnutrition are added to the grand total of deaths averted.[5] Mortality reduction from the expansion of severe acute malnutrition treatment is adjusted to account for the fact that the expansion would happen in parallel with the scale-up of all the other interventions. As noted in chapter 6, in the epidemiological model used in these analyses, mortality resulting from acute malnutrition depends on the prevalence of risk factors such as diarrhea and other infectious diseases. Because interventions implemented to achieve the other three targets could reduce the prevalence of those risk factors, the impact of severe acute malnutrition and its treatment on mortality is less than it would be if the treatment of severe acute malnutrition were scaled up on its own (as modeled in chapter 6). On the basis of the LiST model results, scaling up the treatment of severe acute malnutrition would avert about 30 percent fewer deaths if implemented in conjunction with the other interventions in the package (554,000 over 10 years) than if scaled up on its own (860,000 over 10 years). Therefore, the sum of deaths averted due to stunting (2.8 million), anemia (380,000), and wasting (554,000) equals the cumulative deaths averted of 3.7 million.

In sum, the total investment of $69.9 billion over 10 years is estimated to yield tremendous returns: 3.7 million deaths would be averted and at least 30 million fewer children would be stunted in 2025 compared with the 2015 baseline (table 7.2). In addition, 265 million fewer women would be expected to suffer from anemia in 2025 as compared to the 2015 baseline. Over the 10-year period, an additional 105 million children would be estimated to have been exclusively breastfed for the first six months of life.

In the long run, these outcomes produce more productive workers with higher cognitive and physical work capacities who generate higher earnings. The reductions in morbidity and mortality as a result of these investments are therefore estimated to yield high, positive benefit-cost ratios. With the assumption of a 3 percent discount rate, it is estimated that investing in the stunting, anemia, breastfeeding, and wasting package proposed will generate returns of $10.5, $12.1, $34.7, and $3.6 respectively for every dollar invested (see table 7.3). Using a more conservative 5 percent discount rate also generates positive estimates for benefit-cost ratios.

Table 7.3 Benefit-Cost Ratios of Scaling Up Interventions to Meet All Four Targets, 3 and 5 Percent Discount Rates

Target	3% discount rate Pooled benefit-cost ratio	3% discount rate Median benefit-cost ratio	5% discount rate Pooled benefit-cost ratio	5% discount rate Median benefit-cost ratio
Stunting	10.5	4.0	5.0	1.6
Anemia	12.1	10.6	8.2	7.4
Breastfeeding	34.7	17.5	15.8	7.6
Wasting	3.6	1.8	1.5	0.5

Note: The results in this table are for sample countries.

These benefit-cost ratios should, however, be interpreted with caution. First, aggregating results across countries may distort the results because benefit-cost ratios are driven by country-specific factors such as gross domestic product (GDP), expected economic growth, prevalence of disease, and the effectiveness of interventions in specific contexts.

These figures are conservative estimates. For stunting, cross-generational effects of the interventions were not considered. The literature suggests that mothers' short stature is a risk factor for childhood stunting (Aguayo and Menon 2016). Therefore, preventing stunting in girls, in addition to improving their cognitive ability and productivity, may also decrease the risk of stunting in their children. The estimated benefits from the treatment of severe acute malnutrition capture only deaths averted. It is likely that severe acute malnutrition also has long-term consequences for children's cognitive and physical development and that the treatment of severe acute malnutrition, which mitigates its impact, may have benefits beyond mortality reductions. Fortification of staples with iron will benefit many groups in society in addition to women of reproductive age, including men and children, and thereby generate additional improvements in health, cognition, and economic productivity. Last, the assumed future GDP growth of 3 percent across the sample of countries in these analyses is well below the historical trend of the previous decade, as discussed in chapter 2, and is likely to be a very conservative estimate for the future.

Given the methodological uncertainties in the analyses of benefit-cost projections, the key message is that the aggregate returns on these investments in nutrition are high and positive, but will vary in different country contexts.

Three Potential Packages for Financing: The Full Package, the Priority Package, and the Catalyzing Progress Package

The investment of $70 billion over 10 years needed to scale-up the full package of interventions to reach the global nutrition targets is an admittedly ambitious financial resource mobilization goal, especially given the modest increases in governments' health expenditure in low and middle income countries and plateauing official development assistance (ODA) for health (Dielman et al., 2015). In this environment of constrained resources, some interventions are undoubtedly more cost-effective than others (table 7.4). Furthermore, some of the interventions included in the full package lack global guidelines or established delivery platforms (see table 7.5), and are, thus, not immediately ready to scale-up. These include 1) public provision of complementary foods, 2) balanced energy protein supplementation, 3) prophylactic zinc supplementation, 4) weekly iron and folic acid supplementation for women not attending school, and 5) fortification of rice. Some of these

Table 7.4 Cost per Outcome, by Intervention

Intervention	Total 10-year costs (US$, billions)	Cost per death averted (US$)	Cost per case of stunting averted (US$)	Cost per case-year of anemia averted (US$)	Cost per child exclusively breastfed (US$)
For pregnant women and mothers of infants					
Antenatal micronutrient supplementation	2.59	7,376	3,637	11	n.a.
Infant and young child nutrition counseling (complementary feeding education and breastfeeding promotion combined)	7.64	7,353	467	n.a.	n.a.
Balanced energy-protein supplementation for pregnant women	7.78	37,054	29,949	n.a.	n.a.
Intermittent presumptive treatment of malaria in pregnancy in malaria-endemic regions	0.47	6,594	1,535	62	n.a.
For infants and young children					
Vitamin A supplementation	0.80	4,270	266	n.a.	n.a.
Prophylactic zinc supplementation	15.92	23,642	988	n.a.	n.a.
Public provision of complementary food	14.28	67,787	1,724	n.a.	n.a.
Treatment of severe acute malnutrition	9.1	10,500	n.a.	n.a.	n.a.
Complementary feeding education[a]	4.28	16,122	273	n.a.	n.a.
Breastfeeding promotion[a]	3.36	4,347	4,761	n.a.	54
For all women of reproductive age and general population					
Iron and folic acid supplementation for non-pregnant women	7.51	26,914[b]	n.a.	10	n.a.
Staple food fortification	2.74		n.a.	7	n.a.

Note: n.a. = not applicable.
a. In this analysis of cost per outcome, the two parts of the intervention infant and young child nutrition counseling—complementary feeding education and breastfeeding promotion—are considered separately.
b. This is the combined cost per death averted estimated because it is not possible to estimate the impact on mortality of each of these interventions separately.

Table 7.5 Potential Delivery Platforms for Scaling Up High-Impact Interventions

Intervention	Delivery platform and bottlenecks to scale up
Antenatal micronutrient supplementation[a]	• Currently, iron and folic acid is the preferred supplement, delivered through routine antenatal and postnatal care. These supplements could be substituted with multiple micronutrient supplements if the WHO issues new and updated guidelines.
Infant and young child nutrition counseling	• Community-based nutrition programs • Antenatal and postnatal health care services • Media approaches, social media, and so on
Balanced energy-protein supplementation for pregnant women[a]	• **No large scale-programs currently exist**[b] • Some existing delivery mechanisms through community-based programs (for example, existing public food distribution and rapidly expanding social-protection channels/social safety net programs)
Intermittent presumptive treatment of malaria in pregnancy in malaria-endemic regions	• Antenatal care in malaria-endemic regions only
Vitamin A supplementation for children	• Community-based campaigns • Health facility-based service delivery
Prophylactic zinc supplementation	• **No existing delivery mechanisms**[b] • Potential to use delivery mechanisms such as micronutrient powders (such as Sprinkles) distributed through community-based programs
Public provision of complementary food	• **No existing delivery mechanisms at scale**[b] • Delivery could be based on existing public food distribution/social safety net programs
Treatment of severe acute malnutrition	• Outpatient treatment for uncomplicated cases; inpatient treatment for patients with complications • Existing coverage is low and requires functioning health systems to deliver at scale, hence slower scale-up rate is assumed
Iron and folic acid supplementation for non-pregnant women	• **No examples of scaled delivery mechanisms**[b] • Could be delivered in schools for girls age 15–19 enrolled in school • For other women aged 15–49, could be delivered in the community via community health workers, health facility outpatient visits, and/or via private marketplace
Staple food fortification	• Delivered through the marketplace and via fortified foods in public distribution programs • Fortification platforms/technologies exist for wheat flour and maize flour fortification; rapid scale-up is feasible • **Rice fortification requires different technologies (e.g. coating or extrusion) and is therefore significantly more expensive; further operational research is needed to reduce fortification costs**[b]
Pro-breastfeeding social policies	• Policies, legislation, and monitoring and enforcement of policies related to the Code of Marketing of Breast Milk Substitutes, the WHO Ten Steps integration into hospital accreditation, and protection of maternity leave
National breastfeeding promotion campaigns	• Media and social media channels

a. This intervention will require updated WHO guidance and revised national policies.
b. Bottlenecks to scale up.

interventions may also be expensive, and may benefit from additional operational research before they are ready for full scale-up. Therefore, two alternative packages of interventions are laid out for consideration.

The Priority Package

The first—the "priority package," includes interventions that are most cost-effective, that is, have the lowest cost per health outcome (e.g. case of stunting averted; see table 7.4), and that have well established global policy guidelines and delivery platforms. Based on those two criteria, the priority package includes: 1) antenatal micronutrient supplementation, 2) infant and young child nutrition counseling, 3) intermittent presumptive treatment of malaria in pregnancy in malaria-endemic regions; 4) vitamin A supplementation; 5) treatment of severe acute malnutrition; 6) intermittent weekly iron and folic acid supplementation for girls 15–19 years or age attending school; and 7) fortification of wheat and maize flour with iron and folic acid. These interventions would be scaled up to full program coverage in the first five years and maintained at full coverage levels for the last five years.

This priority package would require about $23 billion over 10 years (see table 7.6) or approximately $2.3 billion annually. Combined with the assumed trend in the underlying determinants of malnutrition, it would result in 50 million

Table 7.6 Total Financing Needs for Immediate Scale-Up of a Set of Priority Interventions
US$, millions

Intervention	Stunting	Breastfeeding	Anemia	Wasting	Total
Antenatal micronutrient supplementation	2,309[a]	n.a.	2,016	n.a.	2,309
Infant and young child nutrition counseling	6,823[a]	4,159	n.a.	n.a.	6,823
Intermittent presumptive treatment of malaria in pregnancy in malaria-endemic regions	416[a]	n.a.	337	n.a.	416
Vitamin A supplementation for children	716[a]	n.a.	n.a.	n.a.	716
Treatment of severe acute malnutrition for children	n.a.	n.a.	n.a.	8,091[a]	8,091
Iron and folic acid supplementation for girls 15–19 years old in school	n.a.	n.a.	622[a]	n.a.	622
Staple food fortification (wheat and maize flour but not rice)	n.a.	n.a.	359[a]	n.a.	359
Pro-breastfeeding social policies	n.a.	111[a]	n.a.	n.a.	111
National breastfeeding promotion campaigns	n.a.	906[a]	n.a.	n.a.	906
Subtotal	**10,264**	**5,176**	**3,334**	**8,091**	**20,353**
Capacity strengthening (assumed to be 9% of subtotal)	924	466	300	728	1,832
Monitoring and evaluation (assumed to be 2% of subtotal)	205	104	67	162	407
Policy development[b]	103	n.a.	33	81	193
Total	**11,496**	**5,745**	**3,734**	**9,062**	**22,785**

Note: n.a. = not applicable.
a. For these interventions, there is overlap in costs associated with more than one target. To avoid double counting, only the higher value was used to calculate the grand total.
b. Policy development is assumed to be 1 percent of the subtotal of all interventions except pro-breastfeeding social policies and national breastfeeding promotion campaigns.

fewer children being stunted in 2025 compared to the 2015 baseline. It would also prevent about 2.3 million deaths in children under five. However, the priority package would fall short of reaching some of the global nutrition targets.

The Catalyzing Progress Package

The second alternative - "catalyzing progress", includes scale-up of all interventions in the priority package, plus a phased approach to scaling up public provision of complementary foods, balanced energy protein supplementation, prophylactic zinc supplementation, weekly iron-folic acid supplementation for women outside of schools, and fortification of rice. It is assumed that, for the latter set of interventions, during the first 5 years, emphasis will be placed on establishing global guidelines and on operational research to develop effective delivery platforms, or to develop less expensive products or more cost-effective technologies (such as for rice fortification). Costs are approximated as the cost of scaling up this set of interventions from 0 to 10 percent coverage only in the first five years. In the subsequent 5 years, it is assumed that the coverage expansion of those interventions will accelerate and reach 60 percent by 2025.

The "catalyzing progress" package would require about $37 billion over 10 years (see table 7.7) or approximately $3.7 billion annually. Combined with the assumed trend in the underlying determinants of malnutrition, it would result in some 58 million fewer children being stunted in 2025 compared to the 2015 baseline. It would also prevent about 2.6 million deaths in children under 5. This would catalyze significant progress toward the global targets, but, it would still not be sufficient to reach all of the global nutrition targets.

Table 7.8 compares the three packages in terms of cost and health outcomes. Overall the priority package and the catalyzing progress package can be considered more cost-effective than the full package with lower costs per death averted (USD 9,900 for the priority package and USD 10,771 for the catalyzing progress package, compared to USD 18,900 for the full package) and lower costs per case of stunting prevented (USD 542 for the priority package and USD 794 for the catalyzing progress package, compared to USD 1,063 for the full package).

Overall, however, the two smaller packages of interventions are less effective than the full package; that is, their impact on the health and nutrition status of women and children is smaller than that of the full package. Under the priority package, 15 million more children will be stunted and 115 million more women will suffer from anemia in 2025 compared to the full package; under the catalyzing progress package 7 million more children will be stunted and 35 million more women will suffer from anemia in 2025 compared to the full package (see table 7.9). Furthermore, 1.4 million fewer deaths in children under five will be prevented under the priority package and 1.1 million fewer deaths under the catalyzing progress package compared to the full package. Consequently, as noted earlier, neither of the two alternative packages is sufficient to reach all of the global targets, albeit the catalyzing progress scenario will come significantly closer.

Table 7.7 Total Financing Needs for Catalyzing Progress Package of Interventions
US$, millions

Intervention	Stunting	Breastfeeding	Anemia	Wasting	Total
Antenatal micronutrient supplementation	2,309[a]	n.a.	2,017	n.a.	2,309
Infant and young child nutrition counseling	6,823[a]	4,159	n.a.	n.a.	6,823
Balanced energy-protein supplementation for pregnant women	2,150[a]	n.a.	n.a.	n.a.	2,150
Intermittent presumptive treatment of malaria in pregnancy in malaria-endemic regions	416[a]	n.a.	337	n.a.	416
Vitamin A supplementation for children	716[a]	n.a.	n.a.	n.a.	716
Prophylactic zinc supplementation for children	4,354[a]	n.a.	n.a.	n.a.	4,354
Public provision of complementary food for children	3,384[a]	n.a.	n.a.	n.a.	3,384
Treatment of severe acute malnutrition for children	n.a.	n.a.	n.a.	8,091[a]	8,091
Iron and folic acid supplementation for girls 15–19 years old in school	n.a.	n.a.	2,490[a]	n.a.	2,490
Staple food fortification (wheat and maize flour but not rice)	n.a.	n.a.	1,002[a]	n.a.	1,002
Pro-breastfeeding social policies	n.a.	111[a]	n.a.	n.a.	111
National breastfeeding promotion campaigns	n.a.	906[a]	n.a.	n.a.	906
Subtotal	*20,152*	*5,176*	*5,846*	*8,091*	*32,753*
Capacity strengthening (assumed to be 9% of subtotal)	1,814	466	526	728	2,948
Monitoring and evaluation (assumed to be 2% of subtotal)	403	104	117	162	655
Policy development[b]	202	n.a.	58	81	317
Total	**22,570**	**5,745**	**6,547**	**9,062**	**36,673**

Note: n.a. = not applicable.
a. For these interventions, there is overlap in costs associated with more than one target. To avoid double counting, only the higher value was used to calculate the grand total.
b. Policy development is assumed to be 1 percent of the subtotal of all interventions except pro-breastfeeding social policies and national breastfeeding promotion campaigns.

Table 7.8 Cost Effectiveness, by Intervention Package

Intervention package	Total 10-year cost (US$, billions)	Cost per death averted (US$)	Cost per case of stunting averted (US$)[a]
Full (meets targets)	69.9	18,900	1,063
Priority	22.8	9,900	542
Catalyzing Progress	37.0	10,771	794

a. Only interventions affecting stunting (see chapter 3) are included in the calculation of cost per case of stunting averted.

Table 7.9 Benefits and Total Financing Needs, by Intervention Package

Global target	Benefit	Priority package	Catalyzing progress package	Full package: All interventions needed to meet targets
		$23 billion total financing need	$37 billion total financing need	$70 billion total financing need
Stunting	Cases of stunting reduced by 2025 (vs 2015)[a]	50 million	58 million	65 million
	Child deaths averted over 10 years	1.5 million	2.1 million	2.8 million
Anemia	Percent reduction in number of women with anemia	28%	45%	50%
	Cases of anemia in women prevented by 2025	150 million	230 million	265 million
	Child deaths averted over 10 years	660,000	740,000	800,000
	Maternal deaths averted over 10 years	7,000	7,000	7,000
Breastfeeding	Percent of babies exclusively breastfed in 2025	54%	54%	54%
	Additional babies breastfed over 10 years	105 million	105 million	105 million
	Child deaths averted over 10 years	520,000	520,000	520,000
Wasting	Number of children treated for severe wasting	91 million	91 million	91 million
	Child deaths averted over 10 years		860,000	860,000
All Targets	Child deaths averted over 10 years	2.3 million	2.6 million	3.7 million

a. Total impact of proposed intervention package combined with other health and poverty reduction efforts.

Discussion

Expanding the coverage of the full package of high-impact nutrition-specific interventions needed to reach the four global nutrition targets would cost about $70 billion over 10 years or $7 billion annually. Estimates presented here indicate that this investment would avert about 3.7 million deaths in children under five, contribute to a reduction in the number of stunted children by about 65 million in 2025 compared with the 2015 baseline, reduce the number of women of reproductive age suffering from anemia in 2025 by about 265 million compared with 2015, and increase the number of infants under six months of age who are exclusively breastfed by 105 million compared with 2015. In addition, 91 million children would be treated for severe wasting.

However, not all of the interventions included in this package are ready for immediate scale-up. Some interventions lack established and effective delivery platforms, for some, there are no global guidelines, and some need more effective technologies. Expanding the coverage of a more limited package of priority interventions that are cost-effective, and for which well-established delivery platforms and guidelines exist would require $23 billion over 10 years (table 7.10) or $2.3 billion annually. An expanded "catalyzing progress" package, which includes the priority package combined with an investment in the development of effective delivery platforms, research and development, and a phased in scale

Table 7.10 Three Scale-up Packages: Total 10-Year Resources Required and Interventions Included

	Priority package	Catalyzing progress package	Full package: All interventions needed to meet targets
Total 10 year Required Resources (billions)	23	37	70
Intervention			
Antenatal micronutrient supplementation	✓	✓	✓
Infant and young child nutrition counseling	✓	✓	✓
Balanced energy-protein supplementation for pregnant women		Phased[a]	✓
Intermittent presumptive treatment of malaria in pregnancy in malaria-endemic regions	✓	✓	✓
Vitamin A supplementation for children	✓	✓	✓
Prophylactic zinc supplementation for children		Phased[a]	✓
Public provision of complementary food for children		Phased[a]	✓
Treatment of severe acute malnutrition for children	✓	✓	✓
Iron and folic acid supplementation:			
• non-pregnant women 15–19 years old in school only	✓	✓	✓
• all non-pregnant women		Phased[a]	✓
Staple Food Fortification:			
• Wheat and maize flour	✓	✓	✓
• Rice		Phased[a]	✓
Pro-breastfeeding social policies	✓	✓	✓
National breastfeeding promotion campaigns	✓	✓	✓

a. Intervention scale up is phased in slowly over 10 years. During 2016-2021, a 10% scale up is assumed during which an emphasis will be put on establishing global guidelines and on operational research to develop effective delivery platforms. In 2021–2025, program expansion is assumed to accelerate and reach 60 percent by 2025.

up for the remaining interventions, would require $37 billion over 10 years or $3.7 billion annually. Both of these alternative packages would be more cost-effective than the full package, with a lower cost per death averted and a lower cost per case of stunting averted. However, overall, they would be less effective in reaching some of the global nutrition targets by 2025.

Several of the interventions contribute to the achievement of multiple targets. For example, the infant and young child nutrition counseling package helps reduce the prevalence of stunting and increases the number of children who are exclusively breastfed. Similarly, antenatal micronutrient supplementation and the intermittent presumptive treatment of malaria in pregnancy in malaria-endemic areas help prevent stunting as well as anemia in pregnant women. Some evidence also suggests a relationship between repeated episodes of acute malnutrition and the risk of stunting (see chapter 6). The analyses presented in the previous chapters demonstrate that scaling up the coverage of the key evidence-based nutrition-specific interventions will help achieve multiple nutrition targets. This in turn suggests that a comprehensive approach to improving the nutrition of children, pregnant women, and adolescent girls and other women of reproductive age may be more efficient and cost-effective than focusing only on a specific aspect of malnutrition (for example, only anemia).

The analyses presented here indicate that, over 10 years, in addition to reaching the global nutrition targets, the scale up of the full package of interventions would prevent about 3.7 million deaths in children under 5 years of age. As discussed in chapter 6, the mortality risks resulting from severe acute malnutrition for children estimated using LiST is lower than that estimated by other authors. It is therefore possible that mortality reductions from the treatment of severe acute malnutrition may be higher. If this is the case, the cost per death averted for the full, priority, and catalyzing progress packages would be lower. The reader should, therefore, consider these to be lower-bound, conservative figures.

The next chapter discusses how the anticipated $70 billion in financing can be raised from domestic budgets, official development assistance, and innovative financing sources to achieve the global nutrition targets.

Notes

1. Note that this intervention is included only for countries in Sub-Saharan Africa, where malaria is endemic.
2. Because the World Health Assembly target related to breastfeeding uses the 0–5-month exclusive breastfeeding indicator to measure progress, the assumption in this analysis is that only one year of infant and young child nutrition counseling would adequately cover the time frame from the third trimester of antenatal care to when an infant reaches six months of age. Although a second year of counseling is recommended, this second year would not have any effect on increasing exclusive breastfeeding.
3. The costs for iron and folic acid supplementation for nonpregnant women include only expected costs for the supplements for all women and the costs of distribution either through the community health system or the hospital system for 70 percent of women and through schools for enrolled girls (girls not enrolled in school are assumed to be supplemented through the health system). An additional 30 percent of women living above the poverty line are assumed to be able to purchase supplements through private sector retailers and pharmacies. This cost is excluded from these estimates.
4. The cost of staple food fortification in these estimates includes only costs to the public sector (that is, domestic government and official development assistance). Not included are the costs to private sector food manufacturing, retail, and marketing, which will be eventually borne by consumers of fortified foods.
5. As indicated in chapter 6, the term *wasting* is used in this report when discussing prevalence rates or reaching the global wasting target. However, because diagnosis is measured by wasting and/or mid-upper arm circumference and/or bilateral pitting edema, the term *acute malnutrition* is most appropriate when referring to treatment. The costs and impact analyses in this report are based specifically on the treatment of severe acute malnutrition.

References

Aguayo, V. M. and P. Menon. 2016. "Stop Stunting: Improving Child Feeding, Women's Nutrition and Household Sanitation in South Asia." *Maternal & Child Nutrition* 12.S1 (2016): 3–11.

Bulti, A., S. Chtiekwe, C. Puett, and M. Myatt. 2015. "How Many Lives Do Our CMAM Programmes Save? A Sampling-Base Approach to Estimating the Number of Deaths Averted by the Nigerian CMAM Programme." Field Exchange 50, August. http://www.ennonline.net/fex/50/deathsavertedcmamnigeria.

Horton, S., M. Shekar, C. McDonald, A. Mahal, and J. Krystene Brooks. 2010. *Scaling Up Nutrition: What Will It Cost?*. Washington, DC: World Bank.

Schofield, C., and A. Ashworth. 1996. "Why Have Mortality Rates for Severe Malnutrition Remained So High?" *Bulletin of the World Health Organization* 74: 223–29.

CHAPTER 8

Financing the Global Nutrition Targets

Mary Rose D'Alimonte, Hilary Rogers, and David de Ferranti

Key Messages

- Approximately $3.9 billion is currently being spent annually on the costed package of interventions by governments in low- and middle-income countries and donors. Assembling the $70 billion of *additional* financing (above current spending on nutrition) that is needed to reach the global nutrition targets is a major challenge, but one that is achievable. Increments of about $7 billion annually on average, on top of current contributions, will be required every year through 2025.
- A continuation of "business as usual"—extrapolating current spending growth trends for nutrition forward—will not be enough. About $13.5 billion in additional financing on top of current investments is expected to be contributed over the next 10 years if "business as usual" continues. However, such a scenario would result in falling far short of the global nutrition targets with a resource gap of $56 billion.
- If governments, official development assistance (ODA), and new innovative financing mechanisms each contribute in alignment with a "global-solidarity" scenario to mobilize the additional resources needed, meeting these targets is feasible.
- The analyses estimated that about $1 billion is currently provided by ODA for nutrition interventions, 53 percent or $531 million of which is allocated to treat severe and acute malnutrition. Another $358 million (36 percent) is allocated to the interventions costed for the stunting target. Much lower amounts are directed to interventions to increase exclusive breastfeeding ($85 million or 8.5 percent) and reduce anemia in women of reproductive age ($78 million or 7.8 percent). Approximately 65 percent of ODA for nutrition is allocated to the 37 highest-burden countries.

The preceding chapters—including the sections on financing needs, benefits, and rationale and evidence for investing in nutrition—lead naturally to the main question addressed in this chapter: how to ensure that sufficient financing will be available to achieve the global nutrition targets? At the heart of that question is another: Who will need to contribute and how much?

Governments,[1] ODA,[2] and other sources[3] all help cover the costs of implementing nutritional interventions in various ways. Success in reaching the targets will depend on how much each of them can contribute in the years ahead. Estimates of current financial contributions, by source, can help inform global efforts to understand what is needed to close gaps and how to mobilize action.

A projected $70 billion of additional financing on top of current contributions is required over the next 10 years, according to the findings presented in chapters 3, 4, 5, and 6, and aggregated across four of the six global nutrition targets (stunting, anemia, breastfeeding, and wasting) in chapter 7.

That $70 billion goal is mapped out over the next 10 years with a scale-up plan beginning with an additional $1.5 billion needed in 2016, ramping up to an additional $9.7 billion per year by 2025. These annual financing needs are in addition to the $3.9 billion the world currently spends on nutrition every year. Thus, the required total—at three and a half times the level of current expenditure by 2025—is a very substantial goal.

This chapter discusses the available evidence of current financing for nutrition and important implications for future financing to achieve the targets. The next section analyzes the *current* levels of investments for nutrition by governments and ODA. It does so by laying out the steps involved in determining that essential baseline, or current level of spending, which is key for understanding what might ensue in subsequent years. The following section then presents and interprets two financing scenarios for the ten-year period until 2025 (first the business-as-usual scenario and then the global-solidarity scenario). The chapter concludes with a discussion of the implications of the results of the analyses.

Current Levels of Spending on Nutrition

Current levels of spending on nutrition globally—through governments, ODA, and other sources—are not immediately obvious from the extant data. This section describes the data sources and methods used to estimate current global investments in the costed package of interventions from governments and ODA.[4]

Domestic Financing from Governments

Assembling good data on how much low- and middle-income countries currently spend on nutrition interventions is complicated by the fact that many countries do not routinely track or report spending on nutrition. As a result, they do not have extensive information on hand on (1) the amount they budget for and spend on nutrition, (2) interventions and programs that are funded, and (3) the sectors funding those interventions. In general, it is widely assumed that governments typically devote relatively modest fractions of their own domestic budgets to nutrition interventions.[5] This report compiles and analyzes publicly available data from the following sources:

- Public Expenditure Reviews for health.
- The World Health Organization's (WHO's) Global Health Expenditure Database, which is a repository for data generated through the System of

Health Accounts (SHA). At the time of this review, 15 countries had reported expenditures on nutritional deficiencies through the SHA (also known as the National Health Accounts).
- Case studies of nutrition budget and expenditure analyses including Tanzania's public expenditure review for nutrition (United Republic of Tanzania, Ministry of Finance 2014), John Snow International's SPRING project nutrition budget analysis in Nepal (SPRING 2016a) and Uganda (SPRING 2016b), and Save the Children UK's budget analyses in Malawi, Zambia, and other countries (Save the Children and CSONA 2015).
- Nutrition budget allocation information reported by 30 Scaling Up Nutrition (SUN) countries in the 2015 *Global Nutrition Report* (IFPRI 2015). These data came from national or sectoral budgets, and were reviewed by researchers to ensure that what was counted as nutrition-specific spending was standardized to match the costed package of interventions across all countries. For integrated programs marked as nutrition-specific (that is, wider maternal and/or child health programs without a clearly identified nutrition component), a lower bound of 10 percent and an upper bound of 50 percent were taken across these programs, assuming that nutrition components of wider maternal and child health programs are rarely over 50 percent of the entire program. In the end, the midpoint of the resulting estimate was taken as the "best" and simplest estimate for all these cases after expert consultation.
- Publicly available financial reports and national budget documents.

From these sources, data on domestic nutrition financing for 31 countries were compiled. The results are presented in appendix D.[6]

Regression models were used to assess the association between domestic nutrition financing and various other variables such as health budgets, gross economic product (GDP), general government expenditure, and regional variations. Government expenditure on health per capita was found to be positively correlated with government expenditure for nutrition per stunted case.[7] Although the sample size was low, this model is intuitive, implying that nutrition financing is concentrated among the countries with higher health spending. This model, based on government health expenditure per capita and applied to all low- and middle-income countries, provided an estimate of about $4.8 billion being spent globally by governments on all nutrition-specific programs in 2015. Further analysis had to be conducted in order to align the baseline with the costed package of interventions.

Although some intervention-level financing data were available for a few countries within the sample of 31 countries—India, Guatemala, Malawi, Mexico, and Tanzania—this level of granularity was mostly not available and had to be estimated in order to align the baseline with the costed package of interventions.

The costed nutrition plans prepared for SUN countries, although they do not provide information on budget allocations or actual spending, offer some insights on the percentage distribution of allocations across nutrition categories (SUN 2014). These costed plans were used only to estimate the *breakdown* of nutrition spending by categories and not for estimating the *total* spending (total spending was estimated using the above-mentioned sources only). For countries with costed nutrition plans, intervention-level breakdowns reflect, albeit not perfectly, how much a country has *planned* to invest in nutrition interventions. A major limitation of this approach is that what is planned often does not adequately reflect what gets financed; however, the approach was thought to be the best approximation of intervention-level financing for nutrition with data currently available.

Additional analyses were performed for India because it is home to the highest absolute global burden of chronic malnutrition, and it is also a lower-middle-income country already spending considerable domestic resources for public health and nutrition schemes. Using the more extensive nutrition-related data available for India, the analysis found that the country contributed approximately $0.9 billion in 2013–14 to the programs and target groups of interest here.[8] The majority is directed toward public provision of complementary food for children through the Integrated Child Development Services scheme, though India also contributes about $50 million annually through the National Health Mission (NHM) for nutrition-specific interventions such as micronutrient supplementation and the treatment of acute malnutrition.

Of the $4.8 billion estimated to be spent for domestic financing for nutrition, the average spending breakdown based on all available data is as follows: 22 percent toward behavior change interventions for good nutrition practices, 2 percent on treatment of acute malnutrition, 7 percent on micronutrient supplementation, 2 percent on fortification, 26 percent on supplementary feeding, 12 percent on governance for nutrition, and 29 percent toward other nutrition programs not aligned with the costed package of interventions (the majority of this includes funding from India as mentioned in note 8).[9] These proportions were applied to country estimates of total nutrition funding in order to estimate funding by intervention.[10] In total, it was estimated that $2.9 billion in government contributions is aligned with the costed package of interventions.

Official Development Assistance

Figures on current nutrition ODA can be obtained from data reported in the Creditor Reporting System (CRS) of the Organisation for Economic Co-operation and Development (OECD) (OECD 2016). The CRS's "purpose codes" make it possible to identify the amounts associated with nutrition interventions, including those relevant for the targeted package of interventions covered in these analyses.

The purpose code 12240 for "basic nutrition" is defined as "Direct feeding programmes (maternal feeding, breastfeeding and weaning foods, child feeding, school feeding); determination of micronutrient deficiencies; provision of vitamin A, iodine, iron, etc.; monitoring of nutritional status; nutrition and food hygiene education; household food security."

The basic nutrition purpose code is often used as a proxy for ODA targeted to nutrition-specific interventions (IFPRI 2016). However, using its current definition, it includes funding for interventions not considered nutrition specific according to the Lancet definition and not included in the costed package of interventions. Also, funding for many nutrition-specific programs can be coded under other purpose codes within health and emergency responses (ACF 2012). To establish an estimate of current ODA for nutrition aligned with the costed package of interventions, project-level line items associated with 16 CRS purpose codes (listed in appendix E) were examined, as described below.

Basic nutrition: Qualitative review of project descriptions. In 2013, a total of $946 million in ODA was disbursed to basic nutrition investments.[11] In order to determine the amount of ODA allocated to the costed package of interventions, project-level line items tied to these disbursements were reviewed and categorized into intervention categories on the basis of qualitative project descriptions. This analysis included all basic nutrition disbursements going to the 60 countries with the highest global burdens of stunting, anemia, breastfeeding, and wasting. Those countries represent 95 percent of the global stunting burden and received 70 percent of all disbursements to basic nutrition in 2013 (representing 945 unique line items).

As shown in figure 8.1, ODA for basic nutrition has been increasing since 2006 and the predominant share goes to African countries. In 2013, the majority of ODA for basic nutrition was allocated directly to recipient countries (80 percent), with another 13 percent allocated to regions to fund multicountry projects (not pictured), and 7 percent was unspecified.[12] Fortunately, donor reporting for basic nutrition has been improving because the amount of unspecified disbursements was 22 percent in 2006, as reported by the CRS.

The qualitative review of projects was conducted on the basis of all available information through the CRS, including through review of project titles and short and long descriptions that are meant to provide a brief description of activities and objectives for the associated funding. Supplementary desk research was undertaken where information directly from the CRS did not provide enough detail to categorize the funding into an intervention category. Researchers used this information to code line items with intervention categories. The full list of intervention categories is shown in appendix E.

During the review, the majority of projects were assigned to more than one intervention category. For example, maternal and child health projects often include both infant and young child nutrition counseling for mothers and supplementation. Because costs vary widely across interventions, it is not accurate to assume funding is split evenly across interventions. Therefore, disbursements

Figure 8.1 Official Development Assistance for Basic Nutrition Disbursed between 2006 and 2013

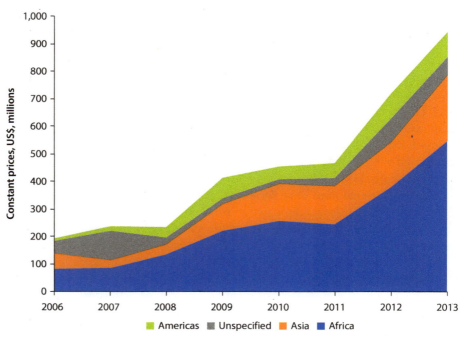

Source: OECD 2016. See note 15 for an explanation of the sources of financing.

were allocated across interventions in accordance with the relative total costs of the interventions in a given country (relative costs were based on estimates from the current analysis).[13]

Validation analyses were conducted for 1 percent of the projects ($n = 12$): a team of five researchers independently coded project disbursements and then verified their results against each other. Coding was found to be reliable across coders.

The qualitative review of projects provided information on which interventions were funded by donors within the 60 countries included in the analyses (shown in appendix E). The average across these 60 countries was used to estimate what interventions are being funded through all other disbursements within the basic nutrition code (that is, recipient countries not included in the analyses and regional disbursements).

Health and emergency response: Rapid keyword search assessment. In addition to the basic nutrition purpose code, ODA for nutrition is also substantial within sectors such as health and emergency response. Indeed, the nutrition content of projects not specifically labeled as nutrition projects can be significant, not least because those other projects are often large overall when compared with nutrition projects. Desk review and stakeholder interviews identified

An Investment Framework for Nutrition • http://dx.doi.org/10.1596/978-1-4648-1010-7

15 additional purpose codes likely to contain funding for nutrition (listed in appendix E). A rapid keyword search was conducted throughout all titles and project descriptions under each purpose code to identify relevant program disbursements.

Within health purpose codes, less than 1 percent to 6 percent of disbursements were related to nutrition. Rapid assessment indicated these investments went toward infant and young child nutrition counseling, treatment of severe acute malnutrition for children, antenatal micronutrient supplementation, vitamin A supplementation for children, and prophylactic zinc supplementation for children. Within emergency response purpose codes, less than 1 percent to 5 percent of disbursements were related to nutrition, all of which went toward the treatment of severe acute malnutrition.

Summary. Using OECD growth projections, ODA disbursements for nutrition were estimated to be $1 billion in 2015. This figure comprises disbursements for the costed package of nutrition interventions across the 16 purpose codes included in the analyses, including about 13 percent through health, 34 percent through emergency response, and 53 percent through basic nutrition.

Adding It All Up: Total Current Financing

Proceeding along the lines described above, the current total level of financing from governments and ODA for the costed package of interventions is estimated to be approximately $3.9 billion annually. Contributions from other sources may exist; however, because of data limitations they are not included.

Figure 8.2 shows the contributions by government and donors across targets. Notably, proportional contributions between governments and donors vary across different interventions and across regions. India alone contributes about a third of the total government contribution for the package of costed interventions across all four targets, which is mainly directed toward one intervention—public provision of complementary food for children through the Integrated Child Development Services scheme (making up the majority of government funding toward the stunting target). ODA presently contributes relatively little to interventions costed for the stunting and anemia targets, compared to governments; however, ODA does play a major role in the treatment of wasting.

Notable patterns in current investments on nutrition can be seen for countries grouped by income level:

- *Low-income countries:* Of the 15 low-income countries with nutrition financing data, the average estimated spending on nutrition interventions is just $0.85 per child under age five (standard deviation = 1.34; appendix E, table E.1). This group consists of the poorest countries with some of the highest rates of stunting globally. There are 35.9 million children under age five living across 30 low-income countries in the world, where the prevalence of stunting ranges from 22 percent in Haiti to as high as 58 percent in Burundi. These countries rely on external assistance for health (that is, ODA) as an

Figure 8.2 Current Financing for the Costed Package of Interventions by Governments and Official Development Assistance in 2015, by Target

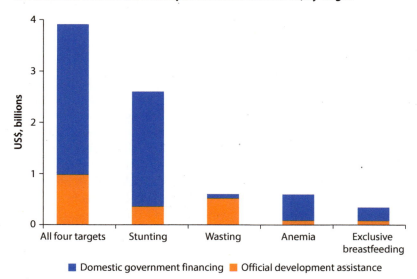

Note: The total amounts across the four targets will not sum to the total of all four targets because of intervention overlap between targets. The column depicting all four targets illustrates current spending for a mutually exclusive package of interventions.

important source of fiscal space (Tandon and Cashin 2010), giving rise to potentially little prioritization of nutrition in the public sector. On the basis of data from the current analysis, low-income countries received 47 percent of all ODA for nutrition in 2013.

- *Lower-middle-income countries:* Of the 13 lower-middle-income countries with data, the average estimated spending on nutrition interventions is $4.66 per child under age five (standard deviation = 8.12; appendix E, table E.1).[14] This group consists of countries with a high nutrition burden but where public financing and delivery systems are typically more advanced than they are in low-income countries, indicating a higher ability to pay for health and nutrition services (Tandon and Cashin 2010). Included in this group are India and Nigeria, the two countries with the highest absolute burden of stunting. They have 58 and 11 million stunted children under age five, respectively. Even without these 2 countries, there are still 51 million children under age five who are stunted in 42 other lower-middle-income countries. On the basis of data from the current analyses, lower-middle-income countries received 47 percent of all ODA for nutrition in 2013.
- *Upper-middle-income countries:* Of the three upper-middle-income countries with data, the average estimated spending on nutrition interventions is $8.15 per child under age five (standard deviation = 3.72; appendix E, table E.1).

This group consists of countries with stable economies and higher public sector income than low-income countries and lower-middle-income countries. Because of their level of development, the double burden of malnutrition is common in these countries: although undernutrition is persistent, overnutrition and obesity are rapidly becoming severe public health concerns (NCD-RisC 2016) and a strong reason for increased financing toward nutrition services. Although many upper-middle-income countries have a low stunting burden, there are still 20 million children stunted across 38 upper-middle-income countries. Almost half of this burden is borne by China and Mexico, two large countries that are among the highest-burden countries in the world. Upper-middle-income countries have stronger public sector health systems and a greater ability to implement nutrition interventions than low-income countries or lower-middle-income countries. Upper-middle-income countries rely less on external financing for health and nutrition. On the basis of data from the current analyses, upper-middle-income countries received 6 percent of all ODA for nutrition in 2013.

Additional insights can be gleaned from looking in more detail at the results for ODA:

- The intervention-level analysis found that, on average, the basic nutrition code funds the following types of programs: behavior change communication for nutrition, including infant and young child nutrition counseling (14 percent of the total), the treatment of acute malnutrition (15 percent), micronutrient supplementation and fortification (9 percent), provision of complementary foods for children (4 percent), research and development (3 percent), system-strengthening initiatives including capacity building (13 percent), and nutrition-sensitive programs such as school feeding (42 percent). Less than 1 percent went to other interventions including deworming and salt iodization.
- In 2015, it was estimated that about $1 billion was disbursed to the costed package of interventions (including funding through basic nutrition, health, and emergency response).[15] This includes $531 million (53 percent) going toward the treatment of severe and acute malnutrition and $358 million (36 percent) going toward the interventions costed for the stunting target. Much lower amounts are directed toward breastfeeding promotion ($85 million or 8.5 percent) and anemia ($78 million or 7.8 percent). Note that the amounts across targets cannot be summed to the total because of some intervention overlap within targets.
- Figure 8.3 shows how the total $1 billion in ODA for nutrition is distributed by region and income group of the recipient country. About 56 percent was disbursed to Sub-Saharan Africa, representing the largest share among regions, where among these African countries 67 percent of ODA for nutrition went to low-income countries. About 65 percent of this funding for nutrition ($647 million) was disbursed to the 37 countries with the highest stunting burdens.

Figure 8.3 Baseline Official Development Assistance Financing for Nutrition, by Region and Income Group

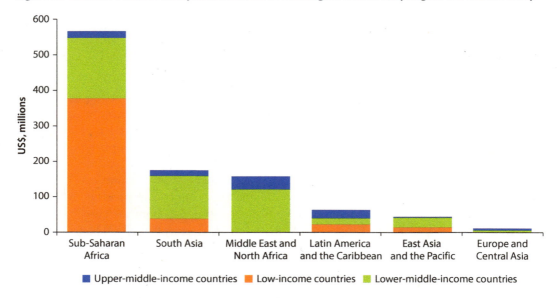

- About 28 percent of total ODA for nutrition goes to five countries, which are spread across three regions. In order from highest to lowest, Ethiopia received $69 million (7 percent of total financing), the Republic of Yemen $67 million (7 percent), Sudan $50 million (5 percent), India $48 million (5 percent), and the Syrian Arab Republic $43 million (4 percent).[16]

Financing the Scale-Up to Reach the Global Targets

The evidence on current levels of nutrition spending has been discussed in the previous section, and the core questions of this chapter as noted at the outset can now be considered: How can the financing needs to achieve the World Health Assembly nutrition targets be mobilized and how to pay for it? This section draws on everything discussed so far as a baseline from which to start, looking closely to determine whether enough financing can plausibly be raised to meet the $70 billion additional financing needed over the 10 years from 2016 to 2025. If this is plausible, the issue is precisely how this can be done—which sources of financing can do more, and how much will be needed from each compared to the baseline starting point.

This section defines and explores two future financing scenarios, one under assumptions of "business as usual" and the other under assumptions of "global solidarity" to meet the World Health Assembly targets for nutrition. The financing scenarios exclude costs to scale up intermittent presumptive treatment of malaria in pregnancy in malaria-endemic regions as well as costs borne by households for food fortification for the following reasons:

- Funding the cost to scale up intermittent presumptive treatment of malaria in pregnancy in malaria-endemic regions ($0.5 billion) is covered by other health initiatives, including the President's Malaria Initiative, the Global Fund to Fight AIDS, TB and Malaria, and to some extent national governments (MCHIP 2012; Thiam, Kimotho, and Gatonga 2013). Funding for this intervention is not likely to be counted as nutrition spending either by governments or donors.
- Household out-of-pocket expenditure on fortified food products is expected to amass to about $19 billion over the 10-year period. These costs are discussed in a previous chapter and are not included in the financing scenario in order to align with the $70 billion cost aggregation borne by the public sector and donors.

The Business-as-Usual Scenario

This scenario looks at trends in nutrition investments based on historical and projected economic growth and current commitments, and assumes that all funding sources continue spending the same proportion of their budgets on nutrition as they do now. Financing for nutrition still increases, but only insofar as overall budgets increase. For example, if a country currently spends 0.7 percent of its general government expenditure on nutrition in 2015, it would spend that same proportion in future years; but that may still imply added support for nutrition if general government expenditure rises as a result of economic growth or other causes. In effect, all baseline investments are maintained annually and additional financing arising from economic growth is added on top of current spending.

Another way of thinking about this scenario is that governments, ODA, and others are assumed to give no more (or less) priority to nutrition in the future than they are giving to it now. That trend would obviously be a very disappointing outcome from the perspective of those seeking faster progress toward reducing the burden of nutritional deficiencies. It is, from that viewpoint, a low-case scenario generating a lower-bound result.

To explore the ramifications of the business-as-usual scenario, the likely trends in government budgets and ODA through 2025 are considered:

- For governments, projections for (1) economic growth (GDP), (2) total government spending, and (3) the share of total spending that goes to health are available for many countries and provide indicative guideposts for how budgets for nutrition are likely to develop. Using data from the International Monetary Fund's World Economic Outlook provides a plausible basis for estimating how governments' spending on nutrition will possibly develop.
- For ODA, future support for nutrition will be sensitive to changes in total, global ODA, which in turn will be sensitive to donor countries' economic growth (GDP). From projections of those variables using OECD-reported data for 2013, estimates for aid for nutrition—for each recipient country—were developed for 2014, 2015, and 2016, using OECD growth rates for those years. The corresponding figures for 2017 through 2025 were projected using the average of the growth rates for 2014–16 (2.08 percent).

The business-as-usual scenario takes into account the commitments that specific sources of ODA made at the Nutrition for Growth Summit in 2013, where $4.15 billion was pledged in support of nutrition-specific programs by 2020 (Nutrition for Growth Secretariat [UK] 2013). It was assumed about half of those commitments are realized ($2.07 billion).[17] That financing is attributed to each target in proportion to current donor investments within the basic nutrition code.[18]

In addition, a very small contribution was assumed to be made by households purchasing nutrition commodities. As discussed in chapter 4, the literature shows that a fraction of nonpregnant women above the poverty line purchase iron and folic acid supplements through private retailers (Bahl et al. 2013) and this is also true for other micronutrient commodities (Leive and Xu 2008; Rannan-Eliya et al. 2012; Siekmann, Timmer, and Irizarry 2012). Although most of the costs to scale up micronutrient supplementation (including iron and folic acid supplementation for nonpregnant women) are borne by the public sector and donors, theoretically some of the scale-up costs would be offset by household spending. Across the 10-year period, it was estimated that households would contribute $748 million toward these out-of-pocket purchases.[19] The same assumption is made for the global solidarity scenario.

The Global-Solidarity Scenario
The global-solidarity scenario was constructed with the explicit objective of demonstrating how the resource gap associated with meeting the global nutrition targets can be closed through a coordinated increase by governments and ODA, supplemented by innovative financing mechanisms. Principles of sustainability and country ability to pay were taken into account. The defining principles of the global-solidarity scenario are shown in table 8.1.[20]

Results from the Two Scenarios
Given the above characterizations of the two scenarios—and the preceding discussion on current levels and required future flows that has led up to this point—we present the bottom-line results and conclusions from the analysis of financing requirements.

The business-as-usual scenario leads to a shortfall of about $56 billion over the next 10 years (figure 8.4). It highlights the magnitude of the significant gap that—if governments, ODA, and others do not do more than continue with what they are doing now—will persist between what is needed to achieve the global nutrition targets and what is projected to be spent in the next decade. The $56 billion figure also calls attention to the stark reality that anything less than a major expansion of financing over and above current trends will not be enough: the targets will not be achieved. Also implicit in these results is the need for swift action: given how large the gap is, failure to ramp up quickly will make it impossible to raise sufficient funds by 2025.

Table 8.1 Financing Principles Used to Close the Resource Gap under the Global-Solidarity Scenario

Principle	Details	Comments
No reduction in current spending on nutrition	The $3.9 billion of current annual financing is continued, so that the additions described below are truly incremental.	If current levels of support cannot be counted on to continue, it would be extremely difficult to close the resource gap.
Countries increase their nutrition spending to reach higher benchmarks	By 2021, governments increase spending on nutrition as a share of total government expenditure linearly to the median in their income group (appendix E, table E.1); those above the benchmark increase spending by 1% per year.	Governments that have been lagging behind their peer countries in prioritizing nutrition will have to step up more if the resource gap is to be closed. ODA and other sources will still be needed to fill in where required.
Countries with higher ability to pay contribute more	Upper-middle-income countries pay 100% of annual additional costs for 2016–25. Lower-middle-income countries pay 70% of the annual additional cost by 2025. Those already above 70% in 2016 stay at that level. Low-income countries pay 50% of the annual additional cost by 2025.	ODA will need to give priority to low- and lower-middle-income countries and focus on supporting the five-year scale-up period. Countries with greater ability to pay—even those with high burdens such as China and Mexico—will completely cover their own costs.
New mechanisms for nutrition financing are optimized	Commitments made by the Power of Nutrition[a] and other innovative financing mechanisms are assumed to be fully realized and distributed among recipient countries proportionally on the basis of stunting burden.	The new mechanisms will help attenuate the cost pressure on governments and ODA. Countries benefitting from The Global Financing Facility[b] and the Power of Nutrition will make maximum use of those new funds.
Private sector engagement	Private sector stakeholders are engaged in the scale-up of food fortification, supply of micronutrient supplements, and other interventions.	Partnerships across stakeholders, including public-private collaboration, will be needed.

a. See www.powerofnutrition.org.
b. For Global Financing Facility, see http://www.worldbank.org/en/topic/health/brief/global-financing-facility-in-support-of-every-woman-every-child.

The global-solidarity scenario (figure 8.5) shows how the financing shortfall can be closed through the following coordinated efforts to mobilize resources from national governments, ODA, and new innovative funding mechanisms such as the Power of Nutrition and the Global Financing Facility (GFF) for reproductive, maternal, neonatal, child, and adolescent health and nutrition.

- Country governments would need to provide an additional $39.7 billion over 10 years from domestic budgets. Figure 8.5 shows an increasing trend from the initial to later years, beginning with an additional $707 million in 2016 and ramping up to an additional $7 billion contributed by all governments by 2025.

Figure 8.4 Business as Usual in Nutrition Financing: A $56 Billion Shortfall

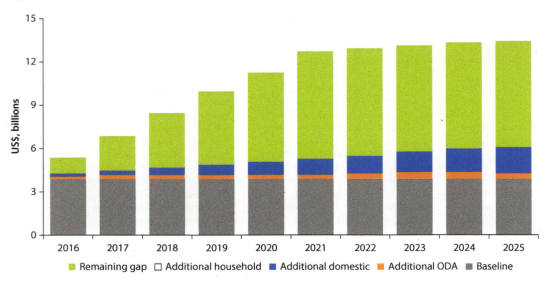

Note: Annual additional household contributions are small relative to other contributions and, as such, are not pictured. Total additional household contributions amount to $748 million across the ten-year period. ODA = official development assistance.

Figure 8.5 The Global-Solidarity Financing Scenario: The $70 Billion Required for Scale-Up Mobilized

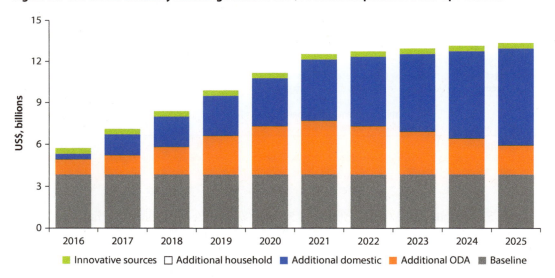

Note: Annual additional household contributions are small relative to other contributions and, as such, are not pictured. Total additional household contributions amount to $748 million across the ten-year period. ODA = official development assistance.

Although this seems a drastic leap, it is worth noting that about 80 percent of this additional $7 billion by the end of 2025 is contributed by middle-income countries.
- Traditional ODA would need to contribute an extra $25.6 billion over the 10 years. Figure 8.5 shows donors contributing to the scale-up phase within the first five years and increasing to a maximum amount of spending at $3.9 billion in additional contributions by 2021. In addition to increased amounts of ODA, donor investments must be refocused to the most effective interventions and high-burden geographies. From 2022 to 2025, donors scale back disbursements in line with country transition plans in a coordinated effort to increase country ownership.
- Innovative sources would contribute another $3.4 billion over the 10 years.

To achieve these goals, high-burden country governments would need to increase the share of their projected spending on health that is directed to nutrition from about 1.0 percent to 2.9 percent. ODA would need to boost expenditures on nutrition from an average of 1.0 percent of total ODA to about 2.8 percent by 2021, after which this could taper back to 1.8 percent by 2025.

All together, closing the resource gap would mean that the $3.9 billion in current annual financing for nutrition interventions would need to rise to $13.5 billion by 2025, a 3.5-fold increase.

Discussion

As noted at the outset of this chapter, mobilizing the $70 billion of additional financing (over and above current spending on nutrition) that is needed to reach the global nutrition targets will be a major challenge, but it is one that is achievable. Meeting that goal is feasible if governments, donors, and others contribute their share in alignment with a "global-solidarity" scenario that is defined and explored in this chapter. On the other hand, a continuation of business as usual, extrapolating current spending growth trends forward, will not be enough; that scenario will result in falling far short of the global nutrition targets. The challenge that exists is clear: a major increase in financial commitments for nutrition will help solve a global problem that has bedeviled humanity since the beginning; anything less will condemn current and future generations to continued unnecessary loss of life and opportunity. Investing in the early years of a child's life—or the first 1,000 days—will save lives and build economic potential. The economic gains that will result from investing in better nutrition are a way to garner increased government commitment to improving nutrition.

Global success is possible. Past experience from other initiatives shows that the dramatic acceleration of financing for the global nutrition targets over a decade is feasible (Kim 2013). Between 2001 and 2011, the global AIDS movement saw funding for prevention and treatment grow from less than $0.5 billion to more than $15 billion—a rate of expansion greater than what is needed to scale up nutrition programs (UNAIDS 2016).

An Investment Framework for Nutrition • http://dx.doi.org/10.1596/978-1-4648-1010-7

Looking forward, the nutrition-financing figures presented in the global-solidarity scenario fit within projections of future global health financing. In terms of development assistance for health, although it has been plateauing in recent years—between 2010 and 2015, development assistance for health grew by just 1.2 percent annually—it is expected to rise to $64.1 billion (95 percent confidence interval; $30.4–161.8 billion) by 2040 (Dieleman, Schneider et al. 2016). Under the global-solidarity financing scenario, the maximum total contribution from donors is about $4.9 billion ($3.9 billion on top of current spending) by 2021. This $4.9 billion would represent approximately 14 percent of total development assistance for health projected for 2021 (Dieleman, Schneider et al. 2016), up from 3 percent in 2015. As such, this would require a significant—but not unachievable—increase in the priority given to nutrition within development assistance for health.

In terms of government health spending, Dieleman, Templin et al. (2016) estimate that per capita health spending will increase by 3.4 percent in upper-middle-income countries, 3.0 percent in lower-middle-income countries, and 2.4 percent in low-income countries annually. Under the global-solidarity financing scenario, upper-middle-income countries pay for 100 percent of the annual additional costs needed to scale up the core package of nutrition interventions in their countries. Lower-middle-income countries and low-income countries pay for 70 percent and 50 percent of annual additional costs by 2025, respectively. In 2025, total contributions for nutrition would represent less than 1 percent of total projected government health spending for upper-middle-income countries, less than 2 percent for lower-middle-income countries, and about 6 percent for low-income countries (Dieleman, Templin et al. 2016).[21]

Decisions on how to allocate resources for health depend on many factors, including burden, cost-effectiveness of interventions, development partner ability and willingness to contribute, intertemporal trade-offs (that is, balancing short-term contributions with longer-term gains such as surveillance and monitoring), and health equity (Dieleman and Haakenstad 2015; Resch, Ryckman, and Hecht 2014). The high burden of malnutrition that exists today, combined with the strong evidence for cost-effective interventions to prevent and treat malnutrition, should be cause for accelerated prioritization of nutrition—not only within health but within all nutrition-relevant sectors. The analyses presented here can help prioritize nutrition within key global health investment frameworks for reproductive, maternal, newborn, and child health that include nutrition as a crosscutting theme (Black et al. 2016; Stenberg et al. 2013).

With a combination of political will, widespread advocacy, and smart investments, it is possible to move toward the global nutrition targets—but only if the global community truly comes together to accelerate and sustain financing and action. What will it take to mobilize sufficient support for a transition to the global-solidarity scenario? A full discussion of that important question requires in-depth commentary that is beyond the scope of this chapter, the main purpose of which is to provide a technical exposition of the basic numbers defining future nutrition financing if the scale-up is to be achieved. Nevertheless, the following points are offered as a point of departure for a larger strategy discussion that will be required.

Advocacy. Advocacy efforts aimed at pushing the nutrition agenda forward will be required at the local, state, national, and international levels. Key policy messages will need to reach all relevant sectors in order to maximize nutrition investment opportunities and leverage funding multisectorally.

Political decision making. To achieve the global nutrition targets by 2025, rapid and prioritized resource mobilization will be necessary. The global-solidarity scenario places a large cost-sharing responsibility on domestic financing from high-burden governments. This is in line with the agreements on sustainable financing from the Financing for Development conference held in Addis Ababa in July 2015. For government contributions to increase, an investment case for nutrition, country by country, will need to be presented to the appropriate political leaders and stakeholders and will need to include the ministries of finance for each country.

The scale-up of nutrition financing requires leaders to commit to increasing nutrition investments and prioritizing nutrition within their budgets. This will be needed both domestically and within external development partner organizations in order to mobilize an additional $70 billion by 2025.

Prioritization. As discussed in an earlier chapter, under constrained resources, priority should be given to the most cost-effective actions that can be scaled up immediately. Increased efforts for research and implementation science could help improve the technical efficiency of interventions (lowering costs and maximizing impact), and maximize service delivery opportunities for interventions.

Widespread implementation. Simply achieving the $70 billion goal in additional financing will not be enough because implementation and capacity constraints are critical components to scale-up. Even with ample financial resources, many other factors—including technical support, delivery systems, and supporting infrastructure—will need to work well in synergy. Considerations of absorptive capacity need due attention.

Monitoring and accountability. All stakeholders will need to be held accountable to their commitments through better resource tracking, analysis, and reporting for financial investments for nutrition. In addition, linking investments with outputs in terms of improved nutrition indicators across all global goals will help to increase targeted, evidence-based programs. Although these analyses represent a first approximation on current investments for nutrition globally, future analyses will depend on continued and improved expenditure tracking systems and better financing data. For governments, this means enhanced focus on tracking resources for nutrition, preferably through an institutionalized financial tracking system that monitors progress toward a costed nutrition plan. For donors, it will be important to consider a way to revise the way ODA for nutrition is coded. As described above, the current basic nutrition code includes more than what is typically considered nutrition-specific, while other health and emergency codes include significant amounts going to nutrition-specific interventions. A revised definition of the basic nutrition code could exclude school feeding schemes, household food security, and other nutrition-sensitive programs; and at the same time a policy marker could be put in place to mark disbursements across sectors and purpose codes that are related to nutrition. Not only will this improve resource tracking for nutrition-specific interventions, but it will also lend itself to tracking nutrition-sensitive investments.

Improvement in underlying determinants of malnutrition. Although these analyses focus on the cost of high-impact, nutrition-specific interventions, it is important to note that, for these programs to be successful, the underlying causes of malnutrition must be addressed through multisectoral nutrition-sensitive programs. Efforts within water, sanitation, and hygiene (WASH); agriculture; poverty reduction and social security; education; and other nutrition-sensitive programs should continue and be enhanced. Cost and financing analysis on nutrition-sensitive programs is warranted for future study, especially assessment of the marginal costs associated with making a program "more" nutrition-sensitive by building in core nutrition-oriented components across sectors.

Notes

1. The word *governments* refers in this chapter to the national authorities of low- and middle-income countries, most of which are in Africa, Asia, and Latin America. Other designations sometimes used here and elsewhere for that same concept include *countries, country governments, aid-recipient countries* or *governments,* and *donor-assisted countries* or *governments. Developing countries,* not used here, is common elsewhere. High-income countries and governments are excluded from these definitions; they are covered under the section on ODA.

2. *ODA* refers to official development assistance and similar kinds of aid. This comprises bilateral assistance agencies (and the high-income countries to which they belong), multilateral organizations, and a wide variety of charitable institutions (not least of which are the large international nongovernmental organizations). Support from consortia of ODA funders, especially the Global Financing Facility (GFF) and the Power of Nutrition, is also important.

3. *Other sources* include households (principally through their purchasing of nutrition-related products and services); the private sector (as investors in nutrition-related ventures, and as buyers and sellers of their outputs, and, less commonly, as charitable supporters); and non-state funders such as nongovernmental organizations that are not funded by bilateral or multilateral aid so are not counted together with the bigger entities under ODA.

4. Funding for nutrition from civil society, nongovernmental organizations, philanthropic organizations, and other sources that is not easily captured could be substantial. There are numerous small and medium-sized nongovernmental organizations in low- and middle-income countries that may not be tracked through donor reporting or through the national treasuries. These kinds of contributions are termed *off-budget* sources and are very difficult to track (SPRING 2016a, 2016b). Unfortunately, there is currently little to no data to estimate their share of global nutrition financing. Accordingly, they were excluded from the current analysis.

5. "Global Harmonization of Budget and Expenditure Analysis Methods for Nutrition." JSI workshop held November 3–4, 2015, in Arlington, VA.

6. Where amounts spent are not obtainable, amounts budgeted are used. Spending often falls short of budget targets, but the difference is generally not worrisomely large for purposes of this analysis. Tanzania's Public Expenditure Review for nutrition finds that 79 percent of the amount budgeted was actually spent (United Republic of Tanzania, Ministry of Finance 2014). The methods and approaches used in this chapter were presented to—and received general support from—various convenings of experts over the course of the study including through the Technical Advisory Group (TAG). For example, at the "Global Harmonization of Budget and Expenditure Analysis Methods for Nutrition" workshop held November 3–4, 2015, in Arlington, VA, there was broad consensus that the methods are appropriate.

7. Government expenditure on health per capita is found to be associated with government expenditure on nutrition per stunted child (r-squared is 0.58; regression coefficient 1.69). Analysis of the residuals finds no significant bias. To minimize any potential impact from extreme outliers (and the possibly incorrect data on them), the lowest-spending country (South Sudan) and the highest-spending country (Costa Rica) were omitted.

8. Nutrition-relevant budget allocation and use data are reported by the Government of India's Ministry of Women and Child Development through Lok Sabha (Unstarred Question No 861, answered on February 2, 2015, in the Lok Sabha database of questions; see Lok Sabha, Parliament of India (2016)). NHM budget documents were downloaded from the NHM, Ministry Health and Family Welfare, Government of India website http://nrhm.gov.in/nrhmin-state.html. About $50 million was spent through NHM on nutrition-specific interventions in 2013–14. In 2013–14, the Government of India released about $1 billion to states for the Supplementary Nutrition Program (SNP) delivered through its Integrated Child Development Services, which states equally match, resulting in about $2 billion for the program. Financing for that program is included in the analysis because the program incorporates complementary food provision to vulnerable households in need. However, some of that funding goes to older children (25 months to 6 years) than the 6–24 months of interest here. On the basis of Government of India–reported beneficiary data of the SNP program, 45 percent of the total is assumed to remain after that exclusion. See Lok Sabha, Parliament of India (2016), Unstarred Question No 1327, answered July 18, 2014.

9. The governance category includes information management, monitoring and evaluation, surveillance, research, coordination and partnership, advocacy, communication, policy development, and system capacity building.

10. In order not to overestimate spending on wasting for countries with low wasting prevalence, it was assumed that countries with a wasting prevalence of less than 5 percent are not investing in the management of acute malnutrition because it likely would not be a priority for those countries. The proportions for the other interventions were then normalized to 100 percent.

11. At the time of analysis, 2013 data were the most recent information available, and the intervention-level analysis was conducted with this dataset. Financing for subsequent years (2014 and 2015) was estimated by applying annual OECD growth rates for each year (1.8 percent and 1.9 percent, respectively). See OECD Data, 2014, Real GDP Forecast, available at https://data.oecd.org/gdp/real-gdp-forecast.htm. Subsequently, 2014 disbursement data became available and were reported as $937 million, which is $26 million lower than predicted on the basis of OECD growth. Because of the two-year lag in CRS reporting and the resource-intense

method to extract intervention-level data, it is not possible to determine whether intervention or recipient country donor prioritization changed between 2013 and 2015. All 2015 figures reported in this chapter for ODA for nutrition are based on the analysis of 2013 data because these were the most recent data at the time of analysis. Future work to track these resources year-on-year is needed for the purposes of monitoring and accountability.

12. In order to estimate how regional disbursements are distributed to countries within the region, the regional disbursement was assumed to be spread across the countries in each region in the same proportions as the amounts directly going to countries. Aid classified as "unspecified" is excluded because it could not be assigned definitely to a country or region.

13. A few categories require special attention. For example, "capacity building" often has to be separated from "research and development," and nutrition interventions pertinent for this study have to be isolated from other types of nutrition-related initiatives. In most cases, the project descriptions provide good pointers for devising assumptions that mirror the reality.

14. Data on Guatemala's current spending on nutrition per child under 5 is almost twice that of the next-highest country (India). Excluding Guatemala as an outlier, the average spending across lower-middle-income countries is $2.79 with a standard deviation of 4.70.

15. This includes $54 million reported by the CRS as disbursed to basic nutrition through the International Development Association (IDA). However, this is a small subset of the total nutrition portfolio from the World Bank Group. As stated by the CRS, "differences between these OECD data (based on World Bank reporting) and data published by the World Bank for economic sectors and themes (i.e., purpose of activities), are due to the use of different classification systems. The taxonomy used by the World Bank provides a disaggregated depiction of World Bank activities more closely aligned to its mandate and business model" (OECD 2015), and it is not possible to track IDA/IBRD contributions to nutrition via OECD/CRS databases. This is further complicated by the fact that IDA/IBRD funds cannot be earmarked for future commitments.

16. The majority of aid going to Syria was for the treatment of severe acute malnutrition.

17. ACTION scorecard indicates many ODA commitments are off track.

18. Because of the nutrition-sensitive investments included in basic nutrition, as well as irrelevant nutrition-specific interventions, only 76 percent ($1.57 billion) of Nutrition for Growth 2013 commitments are attributed to the four targets. This financing is split equally each year for 2013–20, and maintained at that level for 2021–25.

19. Household contributions were generated by calculating the percentage of households that spend regularly on these commodities using UNICEF MICS data, and applying this share to the estimated additional cost. This includes $505 million in out-of-pocket spending for iron and folic acid supplementation for nonpregnant women reported in an earlier chapter, and a relatively modest amount toward all other micronutrient commodities.

20. Note that support for intermittent presumptive treatment of malaria in pregnancy in malaria-endemic regions (total cost = $416 million) is not included in the global-solidarity scenario. That is because financing for that purpose is likely to be forthcoming under other initiatives, possibly related to the sources that are funding this area currently, including the President's Malaria's Initiative and the Global Fund to Fight AIDS, TB and Malaria.

21. Here, total government health expenditure in 2025 was estimated on the basis of reported total health expenditure per capita from Dieleman, Templin et al. (2016) and population estimates from U.N. Population Division, World population prospects, http://esa.un.org/unpd/wpp/Download/Standard/Population/. Note that the average across income groups here is only slightly different than the average 2.9 percent across all income groups reported for the global-solidarity scenario, which was derived from the authors' projections.

References

ACF (Action Against Hunger). 2012. *Aid for Nutrition: Can Investments to Scale Up Nutrition Actions Be Accurately Tracked?* http://www.actionagainsthunger.org/sites/default/files/publications/Aid_for_Nutrition_low_res_final.pdf.

Bahl, K., E. Toro, C. Qureshi, and P. Shaw. 2013. *Nutrition for a Better Tomorrow: Scaling Up Delivery of Micronutrient Powders for Infants and Young Children*. Washington, DC: Results for Development Institute. http://www.resultsfordevelopment.org/nutrition-for-a-better-tomorrow.

Black, R. E., C. Levin, N. Walker, D. Chou, and M. Temmerman for the DCP3 RMNCH Authors Group. 2016. "Reproductive, Maternal, Newborn, and Child Health: Key Messages from Disease Control Priorities 3rd Edition." *The Lancet Online First*. 388 (10061): 2811–24. http://dx.doi.org/10.1016/S0140-6736(16)00738-8.

Dieleman, J. L., and A. Haakenstad. 2015. "The Complexity of Resource Allocation for Health." *The Lancet Global Health* 3 (1): e8–e9. http://dx.doi.org/10.1016/S2214-109X(14)70373-0.

Dieleman, J. L., M. T. Schneider, A. Hakenstad, L. Singh, N. Sadat, M. Birger, A. Reynolds, T. Templin, H. Hamavid, A. Chapin, J. L. Christopher, and M. D. Murray. 2016. "Development Assistance for Health: Past Trends, Associations, and the Future of International Financial Flows for Health." *The Lancet* 387 (10037): 2536–44.

Dieleman, J. L., T. Templin, N. Sadat, P. Reidy, A. Chapin, K. Foreman, A. Haakenstad, T. Evans, C. J. L. Murray, and C. Kurowski. 2016. "National Spending on Health by Source for 184 Countries between 2013 and 2040." *The Lancet* 387 (10037): 2521–35.

IFPRI (International Food Policy Research Institute). 2015. *Global Nutrition Report 2015: Actions and Accountability to Advance Nutrition and Sustainable Development*. Washington, DC: IFPRI.

———. 2016. *Global Nutrition Report 2016: From Promise to Impact: Ending Malnutrition by 2030*. Washington, DC: IFPRI.

Kim, J. Y. 2013. "Time for Even Greater Ambition in Global Health." *The Lancet* 382 (9908): e33–e34.

Leive, A., and K. Xu. 2008. "Coping with Out-of-Pocket Health Payments: Empirical Evidence from 15 African Countries." *Bulletin of the World Health Organization* 86 (11): 849–56C.

Lok Sabha, Parliament of India. 2016. Lok Sabha, List of Questions for ORAL ANSWERS (database of questions). http://164.100.47.192/Loksabha/Questions/questionlist.aspx.

MCHIP (Maternal and Child Health Integrated Program). 2012. *Successes and Challenges for Malaria in Pregnancy Programming: A Three-Country Analysis*.

NCD-RisC (NCD Risk Factor Collaboration). 2016. "Trends in Adult Body-Mass Index in 200 Countries from 1975 to 2014: A Pooled Analysis of 1698 Population-Based Measurement Studies with 19.2 Million Participants." *The Lancet* 387 (10026): 1377–96. http://dx.doi.org/10.1016/S0140-6736(16)30054-X.

Nutrition for Growth Secretariat (UK). 2013. *Nutrition for Growth Commitments: Executive Summary*. https://www.gov.uk/government/uploads/system/uploads/attachment_data/file/207274/nutrition-for-growth-commitments.pdf.

OECD (Organisation for Economic Co-operation and Development). 2015. Creditor Reporting System Database (CRS), (accessed October 19, 2015), https://stats.oecd.org/Index.aspx?DataSetCode=CRS1.

———. 2016. Creditor Reporting System Database (CRS), (accessed September 19, 2016), https://stats.oecd.org/Index.aspx?DataSetCode=CRS1.

Rannan-Eliya, R. P., C. Anuranga, J. Chandrasiri, R. Hafez, G. Kasthuri, R. Wickramasinghe, and J. Jayanthan. 2012. *Impact of Out-of-Pocket Expenditures on Families and Barriers to Use of Maternal and Child Health Services in Asia and the Pacific: Evidence from National Household Surveys of Healthcare Use and Expenditures*. Mandaluyong City, Philippines: Asian Development Bank.

Resch, S., T. Ryckman, and R. Hecht. 2014. "Funding AIDS Programmes in the Era of Shared Responsibility: An Analysis of Domestic Spending in 12 Low-Income and Middle-Income Countries." *Lancet Global Health* 3: e52–61.

Save the Children and CSONA (Civil Society Organization Nutrition Alliance Malawi). 2015. *Unpublished data on Budget Analysis for Nutrition*.

Siekmann, J., A. Timmer, and L. Irizarry. 2012. "Home Fortification Using Market-Based Approaches to Complement Free Public Distribution of Micronutrient Powders (MNP)." 34–38. In *Home Fortification with Micronutrient Powders (MND)*. 34–38. Basel, Switzerland: Sight and Life. https://www.dsm.com/content/dam/dsm/cworld/en_US/documents/home-fortification-with-micronutrient-powders-joint-publication-by-the-world-food-programme-sight-and-life-unicef-cdc-and-hf-tag.pdf.

SPRING. 2016a. *Pathways to Better Nutrition in Nepal: Final Report*. Arlington, VA: Strengthening Partnerships, Results, and Innovations in Nutrition Globally (SPRING) project.

———. 2016b. *Pathways to Better Nutrition in Uganda: Final Report*. Arlington, VA: Strengthening Partnerships, Results, and Innovations in Nutrition Globally (SPRING) project.

Stenberg, K., H. Axelson, P. Sheehan, I. Anderson, A. M. Gülmezoglu, M. Temmerman, et al. 2013. "Advancing Social and Economic Development by Investing in Women's and Children's Health: A New Global Investment Framework." *The Lancet* 383 (9925): 1333–54.

SUN (Scaling Up Nutrition). 2014. *Planning and Costing for the Acceleration of Actions for Nutrition: Experiences of Countries in the Movement for Scaling Up Nutrition*. http://scalingupnutrition.org/wp-content/uploads/2014/05/Final-Synthesis-Report.pdf.

Tandon, A., and C. Cashin. 2010. "Assessing Public Expenditure on Health from a Fiscal Space Perspective." Health, Nutrition and Population Discussion Paper, World Bank, Washington, DC. http://siteresources.worldbank.org/HEALTHNUTRITIONANDPOPULATION/Resources/281627-1095698140167/AssesingPublicExpenditureFiscalSpace.pdf.

Thiam, S., V. Kimotho, and P. Gatonga. 2013. "Why Are IPTp Coverage Targets So Elusive in Sub-Saharan Africa? A Systematic Review of Health System Barriers." *Malaria Journal* 12 (1): 353.

UNAIDS (Joint United Nations Programme on HIV/AIDS). 2016. *Fast-Track Update on Investments Needed in the AIDS Response.* Geneva: UNAIDS.

United Republic of Tanzania, Ministry of Finance. 2014. *Public Expenditure Review of the Nutrition Sector. Main Report.* Innovex. http://scalingupnutrition.org/wp-content/uploads/2014/08/Nutrition-PER-Final-version-April-2014.pdf.

CHAPTER 9

Reaching the Global Targets for Stunting, Anemia, Breastfeeding, and Wasting: Investment Framework and Research Implications

Meera Shekar, Julia Dayton Eberwein, Jakub Kakietek, and Michelle Mehta

Key Messages

- The world needs $70 billion over 10 years to invest in high-impact nutrition-specific interventions in countries that carry the highest burden of stunting, anemia, and wasting, and the lowest rates of breastfeeding. This is in addition to current spending and translates to just over $10 a year per child under age five.
- Although the estimates of what it would take to achieve the global nutrition targets are based on ambitious scale-up assumptions, some countries have shown that rapid scale-up of nutrition interventions can be achieved and can lead to swift declines in stunting and other forms of malnutrition. Rapid declines in stunting have been achieved recently in Bangladesh, Ethiopia, Ghana, Malawi, Peru, Senegal, Tanzania, and Vietnam, among other countries. In fact, the analyses suggest that at least one of the targets—the one for breastfeeding—has the scope to be much more ambitious.
- The benefits of achieving these targets would be enormous. There would be 65 million fewer cases of stunting and 265 million fewer cases of anemia in women in 2025 as compared to the 2015 baseline. In addition, at least 91 million more children would be treated for severe wasting and 105 million additional babies would be exclusively breastfed during the first six months of life over 10 years. Altogether, investing in interventions to reach these targets would also result in at least 3.7 million child deaths averted. Furthermore, these analyses show that significant investments in both the key interventions and other health and poverty reduction efforts are required in order to achieve the targets.
- In an environment of constrained resources, this report lays out two alternative investment packages, with the strong caveat that investing in these sets of interventions would not achieve some of the global targets. A "priority package" of immediately ready to scale interventions would require $23 billion over the next 10 years, $2.3 billion per year, or just over $4 per child. A "catalyzing progress package" would scale up the priority package plus a more phased-in expansion of some of the other interventions to strengthen delivery mechanisms, support for research and program implementation, and invest in better

- technologies, requiring an additional $37 billion over the next 10 years, $3.7 billion per year, or just over $5 per child. Further investments would be needed over time to build up to scaling up the full package.
- The analyses also identify critical areas of research that need to be prioritized by the global community, including determining scalable strategies for delivering high-impact interventions, developing new tools to help countries prioritize the most cost-effective interventions, and understanding how to effectively prevent wasting among children. Better data on annual domestic and official development assistance (ODA) financing would also greatly facilitate future progress tracking.
- Stunting and other forms of malnutrition can be a life sentence, but they must not be accepted as the "new normal." Although political commitment is growing rapidly for investing in the 1,000-day window of opportunity, more is needed to move this agenda from a pet cause to a common cause, and from a political imperative to an economic imperative.
- Given the right investments in "gray-matter infrastructure" at the right time, every child can achieve her full potential. And the payoffs from these investments are durable, inalienable, and portable. An in-depth understanding of current nutrition investments and their impacts, future needs, and ways to mobilize the required financing presented here will pave the way forward for action.

Rationale for Investing in Nutrition

Decades of chronic underinvestment in nutrition have led to progress that is slow and uneven. This underinvestment is a primary reason why malnutrition remains an underlying cause of almost half of all deaths among children under age five, a driver of maternal mortality, and a barrier to more rapid economic development and poverty reduction in scores of countries around the world. Currently, all forms of malnutrition (undernutrition, micronutrient deficiencies, and overweight) cost the global economy an estimated $3.5 trillion per year, or $500 per individual, creating a major impediment for country governments to reduce poverty and create thriving and productive communities (Global Panel 2016). Unlike investments in physical infrastructure, investments to promote optimal nutrition generate benefits that are durable, inalienable, and portable. Why is this so? Ensuring optimum nutrition—particularly early in life—can permanently alter an individual's development trajectory and maximize his or her productive potential. If this window of opportunity is missed, it is missed for life.

As of 2015, nearly 159 million children remain stunted in the world, depriving individuals of their full potential and economies of human capital to drive economic growth (UNICEF, WHO, and World Bank 2015). In addition, nearly 50 million children are wasted, predisposing them to premature death and disability (UNICEF, WHO, and World Bank 2015); 36.3 million children are not exclusively breastfed for the first six months of their lives, depriving them of future cognitive potential, health, and economic opportunities (Victora et al. 2016); and 524 million women of reproductive age and pregnant women remain anemic each year, exposing them to the risk of perinatal mortality as well as consigning them to reduced work capacity and lower productivity (WHO 2008).

In 2012—in an effort to rally the international community around improving nutrition—the World Health Assembly endorsed a *Comprehensive Implementation*

Plan on Maternal, Infant, and Young Child Nutrition (WHO 2014a), including the first-ever global nutrition targets (see table 1.1). These targets aim to boost investments in cost-effective interventions and catalyze progress toward decreasing malnutrition and micronutrient deficiencies. To sustain the momentum, world leaders enshrined some of the World Health Assembly targets within the Sustainable Development Goal (SDG) 2.2, committing to end malnutrition in all its forms by the year 2030. With this in mind, this report aims to identify the financing needs for achieving four of the six World Health Assembly targets: stunting, anemia, breastfeeding, and wasting. It also lays out financing scenarios that can generate the resources—from domestic government, ODA, and innovative financing sources—needed for this purpose.

An Investment Framework for Nutrition

The analyses in the previous chapters show that an additional investment of $70 billion would allow the world to achieve the global targets for stunting, anemia, and breastfeeding, and to scale up the treatment of severe acute malnutrition for children. This investment includes $62.4 billion in direct service delivery costs and an additional $7.5 billion for capacity strengthening, monitoring and evaluation, and policy development.

The benefits of achieving these targets would be enormous (figure 9.1). Sixty-five million cases of stunting and 265 million cases of anemia in women would be prevented in 2025 as compared with the 2015 baseline. In addition, at least 91 million more children would be treated for severe wasting and 105 million additional babies would be exclusively breastfed during the first six months of

Figure 9.1 Benefits of Investing in Global Nutrition Targets

An Investment Framework for Nutrition • http://dx.doi.org/10.1596/978-1-4648-1010-7

life over 10 years. Altogether, investing in these targets would also result in averting at least 3.7 million child deaths. The estimates presented in the previous chapters have focused on nutrition-specific actions. However, the analyses show that significant investments in both the nutrition-specific interventions and nutrition-sensitive actions in agriculture, water and sanitation, and the enabling environment are required to achieve the stunting, breastfeeding, and anemia targets (and probably the wasting target as well).

The analyses confirm that the benefits of investing in preventing malnutrition in children and women vastly outweigh the costs. The benefit-cost ratios presented for the stunting, anemia, and breastfeeding packages are all substantially greater than one, the breakeven point, and this holds true across many different contexts.

Although the estimates of what it would take to achieve the global nutrition targets are based on ambitious scale-up rates, some countries have shown that rapid scale-up of nutrition interventions can be achieved and can lead to swift declines in stunting rates. Rapid declines in stunting have been achieved recently in Bangladesh, China, Ethiopia, Ghana, Kenya, Malawi, Tanzania, and Vietnam, among other countries (figure 9.2). Experiences from two other

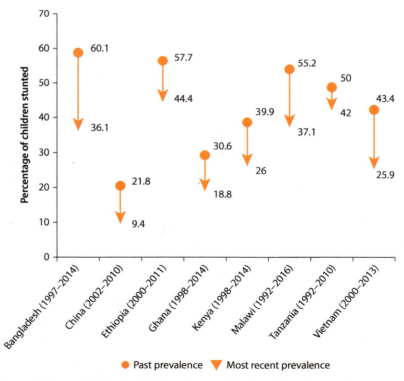

Figure 9.2 Reductions in Prevalence of Stunting, Selected Countries

Source: DHS Program 2016; World Bank 2016b; (for Vietnam only) Viet Nam National Institute of Nutrition, UNICEF, Alive & Thrive 2014.

countries that have achieved remarkable progress, Peru and Senegal, are described in detail in boxes 9.1 and 9.2, respectively. Evidence from Vietnam shows that interventions to promote breastfeeding and to reduce anemia in women can be effective (box 9.3).

The global experience on Vitamin A supplementation is another such example that shows that nutrition outcomes can be achieved with commitment, financing, and capacity building to deliver and sustain programs at scale (box 9.4).

Box 9.1 Peru's Success in Reducing Stunting

If ever anyone doubted that stunting rates could be halved in just one decade, they have only to look to Peru. In 2000, one in three Peruvian children was chronically undernourished. In 2005—five years and millions of dollars later—the numbers remained virtually unchanged at 28 percent of children stunted. But, by 2014, something extraordinary had happened. Stunting fell to only 14 percent, which begs the questions: Just how did Peru do it? What parts of the Peruvian experience are replicable elsewhere?

In 2010, the country awoke to the pressing crisis of child undernutrition. High-level political officials endorsed an effort known as "5x5x5"— which aimed to reduce stunting in children under 5 by 5 percentage points in 5 years and to lessen the resource and health access inequalities between rural and urban areas. With a budding knowledge base on factors influencing nutrition outcomes, a community of practice involving government and stakeholders paved the way for targeting and scaling up nutrition programs. Massive media campaigns put the face of malnutrition into each and every home and health center through radio and television spots and videos, such as *My Future in my First Five Centimeters*. That media effort also promoted the importance of essential health and nutrition services, including child growth promotion and early child development sessions. To support the supply and expansion of high-quality services, a strong monitoring system was linked to a performance incentive mechanism in the Ministry of Finance to redirect resources to the areas where they were most needed and to reward improved coverage and delivery of those services that were assessed to be the most cost-effective in improving child nutrition. A multisectoral effort, spearheaded by the Ministry of Finance and the Prime Minister's office, strengthened the link between the existing conditional cash transfer program *JUNTOS* and the supply of health and nutrition services. This contributed to more than doubling the uptake of regular child health and nutrition checkups in rural areas—from 20 percent in 2008 to 58 percent in 2013.

A further outstanding element of Peru's success is the significance of having annual data on stunting. The power of regular data collection and use cannot be understated in terms of its contribution to enduring political support. As a result of the comprehensive nutrition policy and the trifecta of supply, demand, and accountability, stunting among particularly vulnerable rural populations fell from 44 percent in 2008 to 28 percent in 2014

box continues next page

Box 9.1 Peru's Success in Reducing Stunting *(continued)*

Figure B9.1.1 Key Factors in Peru's Success in Reducing Stunting

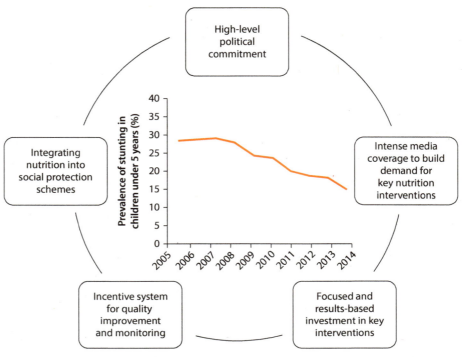

Source: INEI 2015.

(INEI 2015) (figure B9.1.1). Despite leveling economic growth during this period, Peru demonstrated a remarkable effort not only to curb stunting rates but also to create strong commitment and collaboration across sectors to integrate nutrition into social protection programs and, in return, save millions of lives.

Contributed by Alessandra Marini and Omar Arias, World Bank

Box 9.2 Senegal's Nutrition Policy Development Process: A Work in Progress

Senegal has long been plagued by rampant malnutrition. However, prior to 2000, the country's attention was focused primarily on providing humanitarian assistance in the wake of shocks or crises. In 2001, Senegal recognized that the pressing problem of stunting was significantly reducing the cognitive development and growth potential of as many as 30 percent of the nation's children under age five. Three main factors contributed to the country's proactive effort to reduce stunting: high-level political commitment, a multisectoral strategy, and direct and largely government-driven nutrition financing. Under these pillars, the government

box continues next page

Box 9.2 Senegal's Nutrition Policy Development Process: A Work in Progress (continued)

undertook a shift from crisis mitigation to prevention and promotion, cutting program costs dramatically by using local resources and creating an institutional arrangement specifically to fight malnutrition under the Prime Minister's office, which gave voice and responsibility to all those invested. The use of evidence-based programming led to innovative approaches to community mobilization, participation, and, ultimately, ownership over improvements in nutrition programming.

The result of this shift in priorities was impressive. The program scaled up to reach 50 percent of children under age five by 2010 with vital outreach services that included the promotion of exclusive breastfeeding, vitamin A supplementation, and service utilization. In just three years following this scale-up, the prevalence of stunting in children under five fell from 26.5 percent to 18.7 percent (ANSD and ICF International 2012, 2015). Senegal now has one of the lowest rates of stunting in Sub-Saharan Africa. Remarkably, nutrition in Senegal improved even though the economy showed weak and uneven growth, which on average hovered between 1 and 2 percent.

Contributed by Menno Mulder Sibanda and Michelle Mehta, World Bank

---

Box 9.3 The Vietnam Experience: Investing in Breastfeeding Promotion and Anemia Reduction

Vietnam is currently on track to meet at least two of the global targets: increased exclusive breastfeeding and reduced anemia by 2025. The country has proven that investing in the right policies and strategies can significantly improve indicators. In 2010 in Vietnam, nearly one-third of children under five years of age were stunted and fewer than 20 percent of infants under six months of age were exclusively breastfed. Key challenges included general perceptions that women could not produce sufficient breastmilk, the common practice of giving pre-lacteal feeds to newborns, the early introduction of water and other foods, aggressive marketing and widespread availability of infant formula, lack of community and workplace support, and limited health worker commitment and skills to support mothers to breastfeed.

During this time, a social franchise model was successfully implemented to increase breastfeeding counseling for mothers, the government extended maternity leave from four to six months and expanded the ban on the marketing of breastmilk substitutes, and an integrated pro-breastfeeding mass communication campaign was launched—reaching 85 percent of mothers nationwide. This comprehensive strategy changed perceptions, practices, policies, and services toward a more breastfeeding-friendly society (Alive & Thrive 2013). The social franchising model, which covered over 500,000 women in 15 of 58 provinces, raised the rate of exclusive breastfeeding (in children 0–5 months of age) compared with the rate in control sites by 28.3 percent over the 2010–14 period.

Targeted interventions to address micronutrient deficiencies—including supplementation, diet diversification, and food fortification—have also resulted in promising and

box continues next page

Box 9.3 The Vietnam Experience: Investing in Breastfeeding Promotion and Anemia Reduction
(continued)

steady reductions in deficiencies, particularly anemia among women. In the past two decades, the government of Vietnam has prioritized the control and prevention of micronutrient deficiencies through national policies and strategies, including specific policies on prevention of iron deficiency. Since then, Vietnam has seen a steady decline in anemia rates among women of reproductive age to a current prevalence of 14 percent (Stevens et al. 2013).

The Vietnam experience clearly shows that prioritizing the investment in policies and strategies to reduce malnutrition through increased breastfeeding rates and reduced anemia prevalence puts achieving, and even maybe exceeding, the global targets within reach.

Contributed by Dylan Walters and Michelle Mehta, World Bank

Box 9.4 Achieving High Coverage of Nutrition-Specific Interventions: Lessons from Vitamin A Supplementation

Vitamin A supplementation provides a salient example of the potential to achieve sustained, high coverage of evidence-based nutrition programs. Over 95 million children under the age of five globally have compromised immunity as a result of vitamin A deficiency. The semiannual provision of vitamin A capsules is an effective way to reduce vitamin A deficiency and its associated morbidity and mortality.

Vitamin A supplementation can be delivered through routine health facility contacts (for example, well-child and immunization visits for children under age five). However, because of bottlenecks in the provision of public health services (low use, broken supply chains, low-quality health care, and so on), nontraditional mechanisms are necessary to reach vulnerable populations. Vitamin A campaigns serve as an effective means of achieving high and equitable population vitamin A supplementation coverage. Vitamin A campaigns serve to bridge the gap between the needs of the underserved and the formal health sector.

Vitamin A supplementation has a number of features that make it feasible to achieve high population coverage, even in countries that lack well-resourced and high-capacity health systems:

- ***Clear, strong evidence of positive health impact and cost-effectiveness:*** Strong evidence has facilitated political support. Community trials and meta-analyses have demonstrated the positive association between supplementation and decreased mortality (Imdad et al. 2010), while experts routinely cite vitamin A supplementation as one of the most cost-effective nutrition interventions (Horton, Alderman, and Rivera 2008). The analyses in this report support the cost effectiveness of vitamin A supplementation (see table 7.4).
- ***Clearly defined target populations and routine delivery schedules:*** For countries with a high under-five mortality rate, where vitamin A deficiency is defined as a public health problem or that have a history of programming for vitamin A distribution, vitamin A is delivered to all children age 6–59 months on a regular, twice-annual basis.

box continues next page

Box 9.4 Achieving High Coverage of Nutrition-Specific Interventions: Lessons from Vitamin A Supplementation *(continued)*

- **Simplicity of intervention:** Community health volunteers can safely, effectively, and easily deliver vitamin A supplementation without intensive training and through twice-yearly campaigns.

Through integration with child vaccination campaigns or maternal and child health days/weeks, a number of countries have successfully institutionalized the provision of vitamin A supplements and achieved sustained, high coverage (figure B9.4.1). These countries demonstrate that near-universal access to this essential nutrition intervention is possible

Figure B9.4.1 Vitamin A Supplementation Coverage among Children Ages 6–59 months, Selected Countries, 1999–2013

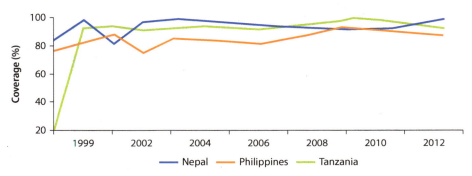

Source: World Bank 2015.

Contributed by Anne Marie Provo, World Bank

Discussion

Although the additional investment of nearly $70 billion over the next 10 years represents a large price tag in absolute terms, it is a miniscule investment in relative terms when compared with other issues the world cares about. For example, the world spends nearly $1.5 billion per day (about $500 billion per year) in untargeted and often unproductive subsidies for agriculture (Potter 2014) in addition to another $543 billion per year (about 1.5 billion per day) on fossil fuel subsidies (IEA 2014). With the right political commitment and economic imperatives, channeling resources toward productive investments such as nutrition is therefore feasible and could yield significant benefits for global and national economies.

Furthermore, even within the health sector, an instructive precedent for building a successful nutrition financing "movement" is available from the recent history of human immunodeficiency virus (HIV) financing. In 1998, when the acquired immune deficiency syndrome (AIDS) epidemic was raging, low- and middle-income countries were spending about $500 million annually to fight HIV. Fifteen years later, with a strong push from civil society organizations representing affected groups as well as governments, nearly $20 billion is being spent each year in these countries on HIV control, more than half of which is from low- and middle-income country governments (UNAIDS 2013). The proposed financing approach for nutrition is somewhat different and must be tailored to the nutrition context, because young children do not have the same voice that HIV-affected groups did. But the argument for investing in children's early years is building rapidly, with support from world leaders, including the president of the World Bank, the African Nutrition Leaders initiative supported by the African Development Bank, and finance ministers and heads of state from several high-burden countries. Therefore, the "global-solidarity" scenario developed in Chapter 8 assumes wherein ODA financing will kick off the effort with a surge of financing (3.5 times current investments) for the first five years, followed by a slower but more sustained scale-up from domestic resources over the second five years.

To provide the $70 billion needed to reach the stunting, anemia, and breastfeeding targets and mitigate the impacts of wasting, national governments will need to mobilize an average of $4 billion more of domestic resources per year, and ODA will need to mobilize an additional $2.6 billion annually over the next 10 years (table 9.1).

The additional financing required under the proposed global-solidarity scenario (see chapter 8) to reach the global target will require large efforts by all stakeholders. For the governments in high-burden countries, it will be challenging to allocate, on average, nearly 2.9 percent of their health budgets to nutrition, an increase from the current average of only 1 percent. Although this level of domestic spending is ambitious, many countries have shown that it is achievable. In order to propose a sustainable financing scenario, the plan is for high-burden countries to gradually scale up their domestic budget shares over 10 years. If they start early and sustain their efforts, and if political commitment translates into budgets, the year-on-year rate of increase is feasible. Countries such as Ethiopia, India, Malawi, and Pakistan are already moving in this direction.

For external financiers, meeting their share of the global-solidarity scenario through ODA will require them to substantially raise their share of development

Table 9.1 Additional Financing Needs to Reach All Four Targets, Selected Years
US$, millions

Source	In 2016	In 2021	In 2025	Total over 10 years
Country governments	707	4,519	7,104	39,676
ODA	622	3,940	2,063	25,628
Other sources[a]	203	570	590	4,608
Total				69,912

Note: ODA = official development assistance.
a. *Other sources* includes innovative financing mechanisms, financing of intermittent presumptive treatment of malaria in pregnancy in malaria-endemic areas (from malaria budgets), and household contributions toward appropriate interventions.

assistance for health devoted to stunting reduction and overall improvement of nutrition outcomes in the early phases. For some donors such as Canada, which already contributes over 11 percent of health ODA to basic nutrition, the challenge will be easier to meet. At present, 13 Organisation for Economic Co-operation and Development (OECD) member countries are providing less than $1 million each in direct aid for nutrition (OECD 2016); they could potentially be encouraged by the evidence presented in this report to make shifts in their policies to prioritize nutrition. New and innovative sources of external financing, including the Global Financing Facility in support of Every Woman Every Child, and the Power of Nutrition, which leverages traditional financing to access new philanthropic and private funding, will also be crucial to help fill the gap.[1]

In an environment of constrained resources, if the world could not afford the $70 billion needed to achieve the targets, but instead could invest in only a subset of interventions, it would have to set priorities. In this context this report lays out two alternative packages for consideration. These scenarios would include scaling up interventions with the highest returns and those that are scalable now (that is, those that maximize both technical and allocative efficiency), with the strong caveat that scaling up a smaller set of interventions will not achieve some of the global targets by 2025. Financing a "priority package" of interventions immediately ready to scale will require an additional investment of $23 billion over the next 10 years, or $2.3 billion per year. When combined with other health and poverty reduction efforts, this priority package would yield significant returns: an estimated 2.3 million lives would be saved, and there would be 50 million fewer cases of stunting in 2025 than in 2015. A slightly more ambitious package of investments, called the "catalyzing progress package" would scale up the priority package plus and more phased-in expansion of the other interventions to strengthen delivery mechanisms and support research and program implementation. It is assumed that, for the latter set of interventions, during the first 5 years, emphasis will be placed on establishing global guidelines and on operational research to develop effective delivery platforms, or to develop less expensive products or more cost-effective technologies (such as for rice fortification). This catalyzing progress package will require an additional $37 billion over the next 10 years, or $3.7 billion per year. When combined with other health and poverty reduction efforts, this package of interventions could yield significant progress towards the global targets: an estimated 2.6 million lives would be saved and there would be 58 million fewer cases of stunting in 2025 than in 2015.

Furthermore, the key to sustainable financing for nutrition lies with ministers of finance in the affected countries, and domestic financing will remain the highest priority as agreed at the Addis Ababa Financing for Development meeting in 2015.

Limitations and Constraints

Several important limitations of the analyses presented in this report should be considered.

Data on unit costs are available only for a limited number of countries and regions, so some analyses are based on extrapolated unit costs. Furthermore, unit cost data are often based on regional or local programs (for example, Puett et al. 2013). It was assumed that the unit cost for large-scale national programs would be similar, but this may not necessarily be the case. Finally, the analyses assume unit costs remain constant over time (with the exception of the costs of treatment of severe acute malnutrition; see chapter 6 for details). It is likely that the unit cost will in fact change over time as a result of the expansion of scale (economies of scale and scope), program maturation and efficiency gains in program delivery, changes in protocols, and other factors. Unfortunately, currently no empirical assessments of nutrition program unit cost changes over time exist either in peer-reviewed or gray literature. This is identified as an area for future work.

Similarly, although data on baseline coverage of some interventions (such as vitamin A supplementation for children) are easily available, for other interventions—including infant and young child nutrition counseling, treatment of severe acute malnutrition, and staple food fortification—data are sparse. Data on breastfeeding and complementary feeding counseling are not routinely collected by flagship surveys (for example, the Demographic and Health Surveys, DHS). Therefore, proxy measures (such as the prevalence of exclusive breastfeeding) had to be used. Data on the treatment of severe acute malnutrition are not collected at all in the DHS or any other standardized survey instruments, even though outpatient treatment of severe acute malnutrition has been recommended as the gold standard for nearly a decade (WHO et al. 2007). As noted in chapter 6, the extrapolation of the coverage data from the coverage monitoring network probably overestimates the current coverage and, consequently, leads to an underestimation of the financial needs.

Robust data on domestic financing for nutrition remain limited despite recent efforts, with data currently available for only 31 countries, and these data are derived mainly from aspirational plans or budgets rather than actual expenditures. Moreover, because domestic government and ODA financing estimates are rarely disaggregated to the intervention level, the numbers presented here are best estimates.

Another limitation is that the estimates of the impact of the interventions are based primarily on results from clinical trials in experimental settings, rather than on large-scale real-world implementation of interventions. Therefore, they likely overestimate the impact the scale-up of the interventions may have on nutrition outcomes, morbidity, and mortality. This is a general limitation of studies using mathematical modeling in the context of public health. However, it is clear that more evidence of effectiveness from large-scale programs is needed to inform nutrition program planning and management.

Evidence regarding wasting prevention is very limited (see chapter 6 for a more in-depth discussion). Consequently, it was impossible to estimate the cost of reaching the wasting target. Instead, the estimates presented include costs for treating severe acute malnutrition (wasting). This is an expensive intervention (approximately $110 per episode per child in Sub-Saharan Africa and $90 in South Asia).

Furthermore, the treatment of wasting represents over 50 percent of the current ODA for nutrition. It is possible that effective wasting prevention interventions may turn out to be more cost-effective than treatment. This is especially likely given the emerging evidence of the long-lasting health and developmental effects of wasting in early childhood (WHO 2014b). However, the current state of evidence is insufficient to determine whether this is indeed the case. As discussed in chapter 6, data on wasting-related mortality are also limited. The approach used here—based on McDonald et al. (2013) analyses of wasting as a risk factor increasing mortality from pneumonia, sepsis, measles, and other conditions—seems to underestimate the impact of wasting on mortality. Alternative estimates, on the other hand, seem to inflate wasting-attributable mortality. More precise, recent, and generalizable (outside of Sub-Saharan Africa) data regarding the impact of wasting on mortality and morbidity are needed to accurately assess cost-effectiveness and benefit-cost ratios of wasting prevention and treatment interventions.

The global estimates presented in this report are based on assumptions that may or may not apply equally to every regional/country context or to fragile and conflict-affected settings. For this reason, the conclusions and recommendations that follow are kept at the global level, with some indications for regional levels.

Following earlier global nutrition cost studies (Horton et al. 2010), an assumption was made that the program cost would account for an additional 12 percent of the total service delivery cost. It is possible that this is an underestimate of actual program costs. For example, a recent study from Kenya shows that program management cost (capacity building, monitoring and evaluation, general program overhead, advocacy) accounted for as much as 60 percent of the direct service delivery cost (UNICEF 2015). At the same time, however, program costs may be lower in other regions where stronger and more efficient health systems require less investment in capacity development, supervision, monitoring, and other program costs than those needed in Sub-Saharan Africa. Systematic examination of actual nutrition program costs in a variety of contexts is urgently needed.

Further limitations include barriers to the immediate scale-up of two of the most expensive interventions—prophylactic zinc supplementation for children and public provision of complementary food for children—that account for 43 percent of total intervention costs. In addition, delivery of iron and folic acid supplementation for nonpregnant women age 15–49 outside of schools and balanced energy-protein supplementation for pregnant women also account for a large share of the total financing needs (about 11 percent). However, to date there is little experience with scaling up these interventions, and World Health Organization guidelines on their delivery are yet to be issued. Because these interventions are highly effective and needed to reach the global targets, it is imperative that development of such guidelines be prioritized. A related issue is the strong need to explore new mechanisms for service delivery at scale that improve upon allocative efficiency—that is, to direct resources toward the most cost-effective interventions and those that contribute to multiple targets. For these reasons, this report presents alternative packages of interventions that are ready for immediate and phased-in scale-up.

The analyses presented in the report show that reaching the stunting and anemia targets will be possible only if improvements in the underlying determinants of malnutrition accompany the nutrition-specific investments identified in the report. Improvements in these underlying determinants may come from so-called nutrition-sensitive actions for which evidence on costs and benefits is very limited, and therefore they are not included in the report. One exception is that water, sanitation, and hygiene (WASH) interventions are included in the stunting analyses (see chapter 3). The interventions are well defined (with the exception of the hygienic disposal of children's stool) and their impact on nutrition outcomes (via diarrhea incidence) is well documented. WASH interventions were excluded from cost and benefit-cost estimates, however, because it is expected that these will be financed under separate financing mechanisms aimed at reaching the SDG WASH targets.

Policy Implications and Recommendations

Three key policy recommendations flow from this report:

1. The world needs $70 billion over 10 years to invest in high-impact nutrition-specific interventions in order to reach the global targets for stunting, anemia, and breastfeeding and to scale up the treatment of severe wasting. This translates to just over $10 per child.

   These investments are expected to have large benefits: 65 million cases of stunting and 265 million cases of anemia in women would be prevented in 2025 as compared with the 2015 baseline. In addition, at least 91 million more children would be treated for severe wasting and 105 million additional babies would be exclusively breastfed during the first six months of life over 10 years. Altogether, achieving these targets would avert at least 3.7 million child deaths. And, importantly, every dollar invested in this package of interventions would yield $10 in economic returns (between $4 and $35). This is in line with previous studies suggesting returns of $18 (Hoddinott et al. 2013).

   In an environment of constrained resources, priority may be given to scaling up a smaller package of highly effective, immediately ready to scale interventions. Therefore, this report lays out two alternative packages for consideration, with the strong caveat that investing in a smaller set of interventions would fall short of reaching some of the global targets by 2025. Financing a "priority package" of interventions immediately ready to scale will require an additional investment of $23 billion over the next 10 years, $2.3 billion per year, or just over $4 per child. A slightly more ambitious package of investments, called the "catalyzing progress" package would scale up the priority package plus a more phased-in expansion of the other interventions to improve delivery mechanisms and program implementation, requiring an additional $37 billion over the next 10 years, $3.7 billion per year, or just over $5 per child. When combined with other health and poverty reduction efforts, these packages of interventions would still yield significant returns: for the priority package, an estimated 2.3 million lives would

be saved and there would be 50 million fewer cases of stunting in 2025 than in 2015, and for the catalyzing progress package an estimated 2.6 million lives would be saved and there would be 58 million fewer cases of stunting in 2025 than in 2015.
2. Even though some of the targets, especially those for reducing stunting and anemia in women, are ambitious and will require concerted efforts in financing, scale-up, and sustained commitment, recent experience from several countries suggests that it is feasible. On the other hand, the target for breastfeeding has scope to be much more ambitious.
3. Some areas of research need to be prioritized:
    (a) *More research on scalable strategies for delivering high-impact interventions* is critical. This includes determining how to address bottlenecks to scaling up, for example through results-based budgeting approaches, or other ways of incentivizing results (World Bank 2016a). Such implementation research will not only facilitate faster scale-up but would also have the potential to increase the technical efficiency and delivery costs for these interventions, thereby reducing future global financing needs.
    (b) Another critical area for future research is *the assessment of allocative efficiency*—that is, identifying the optimum funding allocation among different interventions, or an allocation that maximizes impact under budget constraints. The present analyses show cost per outcome, allowing for only limited comparisons of cost-effectiveness among different interventions for the same targets.
    (c) *Research to improve the technical efficiency of nutrition spending* is also urgently needed. This includes research on new strategies for addressing complex nutritional problems such as stunting and anemia, as well as better technologies to help these solutions scale up more rapidly and at cheaper rates (for example, for rice fortification). Because of the multifactorial nature of anemia, research is under way to get clarity on what fraction of the problem can be addressed by nutrition interventions; these estimates may need to be revised accordingly once results become available. Additionally, some key micronutrient deficiencies are not included in these analyses (that is, iodine), because these were not included in the global targets, even though they have significant impacts on morbidity, mortality, and economic productivity.
    (d) A dedicated effort to *understand which interventions prevent wasting* is urgently needed. It is also essential to learn more about cost-effective strategies for managing moderate acute malnutrition, and whether or not these can contribute toward the prevention of wasting.
    (e) *Strengthening the quality of surveillance data, and building stronger data collection systems for estimating current investments* (from domestic governments and ODA) in nutrition are vital. Not only are improvements needed to better track national-level expenditures for nutrition, but also spending must be closely monitored to track progress, ensure accountability, and identify areas for further efficiency gains, including allocative efficiency.

(f) *Improving unit cost data for interventions in different country contexts.* Further research is needed on the costs of interventions such as maternity leave to support women in the workforce to encourage them to exclusively breastfeed infants for the first six months.

(g) *More evidence is needed on the costs and impacts of nutrition-sensitive interventions*—that is, investments to improve nutrition through agriculture, social protection, and water and sanitation sectors, among others. It is evident that stunting, as well as anemia, are multifactorial and can be improved by increasing the quality, diversity, and affordability of foods; by expanding the control of income by women farmers; and also by reducing exposure to fecal pathogens by improved WASH practices. However, the attributable fraction of the burden that can be addressed by these interventions is unknown. The last five years have seen a proliferation of studies to increase clarity on these issues, as well as on the use of social programs as a platform for reaching the most vulnerable. Future work in this area should take into account such new evidence as studies are published.

As the world stands at the cusp of the new SDGs, with global poverty rates having declined to less than 10 percent for the first time in history, there is an unprecedented opportunity to save children's lives, build future human capital and gray-matter infrastructure, and provide equal opportunity for all children to drive faster economic growth. These investments in nutrition are inalienable and portable and will pay lifelong dividends—not only for the children directly affected but also for us all in the form of more robust societies—that will drive future economies. What happens in the first 1,000 days of early childhood will stay with children for their lifetimes.

Although $7 billion per year may seem to be a large investment, it pales in comparison to the $500 billion per year (nearly $1.5 billion/day) spent on agriculture subsidies (Potter 2014) and $543 billion per year (over $1.5 billion/day) spent on fossil fuel subsidies (IEA 2014).

Stunting and other forms of malnutrition can be a life sentence, but they must not be accepted as the "new normal." Although political commitment is growing

Figure 9.3 A Call to Action

Based on the vast body of evidence presented in this report, the time has come to move investments in nutrition from a pet cause to a common cause ... from a political imperative to an economic imperative.

An Investment Framework for Nutrition • http://dx.doi.org/10.1596/978-1-4648-1010-7

rapidly for investing in the 1,000-day window of opportunity, more efforts are needed to move this agenda from a pet cause to a common cause, and from a political imperative to an economic imperative.

Note

1. See box 1.3 in chapter 1 for more information on the Power of Nutrition and the Global Financing Facility in support of Every Woman Every Child.

References

ANSD (Agence Nationale de la Statistique et de la Démographie) [Senegal] and ICF International. 2012. *Senegal Demographic and Health and Multiple Indicator Cluster Survey (EDS-MICS) 2010–2011*. Calverton, MA: ANSD and ICF International.

———. 2015. *Sénégal: Enquête Démographique et de Santé Continue (EDSContinue 2012–14), Rapport Régional*. Calverton, MA: ANSD and ICF International.

DHS Program. 2016. StatCompiler (BETA): The DHS Program (database), USAID, Washington, DC (accessed June 2016), http://beta.statcompiler.com/

Global Panel (Global Panel on Agriculture and Food Systems for Nutrition). 2016. *The Cost of Malnutrition. Why Policy Action Is Urgent*. London: Global Panel on Agriculture and Food Systems for Nutrition.

Hoddinott, J. H. Alderman, J. R. Behrman, L. Haddad, and S. Horton. 2013. "The Economic Rationale for Investing in Stunting Reduction." *Maternal and Child Nutrition* 9 (Suppl. 2): 69–82.

Horton, S., H. Alderman, and J. Rivera. 2008. *Hunger and Malnutrition*. Copenhagen Consensus 2008: Malnutrition and Hunger. http://www.copenhagen consensus.com/sites/default/files/CP_Malnutrition_and_Hunger_-_Horton.pdf.

Horton, S., M. Shekar, C. McDonald, A. Mahal, and J. Krystene Brooks. 2010. *Scaling Up Nutrition: What Will It Cost?* Directions in Development Series, Washington, DC: World Bank.

IEA (International Energy Agency). 2014. *World Energy Outlook 2014*. Paris: IEA. http://www.worldenergyoutlook.org/weo2014/

Imdad, A.K. Herzer, E. Mayo-Wilson, M. Y. Yakoob, and Z. A. Bhutta. 2010. "Vitamin A Supplementation for Preventing Morbidity and Mortality in Children from 6 Months to 5 Years of Age." *Cochrane Database of Systematic Reviews* 12 (CD008524).

INEI (Instituto National de Estadistica e Informatica). 2015. *Indicadores de Resultados de los Programas Estratégicos, 2007–2014*. Lima, Peru: INEI.

McDonald, C. M., I. Olofin, S. Flaxman, W. W. Fawzi, D. Spiegelman, L. E. Caulfield, R. E. Black, M. Ezzati, and G. Danaei. 2013. "The Effect of Multiple Anthropometric Deficits on Child Mortality: Meta-Analysis of Individual Data in 10 Prospective Studies from Developing Countries." *American Journal of Clinical Nutrition* 97 (4): 896–901.

OECD (Organisation for Economic Co-operation and Development). 2016. *OECD Statistical Database* (accessed 2016), http://stats.oecd.org/.

Potter, G. 2014. "Agricultural Subsidies Remain a Staple in the Industrial World." *Vitalsigns* February 2014. Washington DC: World Watch Institute. Http://Vitalsigns.Worldwatch.Org/Vs-Trend/Agricultural-Subsidies-Remain-Staple-Industrial-World

Puett, C. K. Sadler, H. Alderman, J. Coates, J. L. Fiedler, and M. Myatt. 2013. "Cost-Effectiveness of the Community-Based Management of Severe Acute Malnutrition by Community Health Workers in Southern Bangladesh." *Health Policy and Planning* 28 (4): 386–99.

Stevens, G. A., M. M. Finucane, L. M. De-Regil, C. J. Paciorek, S. R. Flaxman, F. Branca, J. P. Peña-Rosas, Z. A. Bhutta, and M. Ezzati. 2013. "Global, Regional, and National Trends in Hemoglobin Concentration and Prevalence of Total and Severe Anemia in Children and Pregnant and Nonpregnant Women for 1995–2011: A Systematic Analysis of Population-Representative Data." *The Lancet Global Health Blog* 1 (1): e16–e25.

UNICEF (United Nations Children's Fund). 2015. *Costing of Kenya High Impact Nutrition Intervention.* Reference report. Nairobi, Kenya: UNICEF Kenya office.

UNICEF, WHO, and World Bank (United Nations Children's Fund, World Health Organization, and World Bank). 2015. *Joint Child Malnutrition Estimates: Levels and Trends.* Global Database on Child Growth and Malnutrition, http://www.who.int/nutgrowthdb/estimates2014/en/.

UNAIDS (Joint United Nations Programme on HIV/AIDS). 2013. *Global Report: UNAIDS Report on the Global AIDS Epidemic 2013.* Geneva: UNAIDS.

Victora, C., R. Bahl, A. Barros, G. V. A. França, S. Horton, J. Krasevec, S. Murch, M. J. Sankar, N. Walker, and N. C. Rollins. 2016. "Breastfeeding in the 21st Century: Epidemiology, Mechanisms and Lifelong Effect." *The Lancet* 387 (10017): 475–90.

Viet Nam National Institute of Nutrition, UNICEF (United Nations Children's Fund), Alive & Thrive, 2014. *Nutrition Surveillance Profiles 2013.* Ha Noi, Viet Nam.

WHO (World Health Organization). 2008. *Worldwide Prevalence of Anaemia 1993–2005: WHO Global Database on Anaemia.* Geneva: WHO. http://apps.who.int/iris/bitstream/10665/43894/1/9789241596657_eng.pdf.

———. 2014a. *Comprehensive Implementation Plan on Maternal, Infant, and Young Child Nutrition.* Geneva: WHO.

———. 2014b. *Global Nutrition Targets 2025: Wasting Policy Brief.* http://www.who.int/nutrition/topics/globaltargets_wasting_policybrief.pdf.

WHO, WFP, UNSSCN, and UNICEF (World Health Organization, World Food Programme, United Nations System Standing Committee on Nutrition, United Nations Children's Fund). 2007. Community-Based Management of Severe Acute Malnutrition. A Joint Statement by the World Health Organization, the World Food Programme, the United Nations System Standing Committee on Nutrition and the United Nations Children's Fund.

World Bank. 2015. World Development Indicators (database), World Bank, Washington, DC (accessed 2015), http://data.worldbank.org/data-catalog/world-development-indicators.

———. 2016a. *Incentivizing Nutrition: Incentive Mechanisms to Accelerate improved Nutrition Outcomes.* Washington, DC: World Bank.

———. 2016b. *World Development Indicators* (database), (accessed June 2016), http://data.worldbank.org/data-catalog/world-development-indicators.

APPENDIX A

Technical Advisory Group Membership

The Technical Advisory Group (TAG) met on four occasions (March 19, 2015; June 10, 2015; October 7, 2015; and February 22, 2016) to advise the research team (table A.1).

The final meeting of the TAG was a full-day workshop in Washington, DC, where all results were vetted and discussed. The following individuals participated in this meeting: Daniel Arias (Results for Development Institute), Hugh Bagnall-Oakeley (Save the Children), Ammad Bahalim (Global Health Visions), Nora Coghlan (Bill & Melinda Gates Foundation), Helen Connolly (American Institutes for Research), Mary Rose D'Alimonte (Results for Development Institute), Julia Dayton Eberwein (World Bank Group), Luz Maria De-Regil (Micronutrient Initiative), Kaia Engesveen (World Health Organization), Robert Hecht (Results for Development Institute), Augustin Flory (Children's Investment Fund Foundation), Patrizia Fracassi (Scaling Up Nutrition Movement Secretariat, UN Development Programme), Kate Goertzen (1,000 Days), Robert Greener (Oxford Policy Management), Saul Guerrero (Action Against Hunger), Stephanie Heung (Results for Development Institute), Jakub Kakietek (World Bank Group), Priyanka Kanth (World Bank Group), David Laborde (International Food Policy and Research Institute), Ferew Lemma (Ministry of Health, Ethiopia), Kedar Mankad (ONE Campaign), Alyson McColl (GMMB), Sandra Mutuma (Action Against Hunger), Obey Assery-Nkya (Prime Minister's Office, Tanzania), Kelechi Ohiri (Ministry of Health, Nigeria), Clara Picanyol (Oxford Policy Management), Amanda Pomeroy-Stevens (John Snow, Inc.), Danielle Porfido (1,000 Days), Kate Pritchard (GMMB), Ellen Piwoz (Bill & Melinda Gates Foundation), Hilary Rogers (Results for Development Institute), Meera Shekar (World Bank Group), Shan Soe-Lin (Results for Development Institute), Lucy Sullivan (1,000 Days), Dylan Walters (World Bank Group), Neil Watkins (Bill & Melinda Gates Foundation), and William Winfrey (Avenir Health).

Table A.1 TAG Membership

Name	Organization
Victor Aguayo	United Nations Children's Fund
Obey Assery-Nkya	Prime Minister's Office, Tanzania
Robert Black	Johns Hopkins University
Hugh Bagnall-Oakley	Save the Children
Helen Connolly	American Institutes for Research
Luz Maria De-Regil	Micronutrient Initiative
Kaia Engesveen	World Health Organization
Augustin Flory	Children's Investment Fund Foundation
Patrizia Fracassi	Scaling Up Nutrition Movement Secretariat, UN Development Programme
Robert Greener	Oxford Policy Management
Saul Guerrero	Action Against Hunger
Lawrence Haddad	International Food Policy and Research Institute
Rebecca Heidcamp	Johns Hopkins University
Sue Horton	University of Waterloo
David Laborde	International Food Policy and Research Institute
Ferew Lemma	Ministry of Health, Ethiopia
Kedar Mankad	ONE Campaign
Saul Morris	Children's Investment Fund Foundation
Sandra Mutuma	Action Against Hunger, United Kingdom
Obey Assery-Nkya	Prime Minister's Office, Tanzania
Kelechi Ohiri	Ministry of Health, Nigeria
Anne Peniston	U.S. Agency for International Development
Clara Picanyol	Oxford Policy Management
Ellen Piwoz	Bill & Melinda Gates Foundation
Amanda Pomeroy-Stevens	John Snow, Inc.
William Winfrey	Avenir Health

APPENDIX B

Baseline Intervention Coverage Rates, by Target

The tables in this appendix present the percentage of the population that would be covered by the relevant interventions for four targets: stunting, anemia, breast-feeding, and wasting. The full references for the sources of these data are provided in the References section at the end of the appendix.

Table B.1 Stunting Target: Percentage of Target Population Covered by Relevant Intervention at Baseline, by Country

Country	Stunting prevalence	Vitamin A supplementation for children	Complementary feeding education	Public provision of complementary food for children	Infant and young child nutrition counseling	Antenatal micronutrient supplementation	Balanced energy-protein supplementation for pregnant women	Intermittent presumptive treatment of malaria in pregnancy in malaria-endemic regions	Prophylactic zinc supplementation for children
Benin	34.0	48.6	32.2	32.2	40.4	0.0	0.0	15.6	0.0
Bangladesh	36.1	59.5	20.9	20.9	61.0	0.0	0.0	n.a.	0.0
Burundi	57.5	80.7	74.0	74.0	72.5	0.0	0.0	0.0	0.0
Cambodia	32.4	70.9	24.0	24.0	71.4	0.0	0.0	n.a.	0.0
Central African Republic	40.7	78.0	25.2	25.2	19.8	0.0	0.0	0.0	0.0
China	9.4	0.0	40.7	40.7	51.0	0.0	0.0	n.a.	0.0
Congo, Dem. Rep.	42.6	70.4	21.5	21.5	31.9	0.0	0.0	42.6	0.0
Egypt, Arab Rep.	22.3	16.7	41.4	41.4	49.6	0.0	0.0	n.a.	0.0
Eritrea	50.3	38.0	42.5	42.5	25.8	0.0	0.0	0.0	0.0
Ethiopia	40.4	53.1	22.4	22.4	49.8	0.0	0.0	0.0	0.0
Guatemala	48.0	41.7	75.9	75.9	35.3	0.0	0.0	n.a.	0.0
India	38.7	18.1	20.7	20.7	44.2	0.0	0.0	n.a.	0.0
Indonesia	36.4	61.1	41.2	41.2	40.1	0.0	0.0	n.a.	0.0
Kenya	26.0	30.3	38.5	38.5	29.6	0.0	0.0	41.2	0.0
Lao PDR	43.8	59.1	34.4	34.4	25.9	0.0	0.0	n.a.	0.0
Liberia	32.1	60.2	24.5	24.5	27.7	0.0	0.0	63.2	0.0
Madagascar	49.2	72.7	2.7	2.7	48.8	0.0	0.0	71.1	0.0
Malawi	42.4	85.6	18.5	18.5	68.2	0.0	0.0	53.8	0.0
Mexico	13.6	63.0	40.7	40.7	14.7	0.0	0.0	n.a.	0.0
Mozambique	43.1	70.6	83.6	83.6	39.0	0.0	0.0	18.6	0.0

table continues next page

Table B.1 Stunting Target: Percentage of Target Population Covered by Relevant Intervention at Baseline, by Country (continued)

Country	Stunting prevalence	Vitamin A supplementation for children	Complementary feeding education	Public provision of complementary food for children	Infant and young child nutrition counseling	Antenatal micronutrient supplementation	Balanced energy-protein supplementation for pregnant women	Intermittent presumptive treatment of malaria in pregnancy in malaria-endemic regions	Prophylactic zinc supplementation for children
Myanmar	35.1	86.0	41.0	41.0	3.0	0.0	0.0	n.a.	0.0
Nepal	40.5	90.4	57.1	57.1	68.0	0.0	0.0	n.a.	0.0
Niger	40.0	59.6	62.1	62.1	21.7	0.0	0.0	34.8	0.0
Nigeria	0.4	41.3	30.2	30.2	11.5	0.0	0.0	33.7	0.0
Pakistan	45.0	72.1	36.3	36.3	36.4	0.0	0.0	n.a.	0.0
Papua New Guinea	49.5	15.0	57.1	57.1	35.6	0.0	0.0	n.a.	0.0
Philippines	30.3	85.2	55.0	55.0	31.0	0.0	0.0	n.a.	0.0
Rwanda	37.9	92.9	16.8	16.8	83.3	0.0	0.0	72.2	0.0
Sierra Leone	37.9	83.2	22.7	22.7	8.7	0.0	0.0	27.5	0.0
Somalia	25.9	62.0	11.0	11.0	8.0	0.0	0.0	9.0	0.0
Sudan	38.2	60.5	49.4	49.4	6.0	0.0	0.0	0.0	0.0
Tanzania	34.7	60.8	21.3	21.3	45.1	0.0	0.0	26.3	0.0
Timor-Leste	57.7	50.7	0.0	0.0	0.0	0.0	0.0	n.a.	0.0
Uganda	34.2	56.8	23.8	23.8	67.2	0.0	0.0	24.5	0.0
Vietnam[a]	19.4	78.8	41.8	41.8	16.0	0.0	0.0	n.a.	0.0
Yemen, Rep.	46.6	11.0	76.3	76.3	7.6	0.0	0.0	n.a.	0.0
Zambia	40.0	76.5	37.3	37.3	56.0	0.0	0.0	70.2	0.0

Sources: Vitamin A supplementation for children: Most recent Demographic and Health Surveys (DHS) conducted between 2002 and 2014 (as of May 2015), except for the following: Multiple Cluster Indicator Survey (MICS) for Afghanistan, the Central African Republic, Myanmar, Somalia, and Sudan between 2006 and 2012 and FANTA (2014) for Guatemala. Infant and young child nutrition counseling, public provision of complementary food for children, probreastfeeding social policies, and intermittent presumptive treatment of malaria in pregnancy in malaria-endemic regions: Lives Saved Tool default coverage estimates. No data were available on micronutrient supplementation during pregnancy, balanced energy-protein supplementation for pregnant women, or prophylactic zinc supplementation.

Note: n.a. = not applicable.

a. At the time of these analyses, Vietnam stunting prevalence was reported as 19.4 in UNICEF, WHO and World Bank 2015. However, it was later corrected to be 25.9, as indicated in UNICEF, WHO, and World Bank 2016.

Table B.2 Anemia Target: Percentage of Target Population Covered by Relevant Intervention, by Country

Country	Anemia prevalence (%) Nonpregnant women age 15–49 years	Anemia prevalence (%) Pregnant women	Baseline coverage (%) Iron and folic acid supplementation for nonpregnant women	Baseline coverage (%) Antenatal micronutrient supplementation	Baseline coverage (%) Intermittent presumptive treatment of malaria in pregnancy in malaria-endemic regions	Baseline coverage of fortification among staple foods (%) Wheat flour fortification	Baseline coverage of fortification among staple foods (%) Maize flour fortification	Baseline coverage of fortification among staple foods (%) Rice flour fortification	Maximum attainable consumption coverage (%) Wheat flour fortification	Maximum attainable consumption coverage (%) Maize flour fortification	Maximum attainable consumption coverage (%) Rice flour fortification
Bangladesh	43.5	48.0	0.0	0.0	n.a.	0.0	0.0	0.0	50.0	0.0	75.0
Brazil	19.6	32.0	0.0	0.0	n.a.	50.0	0.0	0.0	75.0	0.0	25.0
China	19.5	22.0	0.0	0.0	n.a.	0.0	0.0	0.0	25.0	0.0	50.0
Congo, Dem. Rep.	49.0	49.0	0.0	4.7	14.0	25.0	0.0	0.0	50.0	50.0	0.0
Congo, Rep.	50.7	49.0	0.0	42.9	22.0	50.0	0.0	0.0	50.0	0.0	25.0
Egypt, Arab Rep.	34.5	30.0	0.0	36.1	n.a.	50.0	0.0	0.0	50.0	50.0	25.0
Ethiopia	19.2	23.0	0.0	0.0	0.0	0.0	0.0	0.0	50.0	25.0	0.0
Gabon	50.8	60.0	0.0	56.8	3.0	0.0	0.0	0.0	75.0	25.0	50.0
Ghana	56.4	62.0	0.0	59.4	67.0	50.0	0.0	0.0	25.0	25.0	50.0
India	48.1	54.0	0.0	23.0	n.a.	0.0	0.0	0.0	25.0	0.0	25.0
Indonesia	22.5	30.0	0.0	30.0	n.a.	50.0	0.0	0.0	75.0	25.0	75.0
Iran, Islamic Rep.	28.1	26.0	0.0	0.0	n.a.	50.0	0.0	0.0	75.0	0.0	25.0
Mali	56.2	61.0	0.0	18.3	20.0	50.0	0.0	0.0	25.0	50.0	75.0
Mexico	14.4	21.0	0.0	0.0	n.a.	50.0	0.0	0.0	75.0	75.0	0.0
Myanmar	30.3	33.0	0.0	0.0	n.a.	0.0	0.0	0.0	0.0	0.0	75.0
Nigeria	48.5	58.0	0.0	21.0	15.0	50.0	50.0	50.0	0.0	50.0	25.0
Pakistan	51.1	50.0	0.0	22.1	n.a.	0.0	0.0	0.0	50.0	0.0	0.0
Philippines	25.4	32.0	0.0	47.0	n.a.	50.0	0.0	0.0	25.0	25.0	75.0

table continues next page

Table B.2 Anemia Target: Percentage of Target Population Covered by Relevant Intervention, by Country *(continued)*

Country	Anemia prevalence (%) Nonpregnant women age 15–49 years	Anemia prevalence (%) Pregnant women	Baseline coverage (%) Iron and folic acid supplementation for nonpregnant women	Baseline coverage (%) Antenatal micronutrient supplementation	Baseline coverage (%) Intermittent presumptive treatment of malaria in pregnancy in malaria-endemic regions	Baseline coverage of fortification among staple foods (%) Wheat flour fortification	Baseline coverage of fortification among staple foods (%) Maize flour fortification	Baseline coverage of fortification among staple foods (%) Rice flour fortification	Maximum attainable consumption coverage (%) Wheat flour fortification	Maximum attainable consumption coverage (%) Maize flour fortification	Maximum attainable consumption coverage (%) Rice flour fortification
Senegal	57.5	63.0	0.0	50.0	43.0	50.0	0.0	0.0	25.0	25.0	50.0
South Africa	27.6	30.0	0.0	11.2	n.a.	50.0	50.0	50.0	50.0	75.0	25.0
Tanzania	39.6	61.0	0.0	3.5	33.0	50.0	50.0	50.0	25.0	75.0	25.0
Thailand	23.8	30.0	0.0	0.0	n.a.	0.0	0.0	0.0	0.0	0.0	75.0
Togo	52.7	58.0	0.0	37.1	44.0	50.0	0.0	0.0	25.0	75.0	25.0
Turkey	28.8	28.0	0.0	0.0	n.a.	0.0	0.0	0.0	75.0	25.0	0.0
Uzbekistan	51.7	35.0	0.0	0.0	n.a.	50.0	0.0	0.0	75.0	0.0	0.0
Vietnam	14.1	23.0	0.0	0.0	n.a.	0.0	0.0	0.0	25.0	25.0	75.0

Sources: Anemia prevalence in nonpregnant and pregnant women from Stevens et al. 2013. Iron and folic acid supplementation coverage is assumed to be 0 percent because of lack of data. Antenatal micronutrient coverage, for the purposes of anemia prevention, uses iron supplementation coverage (90+ tablets during pregnancy) from Demographic and Health Surveys (DHS) and Multiple Cluster Indicator Survey (MICS) surveys as a proxy for micronutrient coverage. Intermittent presumptive treatment of malaria in pregnancy in malaria-endemic regions coverage is also from DHS and MICS surveys. Baseline coverage of fortification among staple foods (wheat, maize and rice) is based on the existence of legislation status for foods fortified in respective countries. We assume 0 percent if fortification legislation is in the planning stages, 25 percent for voluntary status, and 50 percent if mandatory fortification is legislated. Data are from GAIN and FFI (Ghauri et al. 2016; Pachon 2016). Maximum attainable consumption coverage displays an estimate for the current level of consumption or demand for the type fortified in each country, or rather a ceiling for coverage of fortification that could realistically be achieved, since not all foods are consumed everywhere (Ghauri et al. 2016; Pachon 2016).

Note: n.a. = not applicable.

Table B.3 Breastfeeding Target: Percentage of Target Population Covered by Relevant Intervention at Baseline, by Country

Country	Exclusive breastfeeding (0–5 months) prevalence	Infant and young child nutrition counseling baseline coverage	Maternity leave cash benefits coverage in practice
Algeria	25.7	21.0	3.2
Bangladesh	55.3	61.0	12.1
Brazil	38.6	27.4	29.1
Chad	3.4	40.3	2.9
China	27.6	11.5	13.4
Congo, Dem. Rep.	47.6	44.2	3.2
Côte d'Ivoire	12.1	3.4	2.4
Djibouti	1.3	1.4	1.6
Dominican Republic	4.7	5.9	10.8
Egypt, Arab Rep.	39.7	49.6	11.6
Ethiopia	52.0	49.8	3.5
Gabon	6.0	4.5	53.4
India	65.0	44.2	1.2
Indonesia	41.5	40.1	2.3
Iraq	19.6	16.0	0.7
Mexico	14.4	14.7	9.5
Myanmar	23.6	3.0	3.4
Nigeria	17.4	16.9	2.2
Pakistan	37.7	36.4	1.1
Philippines	34.0	31.0	39.6
Somalia	5.3	8.8	1.7
Suriname	2.8	0.8	8.5
Tanzania	41.1	45.1	4.0
Tunisia	8.5	5.9	12.3
Turkey	30.1	17.0	14.4
Vietnam	24.3	15.7	15.3
Yemen, Rep.	10.3	7.6	5.3

Sources: Exclusive breastfeeding rates are based on the WHO/UNICEF Global Targets Tracking Tool (WHO 2015), with the exception of India, which is based on the Rapid Survey of Children result from later in 2015 (Government of India and UNICEF 2015). Baseline counseling coverage is based on the LiST default rates used, which are based on DHS survey data for 1-to-5 month exclusive breastfeeding rates. Maternity leave cash benefits coverage rates are based on ILO estimated coverage in practice (ILO 2015). See chapter 5 for more information.

Table B.4 Wasting Target: Percentage of Target Population Covered by Relevant Intervention at Baseline, by Country

Country	Region	Percentage of target population covered by outpatient treatment of severe acute malnutrition
Afghanistan	South Asia	40.14
Bangladesh	South Asia	61.00
Chad	Sub-Saharan Africa	22.95
China	East Asia and Pacific	0.00
Djibouti	Sub-Saharan Africa	0.00
Congo, Dem. Rep.	Sub-Saharan Africa	40.69
Egypt, Arab Rep.	Middle East and North Africa	0.00
Eritrea	Sub-Saharan Africa	0.00
Ethiopia	Sub-Saharan Africa	0.00
India	South Asia	12.20
Indonesia	East Asia and Pacific	0.00
Iraq	Middle East and North Africa	0.00
Mali	Sub-Saharan Africa	31.18
Myanmar	East Asia and Pacific	40.70
Niger	Sub-Saharan Africa	36.16
Nigeria	Sub-Saharan Africa	61.17
Pakistan	South Asia	52.23
Philippines	East Asia and Pacific	33.00
South Sudan	Sub-Saharan Africa	31.14
Sri Lanka	South Asia	0.00
Sudan	Sub-Saharan Africa	63.77
Timor-Leste	East Asia and Pacific	0.00
Vietnam	East Asia and Pacific	0.00
Yemen, Rep.	Middle East and North Africa	61.60

Sources: No country-level estimates of the coverage of the treatment of severe acute malnutrition for children currently exist. To develop baseline coverage, this analysis relies on data from the Coverage Monitoring Network on the percentage of children suffering from severe wasting at subnational levels (for example, districts) for a number of countries. This database is based on information collected from organizations implementing programs in specific subnational geographic locations. For countries where coverage data were available from only one region, these data are used to represent coverage at the national level. For countries where data from multiple regions were available, a population-weighted average is used as a proxy for the national level. It should be noted that this approach likely overestimates the current treatment coverage. For countries without available data, the current coverage of treatment is assumed to be zero.

References

Coverage Monitoring Network (database). http://www.coverage-monitoring.org/ (accessed in 2015).

DHS (Demographic and Health Surveys). "The DHS Program" (accessed in 2015), http://dhsprogram.com/.

FANTA (Food and Technical Assitance III Project). 2014. *Guatemala: Costeo de intervenciones de nutrición en el Primer y Segundo Nivel de atención en el Marco del Convenio de Gestión por Resultados entre el Minfin y el MSPAS*. Guatemala City, Guatemala: Government of Guatemala. http://icefi.org/publicaciones/guatemala-costeo-de-intervenciones-de-nutricion-en-el-primer-y-segundo-nivel-de.

Ghauri, K., S. Horton, R. Spohrer, and G. Garrett. 2016. "Food Fortification Cost Model." Unpublished manuscript. Washington, DC: Global Alliance for Improved Nutrition.

Government of India and UNICEF (United Nations Children's Fund). 2015. *Rapid Survey on Children (RSOC) 2013–14: National Report*. Ministry of Women and Child Development, New Delhi. http://wcd.nic.in/sites/default/files/RSOC%20National%20Report%202013-14%20Final.pdf.

ILO (International Labour Organization). 2015. ILOSTAT Database, Geneva, ILO (accessed May 2, 2015). http://www.ilo.org/ilostat/faces/home/statisticaldata?_afrLoop=39430847112133#%40%3F_afrLoop%3D39430847112133%26_adf.ctrl-state%3Dbakdhzsnf_4.

LiST (Lives Saved Tool). Lives Saved Tool (software tool), Johns Hopkins Bloomberg School of Public Health, Baltimore, MD (accessed in 2015), http://livessavedtool.org/.

MICS (Multiple Indicator Cluster Survey). UNICEF (United Nations Children's Fund, database) (accessed in 2015), http://www.unicef.org/statistics/index_24302.html.

Pachon, H. 2016. "Food Fortification Coverage Data." Unpublished data on food fortification coverage, Food Fortification Initiative, Atlanta, GA.

Stevens, G. A., M. M. Finucane, L. M. De-Regil, C. J. Paciorek, S. R. Flaxman, F. Branca, J. P. Peña-Rosas, Z. A. Bhutta, and M. Ezzati. 2013. "Global, Regional, and National Trends in Haemoglobin Concentration and Prevalence of Total and Severe Anaemia in Children and Pregnant and Nonpregnant Women for 1995–2011: A Systematic Analysis of Population-Representative Data." *The Lancet Global Health*. 1 (1): e16–e25.

UNICEF, WHO, and World Bank (United Nations Children's Fund, World Health Organization, and World Bank). 2015. *Joint Child Malnutrition Estimates: Levels and Trends*. Global Database on Child Growth and Malnutrition. http://www.who.int/nutgrowthdb/estimates2014/en/.

———. 2016. *Joint Child Malnutrition Estimates: Levels and Trends*. Global Database on Child Growth and Malnutrition. http://www.who.int/nutgrowthdb/estimates2015/en/.

WHO (World Health Organization). 2015. Global Targets Tracking Tool (accessed September 15, 2015), http://www.who.int/nutrition/trackingtool/en/.

APPENDIX C

Intervention Unit Costs and Data Sources for Unit Costs

The tables in this appendix present details about the unit cost for each intervention in the analysis. Unit costs are presented for stunting, anemia, exclusive breastfeeding, and wasting. The full references for the sources of these data are provided in the References section at the end of the appendix.

Table C.1 Unit Costs of Interventions to Meet the Stunting Target

Country	Region	Unit cost used in the analyses (2015 US$)[a]	Sources and assumptions
Vitamin A supplementation for children			
Benin, Niger	Sub-Saharan Africa	0.37	Unit cost estimates from Mali; Shekar et al. 2015c
Burundi, Central African Republic, Congo, Dem. Rep., Rwanda	Sub-Saharan Africa	0.55	Unit cost estimates from Congo, Dem. Rep., Shekar et al. 2015a
Eritrea, Ethiopia, Kenya, Somalia, Sudan, Tanzania	Sub-Saharan Africa	0.88	Unit cost estimates from Kenya; Dayton Eberwein et al. (forthcoming)
Liberia, Nigeria, Sierra Leone	Sub-Saharan Africa	0.44	Unit cost estimates from Nigeria; Shekar et al. 2014
Madagascar, Malawi, Mozambique, Zambia	Sub-Saharan Africa	0.94	Unit cost estimates from Zambia; Shekar et al. 2015
Uganda	Sub-Saharan Africa	0.08	Shekar et al. 2015a
Cambodia, China, Lao PDR, Myanmar, Vietnam	East Asia and Pacific	0.03	Unit cost estimates from Vietnam; Alive & Thrive 2013
Indonesia, Papua New Guinea, Timor-Leste	East Asia and Pacific	0.03	Unit cost from Vietnam; Alive & Thrive 2013
Philippines	East Asia and Pacific	4.81	Neidecker-Gonzales, Nestel, and Bouis 2007
Guatemala, Mexico	Latin America and the Caribbean	3.01	Unit cost from Guatemala; Neidecker-Gonzales, Nestel, and Bouis 2007

table continues next page

Table C.1 Unit Costs of Interventions to Meet the Stunting Target *(continued)*

Country	Region	Unit cost used in the analyses (2015 US$)[a]	Sources and assumptions
Egypt, Arab Rep., Yemen, Rep.	Middle East and North Africa	1.40	Africa average unit cost estimate multiplied by the WHO Choice regional multiplier (2.20) from Horton et al. 2010
Bangladesh	South Asia	0.04	Personal communication with the National Nutrition Program. Unit cost for delivery through campaigns twice a year (3.32 Taka per child per year)
India, Pakistan	South Asia	0.09	Unit cost from India; Micronutrient Initiative 2006 (4.04 RS per child)
Nepal	South Asia	2.03	Neidecker-Gonzales, Nestel, and Bouis 2007
Infant and young child nutrition counseling			
Benin, Niger	Sub-Saharan Africa	5.00	Unit cost from Mali; Shekar et al. 2015 Mali
Burundi, Central African Republic, Congo, Dem. Rep., Rwanda	Sub-Saharan Africa	5.00	Unit cost from the Democratic Republic of Congo; Shekar et al. 2015
Eritrea, Ethiopia, Kenya, Somalia, Sudan, Tanzania	Sub-Saharan Africa	6.90	Unit cost from Kenya; Dayton Eberwein et al. forthcoming
Liberia, Nigeria, Sierra Leone	Sub-Saharan Africa	5.00	Unit cost from Nigeria; Shekar et al. 2014
Madagascar, Malawi, Mozambique, Uganda, Zambia	Sub-Saharan Africa	7.25	Unit cost from Zambia; Shekar et al. 2015
Cambodia, China, Indonesia, Lao PDR, Myanmar, Papua New Guinea, Philippines, Timor-Leste, Vietnam	East Asia and Pacific	11.25	Unit cost from Vietnam; Alive & Thrive 2013
Guatemala, Mexico	Latin America and the Caribbean	0.33	Unit cost from Guatemala for breastfeeding promotion and complementary feeding education in primary health care settings; FANTA 2014
Egypt, Arab Rep., Yemen, Rep.	Middle East and North Africa	1.40	Africa average unit cost estimate multiplied by the WHO Choice regional multiplier (2.20) from Horton et al. 2010
Bangladesh, India, Nepal, Pakistan	South Asia	5.13	Menon, McDonald and Chakrabarti 2014; $7.47 per child 6–12 months per year; $2.8 per child 12–24 months per year; on average $5.13 per child 6–24 months per year and $1.67 per pregnant women per child 0–6 months per year; $1.76 per pregnant women (assumes the number of pregnancies is equal to number of children 0–6 months); on average $3.43 per child 0–6 months; inflation adjusted.
In addition to the countries above included in the stunting analysis, the following countries were included in the breastfeeding target			
Chad, Côte d'Ivoire	Sub-Saharan Africa	5.00	Unit cost from Nigeria; Shekar et al. 2014
Djibouti	Sub-Saharan Africa	6.90	Unit cost from Kenya; Dayton Eberwein et al. forthcoming

table continues next page

Table C.1 Unit Costs of Interventions to Meet the Stunting Target *(continued)*

Country	Region	Unit cost used in the analyses (2015 US$)[a]	Sources and assumptions
Gabon	Sub-Saharan Africa	7.25	Unit cost from Zambia; Shekar et al. 2015
Turkey	Europe and Central Asia	13.35	Africa average times the WHO Choice regional multiplier (2.20) from Horton et al. 2010
Suriname	Latin America and the Caribbean	0.70	Unit cost from Guatemala; FANTA 2014
Brazil, Dominican Republic	Latin America and the Caribbean	7.50	Global cost estimate; Horton et al. 2010
Iraq	Middle East and North Africa	7.50	Global cost estimate; Horton et al. 2010
Algeria, Tunisia	Middle East and North Africa	13.35	Africa average unit cost estimate multiplied by the WHO Choice regional multiplier (2.20) from Horton et al. 2010
Public provision of complementary food for children			
Burundi, Central African Republic, Congo, Dem. Rep., Rwanda	Sub-Saharan Africa	40.25	Unit cost from Democratic Republic of Congo; Shekar et al. 2015
Eritrea, Ethiopia, Kenya, Somalia, Sudan, Tanzania	Sub-Saharan Africa	47.99	Unit cost from Kenya; Dayton Eberwein et al. forthcoming
Liberia, Nigeria, Sierra Leone	Sub-Saharan Africa	51.10	Unit cost from Nigeria; Shekar et al. 2014
Madagascar, Malawi, Mozambique, Zambia	Sub-Saharan Africa	87.50	Unit cost from Zambia; Shekar et al. 2015
Uganda	Sub-Saharan Africa	66.50	Shekar et al. 2015 Uganda
Cambodia, China, Indonesia, Lao PDR, Myanmar, Papua New Guinea, Timor-Leste, Vietnam	East Asia and Pacific	36.00	Unit cost from Indonesia; personal communication with the Ministry of Health (2015)
Philippines	East Asia and Pacific	15.84	Personal communication with the Ministry of Health (May 2015): Rice Mongo Instant Blend/Rice Mongo Sesame Blend (P 6.00/pack); 6–11 mos. old: 120 days x P 6.00/pack of CF = P 720.00/child; 12–23 months old: 88 days (weekdays) x P 6.00/pack of CF = P 528.00; average cost per child $15.84.
Guatemala, Mexico	Latin America and the Caribbean	66.23	Africa average unit cost estimate multiplied by the WHO Choice regional multiplier (2.25) from Horton et al. 2010
Egypt, Arab Rep., Yemen, Rep.	Middle East and North Africa	66.23	Africa average unit cost estimate multiplied by the WHO Choice regional multiplier (2.20) from Horton et al. 2010
Bangladesh, India, Nepal, Pakistan	South Asia	29.03	Supplemental food for children 12–26 months; Menon, McDonald, and Chakrabarti 2016

table continues next page

Table C.1 Unit Costs of Interventions to Meet the Stunting Target *(continued)*

Country	Region	Unit cost used in the analyses (2015 US$)[a]	Sources and assumptions
Prophylactic zinc supplementation for children			
Benin, Burundi, Central African Republic, Congo, Dem. Rep., Eritrea, Ethiopia, Kenya, Liberia, Madagascar, Malawi, Mozambique, Niger, Nigeria, Rwanda, Sierra Leone, Somalia, Sudan, Tanzania, Uganda, Zambia	Sub-Saharan Africa	4.61	Based on cost of micronutrient powders (Sprinkles) supplementation for children from the Democratic Republic of Congo (see Shekar et al. 2015). A box of 30 sachets of micronutrient Sprinkles costs $0.86 and each child receives 120 sachets per year; additional 25% for transportation costs $0.31 per child for distribution of kits, identification of beneficiaries, establishment of community health structures, and supervision.
Cambodia, China, Indonesia, Lao PDR, Myanmar, Papua New Guinea, Philippines, Timor-Leste, Vietnam	East Asia and Pacific	4.61	Based on cost of micronutrient powders (Sprinkles) for children from the Democratic Republic of Congo (see Shekar et al. 2015). A box of 30 sachets of micronutrient Sprinkles costs $0.86 and each child receives 120 sachets per year; additional 25% for transportation costs $0.31 per child for distribution of kits, identification of beneficiaries, establishment of community health structures, and supervision.
Guatemala, Mexico	Latin America and the Caribbean	6.19	Based on cost of micronutrient powders (Sprinkles) for children from the Democratic Republic of Congo (see Shekar et al. 2015). A box of 30 sachets of micronutrient Sprinkles costs $0.86 and each child receives 120 sachets per year; additional 25% for transportation costs $0.31 per child for distribution of kits, identification of beneficiaries, establishment of community health structures, and supervision. Unit cost estimate multiplied by the WHO Choice regional multiplier (2.35) from Horton et al. 2010.
Egypt, Arab Rep., Yemen, Rep.	Middle East and North Africa	6.01	Unit cost from the Democratic Republic of Congo; Shekar et al. 2015. Based on cost of micronutrient powders (sprinkles) for children from the Democratic Republic of Congo (see Shekar et al. 2015). A box of 30 sachets of micronutrient Sprinkles costs $0.86 and each child receives 120 sachets per year; additional 25% for transportation costs $0.31 per child for distribution of kits, identification of beneficiaries, establishment of community health structures, and supervision. Unit cost estimate multiplied by the WHO Choice regional multiplier (2.20) from Horton et al. 2010.

table continues next page

Intervention Unit Costs and Data Sources for Unit Costs

Table C.1 Unit Costs of Interventions to Meet the Stunting Target *(continued)*

Country	Region	Unit cost used in the analyses (2015 US$)[a]	Sources and assumptions
Bangladesh, India, Nepal, Pakistan	South Asia	2.40	Based on in-home micronutrient powders (Sprinkles) supplementation costs in Pakistan (Sharieff, Horton, and Zlotkin 2006) Adapted to 120 days a year (one sachet per child per day, 120 sachets per child per year): Includes production: $0.015 per sachet; distribution and overhead: $0.005 per sachet; total cost per sachet: $0.02.

Antenatal micronutrient supplementation

Currently no large-scale antenatal micronutrient supplementation programs exist. The unit costs were approximated on the basis of the unit cost of delivering iron and folic acid supplementation because the delivery platform was assumed to be the same (distribution during antenatal and postnatal visits). We used the iron and folic acid supplementation unit cost from Kenya (Dayton Eberwein et al. forthcoming) and replaced the cost of the iron and folic acid supplement with the cost of a supplement that included 13 essential minerals in the following formulation: Retinol (vitamin A) 800RE; vitamin E 10 mg; vitamin D 200 International Units (5mcg); vitamin B1 1.4 mg; vitamin B2 1.4 mg; niacin 18 mg; vitamin B6 1.9 mg; vitamin B12 2.6 mcg; folic acid 400 mcg; vitamin C 70 mg; iron 30 mg (as ferrous fumarate or ferrous sulphate); zinc 15 mg; copper 2 mg; selenium 65 mcg; iodine 150 mcg. The supplement cost was extracted from the UNICEF supply catalogue, accessed 2015 (UNICEF 2015). The pack costs $13.57 and the cost per tablet was $0.01357. As compared with the costs for providing iron and folic acid supplementation, the multiple micronutrient tablet increased the cost by $1.29 per pregnant women. We assumed that a similar increase would apply to all countries in the sample (because it is a result of substituting one input for another while keeping all other costs constant). We therefore calculated the cost of antenatal micronutrient supplementation as the country iron and folic acid supplementation cost plus the additional $1.29 for substituting the currently used iron and folic acid supplement with antenatal micronutrient supplement. The table below lists sources for iron and folic acid supplementation unit costs.

Country	Region	Unit cost	Sources
Benin, Niger	Sub-Saharan Africa	2.56	Unit cost from Mali; Shekar et al. 2015
Burundi, Central African Republic, Congo, Dem. Rep., Rwanda	Sub-Saharan Africa	3.29	Unit cost from Democratic Republic of Congo; Shekar et al. 2015
Eritrea, Ethiopia, Kenya, Somalia, Sudan, Tanzania	Sub-Saharan Africa	4.04	Unit cost from Kenya; Dayton Eberwein et al. forthcoming
Liberia, Nigeria, Sierra Leone	Sub-Saharan Africa	3.08	Unit cost from Nigeria; Shekar et al. 2014
Madagascar, Malawi, Mozambique, Zambia	Sub-Saharan Africa	3.40	Unit cost from Zambia; Shekar et al. 2015
Uganda	Sub-Saharan Africa	4.04	Shekar et al. 2015 Uganda
Cambodia, China, Indonesia, Lao PDR, Myanmar, Papua New Guinea, Timor Leste, Vietnam	East Asia and Pacific	2.12	Unit cost from Vietnam adjusted for iron-folic acid supplementation; Casey et al. 2011
Philippines	East Asia and Pacific	3.54	Personal communication with Ministry of Health (May 2015)
Guatemala, Mexico	Latin America and the Caribbean	7.55	Africa average unit cost estimate multiplied by the WHO Choice regional multiplier (2.35) from Horton et al. 2010
Egypt, Arab Rep., Yemen, Rep.	Middle East and North Africa	7.07	Africa average unit cost estimate multiplied by the WHO Choice regional multiplier (2.20) from Horton et al. 2010
Bangladesh	South Asia	2.04	Personal communication with the Ministry of Health and Family Welfare (May 2015)
India, Nepal, Pakistan	South Asia	1.80	Unit cost from India; Menon, McDonald, and Chakrabarti 2016

table continues next page

Table C.1 Unit Costs of Interventions to Meet the Stunting Target *(continued)*

Country	Region	Unit cost used in the analyses (2015 US$)[a]	Sources and assumptions
In addition to the countries above included in the analysis for the stunting target, the following countries were included in the analysis for the anemia target			
Ghana, Mali, Senegal, Togo	Sub-Saharan Africa	3.08	Unit cost from Nigeria; Shekar et al. 2014
Congo, Dem. Rep., Gabon	Sub-Saharan Africa	3.29	Unit cost from Democratic Republic of Congo; Shekar et al. 2015
South Africa	Sub-Saharan Africa	4.04	Unit cost from Kenya; Dayton Eberwein et al. forthcoming
Thailand	East Asia and Pacific	2.12	Vietnam cost (unit cost data on iron and folic acid supplementation); Casey et al. 2011
Turkey, Uzbekistan	Europe and Central Asia	7.07	Africa average with the regional multiplier of 2.20 from Horton et al. 2010
Brazil	Latin America and the Caribbean	7.55	Africa average with the regional multiplier of 2.35 from Horton et al. 2010
Iran, Islamic Rep.	Middle East and North Africa	1.80	India costs; Menon, McDonald, and Chakrabarti 2016
Balanced energy-protein supplementation for pregnant women			
Benin, Burundi, Central African Republic, Congo, Dem. Rep., Eritrea, Ethiopia, Kenya, Liberia, Madagascar, Malawi, Mozambique, Niger, Nigeria, Rwanda, Sierra Leone, Somalia, Sudan, Tanzania, Uganda, Zambia	Sub-Saharan Africa	25.00	Global cost; Bhutta et al. 2013
Cambodia, Indonesia, Lao PDR, Myanmar, Papua New Guinea, Philippines, Timor-Leste, Vietnam	East Asia and Pacific	54.72	Unit cost from Indonesia; personal communication with the Ministry of Health (May 2015)
China	East Asia and Pacific	25.00	Global cost; Bhutta et al. 2013
Guatemala, Mexico	Latin America and the Caribbean	25.00	Global cost; Bhutta et al. 2013
Egypt, Arab Rep., Yemen, Rep.	Middle East and North Africa	25.00	Global cost; Bhutta et al. 2013
Bangladesh, India, Nepal, Pakistan	South Asia	16.93	Unit cost from India; Menon, McDonald, and Chakrabati 2016
Intermittent presumptive treatment of malaria in pregnancy in malaria-endemic regions			
Benin, Burundi, Central African Republic, Congo, Dem. Rep., Eritrea, Ethiopia, Kenya, Liberia, Madagascar, Malawi, Mozambique, Niger, Nigeria, Rwanda, Sierra Leone, Somalia, Sudan, Tanzania, Uganda, Zambia	Sub-Saharan Africa	2.18	Global cost; White et al. 2011
In addition to the countries above included in the analysis for the stunting target, the following countries were included in the analysis for the anemia target			
Congo, Rep., Gabon, Ghana, Mali, Senegal, South Africa, Togo	Sub-Saharan Africa	2.18	Global cost, White et al. 2011

Note: mcg = micrograms; CF = complementary food; P = Philippine peso.
a. All unit costs from the literature were converted into U.S.$ and inflated to 2015 values.

Intervention Unit Costs and Data Sources for Unit Costs

In addition to unit costs for antenatal micronutrient supplementation detailed in table C.1, the following unit costs were used for the anemia costing analysis.

Table C.2 Unit Costs of Interventions to Meet the Anemia Target

In addition to unit costs for antenatal micronutrient supplementation detailed in table C.1, the following unit costs were used for the anemia costing analysis

Iron and folic acid supplementation for nonpregnant women		Unit cost used in the analyses (2015 US$)			
Country	Region	In-school program delivery + supplement	Community health system delivery + supplement	Hospital/clinic system delivery + supplement	Private retailer distribution of supplement with markup
Bangladesh	South Asia	0.46	0.22	1.49	0.24
Brazil	Latin America and the Caribbean	0.63	0.35	2.28	0.24
China	East Asia and Pacific	0.63	1.60	2.07	0.24
Congo, Dem. Rep.	Sub-Saharan Africa	0.46	0.21	1.78	0.24
Congo, Rep.	Sub-Saharan Africa	0.46	0.21	1.78	0.24
Egypt, Arab Rep.	Middle East and North Africa	0.63	0.44	0.54	0.24
Ethiopia	Sub-Saharan Africa	0.46	0.21	1.78	0.24
Gabon	Sub-Saharan Africa	0.46	0.21	1.80	0.24
Ghana	Sub-Saharan Africa	0.46	0.21	1.80	0.24
India	South Asia	0.46	0.22	1.49	0.24
Indonesia	East Asia and Pacific	0.63	0.28	1.11	0.24
Iran, Islamic Rep.	Middle East and North Africa	0.63	1.01	5.54	0.24
Mali	Sub-Saharan Africa	0.46	0.21	1.80	0.24
Mexico	Latin America and the Caribbean	0.63	1.76	2.28	0.24
Myanmar	East Asia and Pacific	0.63	0.28	1.49	0.24
Nigeria	Sub-Saharan Africa	0.46	0.21	1.80	0.24
Pakistan	South Asia	0.46	0.22	0.54	0.24
Philippines	East Asia and Pacific	0.63	0.28	2.07	0.24
Senegal	Sub-Saharan Africa	0.46	0.21	1.78	0.24
South Africa	Sub-Saharan Africa	0.46	0.21	1.80	0.24
Tanzania	Sub-Saharan Africa	0.46	0.21	1.78	0.24
Thailand	East Asia and Pacific	0.63	0.87	1.11	0.24
Togo	Sub-Saharan Africa	0.46	0.21	1.80	0.24
Turkey	Europe and Central Asia	0.63	1.78	2.31	0.24
Uzbekistan	Europe and Central Asia	0.63	1.78	2.31	0.24
Vietnam	East Asia and Pacific	0.63	0.28	2.07	0.24

Staple food fortification		Unit cost used in the analyses (2015 US$)		
Country	Region	Wheat flour fortification	Maize flour fortification	Rice fortification
Bangladesh	South Asia	0.20	n.a.	1.41
Brazil	Latin America and the Caribbean	0.20	n.a.	0.08

table continues next page

An Investment Framework for Nutrition • http://dx.doi.org/10.1596/978-1-4648-1010-7

Table C.2 Unit Costs of Interventions to Meet the Anemia Target *(continued)*

	Staple food fortification		Unit cost used in the analyses (2015 US$)	
Country	Region	Wheat flour fortification	Maize flour fortification	Rice fortification
China	East Asia and Pacific	0.20	n.a.	1.68
Congo, Dem. Rep.	Sub-Saharan Africa	0.15	0.15	n.a.
Congo, Rep.	Sub-Saharan Africa	0.15	0.15	0.08
Egypt, Arab Rep.	Middle East and North Africa	0.29	0.15	0.08
Ethiopia	Sub-Saharan Africa	0.21	0.15	n.a.
Gabon	Sub-Saharan Africa	0.15	0.15	0.55
Ghana	Sub-Saharan Africa	0.06	0.15	0.55
India	South Asia	0.17	n.a.	0.08
Indonesia	East Asia and Pacific	n.a.	0.15	1.41
Iran, Islamic Rep.	Middle East and North Africa	0.20	n.a.	0.08
Mali	Sub-Saharan Africa	0.15	0.15	1.41
Mexico	Latin America and the Caribbean	0.20	0.15	n.a.
Myanmar	East Asia and Pacific	n.a.	n.a.	1.41
Nigeria	Sub-Saharan Africa	0.06	0.15	0.08
Pakistan	South Asia	0.20	n.a.	n.a.
Philippines	East Asia and Pacific	0.20	0.15	1.41
Senegal	Sub-Saharan Africa	0.08	0.15	0.55
South Africa	Sub-Saharan Africa	0.15	0.30	0.08
Tanzania	Sub-Saharan Africa	0.08	0.15	0.08
Thailand	East Asia and Pacific	n.a.	n.a.	1.41
Togo	Sub-Saharan Africa	0.15	0.15	0.08
Turkey	Europe and Central Asia	0.20	0.15	n.a.
Uzbekistan	Europe and Central Asia	0.20	n.a.	n.a.
Vietnam	East Asia and Pacific	0.20	0.15	1.41

Note: Unit costs for antenatal micronutrient supplementation are detailed in table C.1. All unit costs from the literature were converted into U.S.$ and inflated to 2015 values. n.a. = not applicable.

Sources for iron and folic acid supplementation for nonpregnant women: The unit costs of four different delivery platforms for nonpregnant women each include the cost of a supplement at $0.12 per woman per year from the OneHealth Tool manual (Futures Institute 2013) plus a 10 percent transportation cost. In addition, the cost of delivery through school-based programs for the girls age 15–19 enrolled in secondary school (World Bank 2016) includes an additional program cost of $0.33 for the Sub-Saharan Africa and South Asia regions and $0.50 for other regions in the sample (WHO 2011). It was assumed that the cost of iron and folic acid supplements purchased through private retailers would include an 84 percent markup, similar to the markup found by Bahl et al. (2013) for multiple micronutrient supplements, totaling $0.24 per woman per year. The distribution of iron and folic acid supplements to a woman through community health or hospital/clinic consultation is estimated to require two consultations per year of five minutes each. Therefore, human resources for health costs are estimated by multiplying the time allocation for all annual consultations by salary estimates for community health workers, which range from $80 to $917 per month (Casey et al. 2011; Dahn et al. 2015; Maternal and Child Health Integrated Program 2011), and nurse salaries, which range from $3,047 to $40,265 per annum in sample countries (WHO 2005). See chapter 4 for more detail.

Sources for staple food fortification: Unit cost of staple food fortification per person per year were drawn either from the Global Alliance for Improved Nutrition (GAIN) costing model (Ghauri et al. 2016) for wheat and maize fortification or from Alavi et al. (2008) for rice fortification. For countries for which estimates did not exist, the best possible proxies were used. In an attempt to take into account dietary differences across populations, the available data from GAIN costing model or Food Fortification Initiative (FFI) suggested that there is, respectively, no low or moderate demand for consumption for each particular type of food staple in each country, so the per capita fortification unit costs are lowered to 0 percent, 25 percent, and 50 percent.

Intervention Unit Costs and Data Sources for Unit Costs

In addition to the unit costs for infant and young child nutrition counseling listed in table C.1, the following unit costs were used for the breastfeeding costing analysis.

Table C.3 Unit Costs of Interventions to Meet the Breastfeeding Target

In addition to the unit costs for infant and young child nutrition counseling listed in table C.1, the following unit costs were used for the breastfeeding costing analysis

Country	Region	National breastfeeding promotion campaigns	Pro-breastfeeding social policies
Djibouti, Gabon	Sub-Saharan Africa	800,000	200,000
Chad, Côte d'Ivoire, Somalia, Tanzania	Sub-Saharan Africa	2,400,000	600,000
Congo, Dem. Rep., Ethiopia, Nigeria	Sub-Saharan Africa	4,000,000	1,000,000
Myanmar, Philippines, Vietnam	East Asia and Pacific	4,000,000	1,000,000
China, Indonesia	East Asia and Pacific	8,000,000	2,000,000
Turkey	Europe and Central Asia	4,000,000	1,000,000
Dominican Republic, Surname	Latin America and the Caribbean	800,000	200,000
Brazil, Mexico	Latin America and the Caribbean	4,000,000	1,000,000
Algeria, Iraq, Tunisia, Yemen, Rep.	Middle East and North Africa	2,400,000	600,000
Egypt, Arab Rep.	Middle East and North Africa	4,000,000	1,000,000
Bangladesh, Pakistan	South Asia	4,000,000	1,000,000
India	South Asia	8,000,000	2,000,000

Source: Alive and Thrive 2013, 2014; Walters et al. 2016.
Note: All unit costs from the literature were converted into US$ and inflated to 2015 values. More detail on assumptions used about current coverage and implementation of pro-breastfeeding social policies is described in chapter 5.

Table C.4 Unit Costs of Interventions to Treat Severe Acute Malnutrition

Country	Region	Unit cost used in the analyses (2015 US$)[a]	Sources and assumptions
Chad, Mali, Niger	Sub-Saharan Africa	135.33	Unit cost from Mali; Shekar et al. 2015
Djibouti, Eritrea, Republic of South Sudan, Sudan	Sub-Saharan Africa	95.17	Based on Dayton Eberwein et al. forthcoming. Assumptions: 100% receive outpatient treatment ($83.32 [82% inputs]); in addition, 15% of children have complications and need additional inpatient treatment ($79.03 per case). Total unit cost: 83.32 + 79.03*0.15 = 95.17
Congo, Dem. Rep.	Sub-Saharan Africa	162.00	Shekar et al. 2015

table continues next page

Table C.4 Unit Costs of Interventions to Treat Severe Acute Malnutrition (continued)

Country	Region	Unit cost used in the analyses (2015 US$)[a]	Sources and assumptions
Ethiopia	Sub-Saharan Africa	147.74	Tekeste et al. 2012
Nigeria	Sub-Saharan Africa	160.00	UNICEF Nigeria 2015
China, Indonesia, Myanmar, Philippines, Timor-Leste, Vietnam	East Asia and Pacific	57.49	Unit cost from Vietnam; Alive and Thrive 2013, Assumptions: 2013 cost per case without complications: VND 1,252,197 (US$55.69) and with complications: VND 1,435,897 (US$63.85); assume 15% of cases are with complications; weighted average unit cost is VND 1,270,567 (US$56.5); assume exchange rate of US$1 = VND 22,727.27 [12/1/2015]
Egypt, Arab Rep., Iraq, Yemen, Rep.	Middle East and North Africa	218.90	Average from Africa: Assumed that input (RUTF) cost will not be different from the African average ($70); noninput costs (e.g., labor) were adjusted by WHO CHOICE multiplier of 2.20; (137.68 − 70) * 2.20 + 70 = 218.9
Afghanistan, Pakistan	South Asia	158.15	Unit cost from Pakistan; UNICEF 2012
Bangladesh	South Asia	179.97	Puett et al. 2013
India, Sri Lanka	South Asia	107.38	Unit cost from India; Menon, McDonald, and Chakrabati 2016

Note: RUTF = ready-to-use therapeutic food; VND = Vietnamese dong.
a. All unit costs from the literature were converted into U.S.$ and inflated to 2015 values.

References

Alavi, S., B. Bugusu, G. Cramer, O. Dary, T.-C. Lee, L. Martin, J. McEntire, and E. Wailes. 2008. *Rice Fortification in Developing Countries: A Critical Review of the Technical and Economic Feasibility*. Washington, DC: Academy for Educational Development.

Alive and Thrive. 2013. *Vietnam Costing Study: Implementation Expenditure and Costs*. Hanoi, Vietnam: Alive and Thrive.

———. 2014. "Country Brief: Program Approach and Results in Vietnam, June 2009 to December 2014." Hanoi: Alive & Thrive. http://aliveandthrive.org/countries/viet-nam/.

Bahl, K., E. Toro, C. Qureshi, and P. Shaw. 2013. *Nutrition for a Better Tomorrow: Scaling Up Delivery of Micronutrient Powders for Infants and Young Children*. Washington, DC: Results for Development Institute.

Bhutta, Z. A., J. K. Das, A. Rizvi, M. F. Gaffey, N. Walker, S. Horton, et al. 2013. "Evidence-Based Interventions for Improvement of Maternal and Child Nutrition: What Can Be Done and at What Cost?" *The Lancet* 382 (9890): 452–77.

Casey, G. J., D. Sartori, S. E. Horton, T. Q. Phuc, L. B. Phu, D. T. Thach, T. C. Dai, G. Fattore, A. Montresor, and B.-A. Biggs. 2011. "Weekly Iron-Folic Acid Supplementation with Regular Deworming Is Cost-Effective in Preventing Anaemia in Women of Reproductive Age in Vietnam." *PLoS One* 6 (9): e23723.

Dahn, B., A. Woldemariam, H. Perry, A. Maeda, D. von Glahn, R. Panjabi, N. Merchant, K. Vosburg, D. Palazuelos, C. Lu, John Simon, J. Pfaffmann, D. Brown, A. Hearst,

P. Heydt, and C. Qureshi. 2015. "Strengthening Primary Health Care through Community Health Workers: Investment Case and Financing Recommendations." http://www.healthenvoy.org/wp-content/uploads/2015/07/CHW-Financing-FINAL-July-15-2015.pdf.

Dayton Eberwein, J., J. Kakietek, D. de Beni, G. Moloney, A. Pereira, J. K. Akuoku, M. Volege, S. Matu, and M. Shekar. Forthcoming. "Scaling Up Nutrition in Kenya: What Will It Cost?" Health, Nutrition and Population (HNP) Discussion Paper. World Bank, Washington, DC.

FANTA (Food and Technical Assitance III Project). 2014. *Guatemala: Costeo de intervenciones de nutrición en el Primer y Segundo Nivel de atención en el Marco del Convenio de Gestión por Resultados entre el Minfin y el MSPAS*. Guatemala City, Guatemala: Government of Guatemala. http://icefi.org/publicaciones/guatemala-costeo-de-intervenciones-de-nutricion-en-el-primer-y-segundo-nivel-de.

Futures Institute. 2013. *OneHealth Model: Intervention Treatment Assumptions*. Glastonbury: Futures Institute. http://avenirhealth.org/Download/Spectrum/Manuals/Intervention percent20Assumptions percent202013percent209 percent2028.pdf.

Ghauri, K., S. Horton, R. Spohrer, and G. Garrett. 2016. "Food Fortification Cost Model." Unpublished manuscript. Washington, DC: Global Alliance for Improved Nutrition.

Horton, S., M. Shekar, C. McDonald, A. Mahal, and J. K. Brooks. 2010. *Scaling Up Nutrition: What Will It Cost?* Directions in Development Series. Washington, DC: World Bank.

Maternal and Child Health Integrated Program. 2011. *Community-Based Distribution for Routine Iron/Folic Acid Supplementation in Pregnancy*. Washington, DC: MCHIP. http://www.mchip.net/node/632.

Menon, P., C. M. McDonald, and S. Chakrabarti. 2016. "Estimating the Cost of Delivering Direct Nutrition Interventions at Scale: National and Subnational Level Insights from India." *Maternal & Child Nutrition* 12 (S1): 169–85.

Micronutrient Initiative. 2006. *India Micronutrient National Investment Plan 2007–2011*. New Delhi: Micronutrient Initiative.

Neidecker-Gonzales, O., P. Nestel, and H. Bouis. 2007. "Estimating the Global Costs of Vitamin A Capsule Supplementation: A Review of the Literature." *Food and Nutrition Bulletin* 28 (3): 307–16.

Pachon, H. 2016. "Food Fortification Coverage Data." Unpublished Data. Atlanta: Food Fortification Initiative.

Puett, C., K. Sadler, H. Alderman, J. Coates, J. L. Fiedler, and M. Myatt. 2013. "Cost-Effectiveness of the Community-Based Management of Severe Acute Malnutrition by Community Health Workers in Southern Bangladesh." *Health Policy and Planning* 28 (4): 386–99.

Sharieff, W., S. E. Horton, and S. Zlotkin. 2006. "Economic Gains of a Home Fortification Program: Evaluation of 'Sprinkles' from the Provider's Perspective." *Canadian Journal of Public Health* 97 (1): 20–3.

Shekar, M., Z. Hyder, A. Subandoro, J. Dayton Eberwein, K. Kakietek, A. L. Pereira, and J. K. Akuoku. 2015a. "Scaling Up Nutrition in Uganda: What Will It Cost?" Unpublished. Washington, DC: World Bank.

Shekar, M., Z. Hyder, A. Subandoro, J. Dayton Eberwein, K. Kakietek, A. L. Pereira, R. Sunkutu, and J. K. Akuoku. 2015b. "Scaling Up Nutrition in Zambia: What Will It Cost?" Unpublished. Washington, DC: World Bank.

Shekar, M., M. Mattern, P. Eozenou, J. Dayton Eberwein, J. K. Akuoku, E. Di Gropello, and W. Karamba. 2015c. "Scaling Up Nutrition for a More Resilient Mali: Nutrition Diagnostics and Costed Plan for Scaling Up." Health, Nutrition and Population (HNP) Discussion Paper. Washington, DC: The World Bank Group.

Shekar, M., M. Mattern, L. Laviolette, J. Dayton Eberwein, W. Karamba, and J. K. Akuoku. 2015d. "Scaling Up Nutrition in the DRC: What Will It Cost?" Health, Nutrition and Population (HNP) Discussion Paper. Washington, DC: The World Bank Group.

Shekar, M., C. McDonald, A. Subandoro, J. Dayton Eberwein, M. Mattern, and J. K. Akuoku. 2014. "Costed Plan for Scaling Up Nutrition: Nigeria." Health, Nutrition and Population (HNP) Discussion Paper. Washington, DC: The World Bank Group.

Tekeste, A., M. Wondafrash, G. Azene, and K. Deribe. 2012. "Cost Effectiveness of Community-Based and In-Patient Therapeutic Feeding Programs to Treat Severe Acute Malnutrition in Ethiopia." *Cost Effectiveness and Resource Allocation* 10 (4): 1.

UNICEF (United Nations Children's Fund). 2012. *Evaluation of Community Management of Acute Malnutrition (CMAM) Pakistan Country Case Study.* New York: UNICEF.

———. 2015. "UNICEF Supply Catalogue" (accessed 2015), https://supply.unicef.org/unicef_b2c/app/displayApp/(cpgsize=5&layout=7.0-12_1_66_68_115_2&uiarea=2&carea=4F0BC9C3A0B90688E10000009E711453&cpgnum=1)/.do?rf=y.

UNICEF Nigeria. 2015. "In Nigeria, Saving Lives and Investing in the Future," September. http://www.unicef.org/infobycountry/nigeria_83094.html.

Walters, D., S. Horton, A. Y. M. Siregar, P. Pitriyan, N. Hajeebhoy, R. Mathisen, L. T. Phan, and C. Rudert. 2016. "The Cost of Not Breastfeeding in Southeast Asia." *Health Policy and Planning* 31 (8): 1107–16.

White, M. T., L. Conteh, R. Cibulskis, and A. C. Ghani. 2011. "Costs and Cost-Effectiveness of Malaria Control Interventions: A Systematic Review." *Malaria Journal* 10 (1): 1.

WHO (World Health Organization). 2005. Choosing Interventions that Are Cost-Effective (WHO-CHOICE), WHO, Geneva (accessed 2015), http://www.who.int/choice/costs/prog_costs/en/.

———. 2011. *Weekly Iron and Folic Acid Supplementation Programmes for Women of Reproductive Age: An Analysis of Best Programme Practices.* Geneva: WHO. http://www.wpro.who.int/publications/PUB_9789290615231/en/.

World Bank. 2016. World Development Indicators (database), World Bank, Washington, DC (accessed January 3, 2016), http://data.worldbank.org/data-catalog/world-development-indicators.

APPENDIX D

Current Government Investments in Nutrition

Table D.1 presents estimates of government investments on nutrition specific programs by source, indicating where expenditure data versus budget data were available. These data were compiled through a systematic review of all available data on government nutrition financing, as described in chapter 8.

Although access to data on government financing for nutrition is limited, efforts to track government investments in nutrition have been growing as a result of promotion by the Scaling Up Nutrition (SUN) Movement and other platforms advocating for countries to build an investment case for nutrition. Data availability has come a long way forward over the last few years. However, many limitations in the quantity and quality of government nutrition financing data still exist. With the paucity of domestic expenditure data in the public domain, it is impossible to get a precise estimate of what is actually spent on nutrition programming. Even when data on nutrition budget allocations and expenditures do exist, the granularity of this information at the program and project level is commonly not accessible. More research is needed in this area, along with capacity building to ensure financial tracking systems are established within countries and used to monitor progress toward national nutrition plans.

Table D.1 Estimates of Government Expenditure on Nutrition Programs, Various Sources

Country	Source	Type of financing data	Most recent data year	Total GEN (US$, millions)[a]	GEN per stunted child under five (US$)[b]	GEN per child under five (US$)[b]	GEN as a share of GGE (%)[b]	GEN as a share of GHE (%)[b]
Low-income countries (n = 15)				53.34	2.09	0.85	0.15	1.38
Benin	GHED	Expenditure	2012	0.37	0.65	0.22	0.02	0.20
Burkina Faso	GHED	Expenditure	2013	1.00	1.02	0.32	0.03	0.22
Burundi	GHED	Expenditure	2012	9.00	9.09	4.49	1.02	8.18
Cambodia	GHED	Expenditure	2012	0.20	0.35	0.11	0.01	0.09
Comoros	GNR adjusted	Approved budget allocation	2014	0.06	1.75	0.54	0.03	0.47
Congo, Dem. Rep.	GHED	Expenditure	2013	3.00	0.53	0.24	0.05	0.54
Ethiopia	GHED	Expenditure	2008	2.23	0.38	0.15	0.03	0.17
Haiti	GHED	Expenditure	2012	0.03	0.10	0.02	0.00	0.05
Madagascar	GNR adjusted	Approved budget allocation	2014	1.01	0.62	0.27	0.05	0.34
Malawi	Save the Children budget analysis	Approved budget allocation	2014	0.81	0.66	0.28	0.04	0.44
Nepal	GNR adjusted & SPRING	Approved budget allocation	2014	1.75	1.64	0.62	0.05	0.34
Niger	GHED	Expenditure	2013	12.00	7.57	3.01	0.58	6.73
South Sudan	GNR adjusted	Approved budget allocation	2012	0.01	0.01	0.00	0.00	0.01
Tanzania	PER	Expenditure	2012	21.30	6.70	2.37	0.28	2.82
Uganda	GHED	Expenditure	2012	0.57	0.25	0.08	0.01	0.06

table continues next page

Table D.1 Estimates of Government Expenditure on Nutrition Programs from Various Sources *(continued)*

Country	Source	Type of financing data	Most recent data year	Total GEN (US$, millions)[a]	GEN per stunted child under five (US$)[b]	GEN per child under five (US$)[b]	GEN as a share of GGE (%)[b]	GEN as a share of GHE (%)[b]
Lower-middle income countries (n = 13)								
Bangladesh	GNR adjusted	Approved budget allocation	2014	2,240.37	11.85	4.67	0.14	1.55
Cameroon	GHED	Expenditure	2011	45.00	8.11	2.96	0.18	1.84
Côte d'Ivoire	GHED	Expenditure	2013	0.06	0.05	0.01	0.00	0.01
Guatemala	Budget analysis	Expenditure	2014	1.91	1.89	0.56	0.03	0.32
India	Budget analysis	Approved budget allocation; Expenditures	2014	63.11	66.16	27.20	0.81	4.48
Indonesia	Budget analysis	Approved budget allocation; Expenditures	2013	2,060.46	33.13	16.86	0.41	8.59
Kenya	GHED	Expenditure	2015	18.96	2.16	0.83	0.01	0.19
Lesotho	GNR adjusted	Approved budget allocation	2013	5.02	2.73	0.69	0.04	0.49
Mauritania	GHED	Expenditure	2014	1.39	15.28	5.25	0.09	0.62
Pakistan	GNR adjusted	Approved budget allocation	2013	1.63	12.91	2.71	0.11	2.11
Philippines	GNR adjusted	Approved budget allocation	2014	16.06	1.50	0.75	0.03	0.66
	GNR adjusted	Approved budget allocation	2012	22.06	6.60	1.89	0.05	0.63

table continues next page

Table D.1 Estimates of Government Expenditure on Nutrition Programs from Various Sources *(continued)*

Country	Source	Type of financing data	Most recent data year	Total GEN (US$, millions)[a]	GEN per stunted child under five (US$)[b]	GEN per child under five (US$)[b]	GEN as a share of GGE (%)[b]	GEN as a share of GHE (%)[b]
Vietnam	GNR adjusted	Approved budget allocation	2014	3.53	2.39	0.50	0.01	0.08
Zambia	Save the Children budget analysis	Approved budget allocation	2014	1.18	1.08	0.41	0.02	0.16
Upper-middle-income countries (n = 3)				227.82	54.50	8.14	0.03	0.23
Brazil	Budget analysis	Approved budget allocation	2015	57.21	48.10	3.88	0.01	0.05
Mexico	Budget analysis	Approved budget allocation	2014	118.85	75.11	10.73	0.03	0.28
South Africa	Budget analysis	Approved budget allocation	2015	51.76	40.28	9.83	0.05	0.35
All low- and middle-income countries (n = 31)				2,521.53	11.25	3.16	0.13	1.34

Note: GEN = government expenditure on nutrition; GGE = general government expenditure; GHE = government health expenditure; GHED = Global Health Expenditure Database (WHO 2015); GNR = *Global Nutrition Report* (IFPRI 2014); PER = public expenditure review; SPRING = Strengthening Partnerships, Results, and Innovations in Nutrition Globally. *GNR adjusted* means that the reported figure was adjusted by an internal standardization process to be able to compare data points (described in chapter 8).

a. Income group categories are reported as totals across income groups.
b. Income group categories are reported as averages across income groups.

References

IFPRI (International Food Policy Research Institute). 2014. *Global Nutrition Report 2014*. Washington, DC: IFPRI.

SPRING. 2016. *Pathways to Better Nutrition in Nepal: Final Report*. Arlington, VA: Strengthening Partnerships, Results, and Innovations in Nutrition Globally (SPRING) project.

SPRING. 2016. *Pathways to Better Nutrition in Uganda: Final Report*. Arlington, VA: Strengthening Partnerships, Results, and Innovations in Nutrition Globally (SPRING) project.

United Republic of Tanzania, Ministry of Finance. 2014. *Public Expenditure Review of the Nutrition Sector: Main Report*. Innovex. http://scalingupnutrition.org/wp-content/uploads/2014/08/Nutrition-PER-Final-version-April-2014.pdf.

WHO (World Health Organization). 2015. Global Health Expenditure Database (accessed September 18, 2015), http://apps.who.int/nha/database.

APPENDIX E

Current Official Development Assistance for Nutrition across Aid Categories

All data on donor funding for nutrition were extracted from the Creditor Reporting System (CRS) of the Organisation for Economic Co-operation and Development (OECD).

Table E.1 provides a summary of all the purpose codes included in this analysis. As discussed in chapter 8, the basic nutrition purpose code does not capture all official development assistance (ODA) for nutrition, so multiple purpose codes within health and emergency relief—identified by stakeholders as most likely purpose codes to contain nutrition programs—were explored. The following section describes in more detail the methods used for exploring the other purpose codes.

Capturing Nutrition Investments within the CRS Purpose Code for Basic Nutrition

Chapter 8 described the methods used to track intervention-level disbursements within the basic nutrition purpose code. Table E.2 presents the results of this analysis by showing the breakdown of how disbursements for basic nutrition to the 60 highest-burden countries are distributed between interventions.

Capturing Nutrition Investments within CRS Purpose Codes for Health

In practice, nutrition interventions are often delivered through maternal and child health programs and other health initiatives, and ODA for these programs is most often coded under health. To that end, this study analyzed ODA disbursement data under six health codes: basic health care, reproductive health, health education, health personnel development, infectious disease, and personnel development for population and reproductive health. These six were chosen through consultations with nutrition financing experts, donors, and nutrition advocates, and desk research.

Table E.1 Summary of Purpose Codes Included in the Analysis

Purpose code	Purpose code name	Total disbursements in 2013 (US$, millions)	Screening method used	Percent of projects screened under the purpose code using the related method	Percent of disbursements found to be aligned with the costed package of interventions
12240	Basic nutrition	946	Project-level categorization	70 (n = 945)	53.0[a]
12220	Basic health care	3,217	Keyword search	100	0.9
12250	Infectious disease control	1,369	Keyword search	100	<0.01
12261	Health education	167	Keyword search	100	1.5
12281	Health personnel development	107	Keyword search	100	2.4
13020	Reproductive health care	1,678	Keyword search	100	5.7
13081	Personnel development for population & reproductive health	68	Keyword search	100	0.0
51010	General budget support-related aid	9,629	Keyword search	100	0.0
52010	Food aid/food security programs	1,290	Keyword search	100	2.0
53030	Import support (capital goods)	315	Keyword search	100	0.0
53040	Import support (commodities)	58	Keyword search	100	0.0
72010	Material relief assistance and services	7,405	Keyword search	100	1.2
72040	Emergency food aid	3,835	Keyword search	100	5.3
72050	Relief coordination; protection and support services	835	Keyword search	100	0.5
73010	Reconstruction relief and rehabilitation	625	Keyword search	100	0.0
74010	Disaster prevention and preparedness	1,017	Keyword search	100	0.2%

Source: Compiled by authors based on 2013 disbursement data from the Creditor Reporting System (CRS) of the Organisation for Economic Co-operation and Development (OECD) (OECD 2016).
a. Remaining disbursements within the basic nutrition code went toward interventions not included in the costed package of interventions (including deworming and salt iodization), nutrition-sensitive interventions such as school feeding, and unspecified disbursements.

Table E.2 Average Segmentation of Basic Nutrition (Purpose Code 12240) Disbursements in 2013, by Intervention/Activity in 60 Countries

Intervention category	Average allocation (%)
Infant and young child nutrition counseling	13.7
Treatment of acute malnutrition	15.2
Deworming	0.5
Supplementation	
Iron and folic acid for pregnant women	0.6
Micronutrient powders for children and pregnant women	0.7
Therapeutic zinc and oral rehydration solution	3.6
Vitamin A for children	1.3
Public provision of complementary food	4.1
Salt iodization	0.2
Staple food fortification	2.7
Research and development	2.6
System strengthening	12.7
Nutrition-sensitive[a]	42.1

Source: Compiled using 2013 disbursement data from the Creditor Reporting System (CRS) of the Organisation for Economic Co-operation and Development (OECD) (OECD 2016).
a. Nutrition-sensitive includes school feeding programs, household food security interventions, food safety programs, women's empowerment interventions, and other nutrition-sensitive programs.

A keyword search for "nutrition" was conducted within project titles and short/long descriptions of the additional health codes (table E.1).[1] For purpose codes for basic health care, reproductive health, health education, and health personnel development, projects containing the word nutrition represented 1 to 6 percent of total disbursements to that code. No mention of nutrition was found within the code for personnel development for population and reproductive health.

A rapid assessment of project descriptions indicated that the majority of these disbursements were linked to the following interventions: infant and young child nutrition counseling, treatment of severe acute malnutrition for children, antenatal micronutrient supplementation, vitamin A supplementation for children, and prophylactic zinc supplementation for children. In order to disaggregate the estimated nutrition disbursement by the interventions included in the health code, the same relative-cost weighting method that was used for the basic nutrition code analysis, as described in chapter 8, was employed.

Capturing Nutrition Investments within CRS Purpose Codes for Emergency Relief and Food Aid

A similar methodology was used for the additional health codes on emergency and food aid codes. Keyword searches for "nutrition," "community based management of acute malnutrition," "severe acute malnutrition," "ready to use therapeutic foods," and all acronyms used to describe these terms were conducted across project descriptions. The following purpose codes were included: general budget support-related aid, food aid/food security programs, import support, material relief assistance and services, emergency food aid, relief coordination, reconstruction relief and rehabilitation, and disaster prevention and preparedness. No mention of the keywords was found in general budget support-related aid or import support (capital goods and commodities), so these codes were removed from the rest of the analysis.

Table E.1 shows that from less than 1 percent to a maximum of 5 percent of disbursements to these purpose codes were captured within the keyword search. Rapid assessment of project descriptions indicated that all disbursements were targeted toward the treatment of severe acute malnutrition for children.

Searching for Food Fortification

The agriculture sector code (311) was analyzed to search for funding for food fortification efforts. No additional financing for staple food fortification was found within this code.

Note

1. When downloaded, data had been last updated by the OECD CRS on October 19, 2015.

Reference

OECD (Organisation for Economic Co-operation and Development). 2016. Creditor Reporting System Database (CRS). https://stats.oecd.org/Indix.aspx?DataSetCode=CRS1

Environmental Benefits Statement

The World Bank Group is committed to reducing its environmental footprint. In support of this commitment, we leverage electronic publishing options and print-on-demand technology, which is located in regional hubs worldwide. Together, these initiatives enable print runs to be lowered and shipping distances decreased, resulting in reduced paper consumption, chemical use, greenhouse gas emissions, and waste.

We follow the recommended standards for paper use set by the Green Press Initiative. The majority of our books are printed on Forest Stewardship Council (FSC)–certified paper, with nearly all containing 50–100 percent recycled content. The recycled fiber in our book paper is either unbleached or bleached using totally chlorine-free (TCF), processed chlorine–free (PCF), or enhanced elemental chlorine–free (EECF) processes.

More information about the Bank's environmental philosophy can be found at http://www.worldbank.org/corporateresponsibility.